Introduction to Therapeutic Play

Other titles in the series

Patterns of Adoption
D. Howe
0-632-04149-8

Family Group Conferences in Child Welfare
P. Marsh and G. Crow
0-632-04922-7

Neglected Children: issues and dilemmas
O. Stevenson
0-632-04146-3

Young Carers and their Families
S. Becker, C. Dearden and J. Aldridge
0-632-04966-9

Child Welfare in the UK
Edited by O. Stevenson
0-632-04993-6

Also available from Blackwell Science

Child and Family Social Work
Editor: Professor David Howe
ISSN 1356-7500

Child and Family Social Work is a major international journal for all those concerned with the social and personal well-being of children and those who care for them. The Journal publishes original and distinguished contributions on matters of research, theory, policy and practice in the field of social work with children and their families. It aims to give international definition to the discipline and practice of child and family social work.

Child and Family Social Work is published quarterly

WORKING TOGETHER FOR CHILDREN,
YOUNG PEOPLE AND THEIR FAMILIES

SERIES EDITOR: PROFESSOR OLIVE STEVENSON

Introduction to Therapeutic Play

Jo Carroll
Play Therapist

**Blackwell
Science**

© 1998 by
Blackwell Science Ltd
Editorial Offices:
Osney Mead, Oxford OX2 0EL
25 John Street, London WC1N 2BL
23 Ainslie Place, Edinburgh EH3 6AJ
350 Main Street, Malden
 MA 02148 5018, USA
54 University Street, Carlton
 Victoria 3053, Australia

Other Editorial Offices:

Blackwell Wissenschafts-Verlag GmbH
Kurfürstendamm 57
10707 Berlin, Germany

Blackwell Science KK
MG Kodenmacho Building
7–10 Kodenmacho Nihombashi
Chuo-ku, Tokyo 104, Japan

First published 1998

Set in 10/12 pt Sabon
by DP Photosetting, Aylesbury, Bucks
Printed and bound in Great Britain by
Hartnolls Ltd, Bodmin, Cornwall

DISTRIBUTORS

Marston Book Services Ltd
PO Box 269
Abingdon
Oxon OX14 4YN
(*Orders:* Tel: 01235 465500
 Fax: 01235 465555)

USA
 Blackwell Science, Inc.
 Commerce Place
 350 Main Street
 Malden, MA 02148 5018
 (*Orders:* Tel: 800 759 6102
 617 388 8250
 Fax: 617 388 8255)

Canada
 Copp Clark Professional
 200 Adelaide Street West, 3rd Floor
 Toronto, Ontario M5H 1W7
 (*Orders:* Tel: 416 597-1616
 800 815-9417
 Fax: 416 597-1617)

Australia
 Blackwell Science Pty Ltd
 54 University Street
 Carlton, Victoria 3053
 (*Orders:* Tel: 03 9347 0300
 Fax: 03 9347 5001)

A catalogue record for this title
is available from the British Library

ISBN 0-632-04148-X

For

John

Contents

Foreword
by Professor Olive Stevenson

This is the first book to be published in the new series *Working Together for Children, Young People and Families*. It concerns direct work with children in difficulty; nothing could be more important and timely. The author expresses her intentions sensitively when she says:

> 'For those who live with troubled children or try to teach them when their minds are full of sadness, this book aims to offer some understanding of the processes of therapy. Therapy should not be mysterious...'

This book, then, demystifies therapeutic play, explaining its assumptions and techniques. The need for more effective intervention to help children who have been hurt and damaged is urgent. Too often in recent years, 'risk assessments', with or without removal from home, have left children unprotected from their own inner turmoil, with disastrous consequences for their behaviour and capacity to form relationships. For example, we have only to look at the mounting evidence of 'child on child abuse' to see examples of earlier trauma being re-enacted in destructive ways.

However, we have a problem and I hope this book will stimulate thought about its resolution. As Jo Carroll implies, 'therapy' can easily be reified and can be viewed as an esoteric activity from which 'ordinary' social workers or other professionals back away. It is obviously vital (and the book stresses this) that training, supervision and consultation should be available for those who engage in this delicate work. Yet, as the Appendix shows, training courses are at present few and far between and not in the mainstream of post-qualifying education in child welfare.

What is now needed is a review of the place of therapeutic play in the range of interventions available and a consideration of the implications for developments in education and training at basic and post-qualifying levels. Specifically, we have to work out what those outside the small group of full-time therapists can take from that expertise, without risk of dabbling unhelpfully in children's psychic experiences. Play is a natural medium for the expression of children's feelings and, to a degree, understanding of it can be available to a range of helping professionals. How can we utilise the kinds of insights available in this book to help the thousands of children who cannot have (and may not need) prolonged intensive therapy but who would benefit from a more limited exploration? How can we inculcate in those who care for children in difficulty the notion that the door to children's emotions should not be closed?

My working lifetime in the field of child welfare has seen shifts in fashions and emphases. My own training was much influenced by psychodynamic theory and practice, carried forward by my generation of educators into periods of child observation in the curriculum, discussion of 'communicating with children' and so on. Somewhere along the line, we lost this and other preoccupations became dominant. Recently, there have been welcome indications of a reintroduction of such elements. But 'observation or assessment' is not enough; it has to be utilised within a relationship.

This book is a significant contribution to a debate of great importance and to an area of practice which is critical to the well being of children.

Olive Stevenson
Professor Emeritus of Social Work Studies

Preface

When I began working with children 15 years ago, I looked for a book which brought together the range of therapeutic interventions in an easily accessible form. When I was unable to find such a book, my supervisor suggested that I write it. Although this was a throwaway remark at the time, it was a passing thought which eventually grew into this book.

The past 20 years has seen a growing recognition of the distress of children who experience abuse or rejection. Disturbances within their families can leave them bewildered, and their emotional and behavioural responses illustrate the extent of their unhappiness. In addition, practitioners have grown increasingly aware of the emotional needs of disabled children, or those who are traumatised by disasters.

I have aimed to provide a cohesive guide to the disparate approaches to therapeutic work with children who have experienced a wide range of misfortunes. These extend from the non-directive play therapy techniques of Axline and Moustakas to the focused interventions of James and Oaklander. Many of these techniques were developed in America and Canada, but practitioners throughout the world are now seeking to develop their skills to meet the needs of disturbed and bewildered children. I hope that readers will find this book practically helpful as they rise to the challenge of reaching out to these troubled children.

Acknowledgements

I must begin by thanking all those children who have taught me about the practice of play therapy, and shared their pain and their courage with me. Many are mentioned in this book; all have enlarged my understanding.

I am grateful to Lisa Field, from Blackwell Science Ltd, and to Griselda Campbell and Olive Stevenson, who have nurtured this book from draft to final copy.

I would also like to thank Hazel Spurrier and her staff at the Post Graduate Library at Princess Margaret Hospital in Swindon; without their willingness and enthusiasm to search for obscure material I would have been unable to complete the research that has resulted in this book.

I am indebted to friends and professional colleagues who have been generous with their support, particularly Linnet McMahon, Judy Russ, and Carolyn Caldwell. Elizabeth Hardcastle and Lucy Grafen have supervised my clinical practice with wisdom and patience, and extended my understanding of the process of survival for both child and therapist. Colleagues in the Therapy Supervision Group at the Five Rivers Project have been unstinting in their unconventional support. Kenny Odart's copies of children's drawings, his help with proof reading, and common sense when I was in danger of losing mine, have been invaluable.

I wish to express my appreciation to Elianna Gil, who gave permission for me to discuss a child she presented at a Conference at Reading University in 1994.

Sadly, neither my husband nor my mother lived to see this book published; their belief in me has continued to sustain me after their deaths. Most importantly, I must thank my daughters Anna and Tessa; this book has been as much a part of their lives as it has mine. Without their patience (and many delayed suppers) this book would never have been completed.

Many of the issues explored in this book were first considered in my paper Reaching Out to Aggressive Children, in the *British Journal of Social Work* 25, pp. 37–53 (1995). This material is included by kind permission of Oxford University Press.

Author's note

All identifying features of the children discussed in this book have been
changed to preserve anonymity. 'Kelly' is a 'composite child', an
amalgamation of several children.

Chapter 1

Therapeutic Play

Introduction

The rapid expansion of interest in play as a therapeutic intervention in recent years has led to a growing repertoire of play techniques. This coincides with an acknowledgement that children who have experienced abuse need skilled help to enable them to recover and lead fulfilling lives. Not only are a caring environment and professional cohesion essential, but attention to individual circumstances and distress is required to help this child in his or her unique circumstances. Practitioners are united in their search for methods to reach and restore these children.

A variety of approaches have been developed in recent years, all aimed at healing troubled children. Techniques range from the intensity of child psychotherapy to focused, short-term interventions to alleviate a particular problem. Accurate assessment, and an understanding of the numerous techniques available, will enable practitioners to select that method best suited to this child.

Therapeutic play

In spite of the recognition of the value of play as a therapeutic tool, there remains a lack of understanding among referring agencies as to the process of therapy and the nature of the techniques involved. It is common to be given lengthy details of a child's circumstances and difficulties, and then to be asked: 'What do you actually do?'

This book is about what I do in my efforts to help troubled children. I crawl around the floor with them; I paint and draw and glue with them; I become part of fantasy worlds in which I can be happy or miserable, powerful or helpless; I play with tea-sets and soldiers and farm animals and snakes. I struggle to understand the feelings and experiences that prompt such play, and to share these with each child. This is how I spend much of my time; it does not describe the process of healing prompted by such play.

Until recently, there has been no clear definition of play therapy.

However, this has lately been clarified by the British Association of Play Therapists, who define play therapy as:

> 'The dynamic process between child and play therapist, in which the child explores, at his or her own pace and with his or her own agenda, those issues past and current, conscious and unconscious, that are affecting the child's life in the present. The child's inner resources are enabled by the therapeutic alliance to bring about growth and change. Play therapy is child-centred, in which play is the primary medium and speech the secondary medium.'

> (Association of Play Therapists Newsletter, 1995)

This includes any activity which enables the child to use the materials provided to explore his or her circumstances and express feelings. It excludes methods such as life story work which, although validating the feelings and difficulties of the child, is essentially adult-led. Child-centred, or non-directive, play therapy is a highly skilled technique; training and supervision are essential.

Throughout this book, the term *play therapy* is used to describe a child-centred approach, and *play therapists* are those trained to practise this form of intervention. Unqualified practitioners, engaged in play work with children, are termed *play workers*. *Workers*, *therapists* or *practitioners* refer to all those involved in therapeutic play with children.

Some play therapists adhere closely to child-centred principles. Many take a more eclectic approach, including more focused techniques when these best meet the needs of an individual child. A full assessment of each child leads naturally to employing those interventions which are most helpful in each situation.

In this book I try to bring together the wide range of play techniques available to practitioners; and to indicate the content of a thorough assessment which can lead to the selection of an appropriate intervention for each child. Social workers, resource centre workers, residential workers, early years workers, occupational therapists – anyone who uses play to help children will find methods to assist them here. This is not a book of solutions, but of practical ideas. Whilst stressing the need for appropriate training and supervision, it hopes to bring therapeutic play techniques within the reach of anyone who can suspend adult thinking and view the world through the eyes of a child.

This book concentrates on therapeutic play with individual children. Many techniques can be adapted for groups of children (Axline, 1969; Oaklander, 1969; McMahon, 1992; Jennings, 1993); Griff (1983) and Ariel (1992) extend this work to play therapy for families. It is beyond the scope of this book to discuss these approaches.

For those who live with troubled children, or try to teach them when their minds are full of sadness, this book aims to offer some understanding of the process of therapy. Therapy should not be mysterious, carried on behind closed doors from which the child emerges cured. Good communication between the practitioner and all who care for the child is essential. Therapy takes place in the context of other day-to-day events in the child's life, and therefore everyone concerned for him or her must work in partnership.

Many children described in this book have been abused; social workers will be familiar with their difficulties. However, there are other life events that make children unhappy. Parents separate; siblings die; children struggle with the consequences of disability or surgery. With the current emphasis on the plight of the abused child there is a risk that the suffering of the other children will go unrecognised. All children, whatever their circumstances, and whatever makes them unhappy, have the right to be listened to, and the right to appropriate help.

The range of techniques

There is now a wide range of treatments which fall under the umbrella of play therapy. Schaefer & O'Connor discuss a variety of techniques, and advocate an eclectic approach:

'To use play therapy in a prescriptive way ... means to choose a specific strategy for each child patient from the wide array of theories, techniques, and variations now encompassed by this particular category of therapy.'

(1983: p.1)

Current thinking in Britain has narrowed the definition of play therapy to concentrate on a child-centred approach, attaching importance to the value of enabling children to set their own agendas. However, the premise that the intervention selected should meet the needs of each individual child remains valid.

The range of techniques available to practitioners can be expressed as a continuum, with the most intensive intervention at one end, and less intrusive, short-term work at the other (see Fig. 1.1).

Although I discuss these approaches under separate headings, they are not as distinguishable as such classifications suggest. Practitioners who can draw on the ideas of child psychotherapists, which offer an understanding of the child's inner world, who can employ short-term, focused approaches when they would bring speediest results, and can utilise non-directive techniques for children unable to respond to active methods, bring a wealth of knowledge and skill to their practice.

Some writers promote one approach to therapy with children, although they draw on the ideas of other practitioners (Oaklander, 1969; Cattanach, 1992; West, 1992; Wilson *et al.*, 1992; Jennings,

Fig. 1.1 A continuum of interventions.

1993). Others classify children according to presenting problems, and develop an approach which they feel effective for specific disorders (Schaefer & O'Connor, 1983, Part 4; Hellendoorn *et al.*, 1994).

However, these authors agree that play is an effective, and appropriate, medium of communication for most children. There are no disagreements with Amster's comments:

> 'Essentially, play is an activity a child comprehends and in which he is comfortable; an integral part of his world, his method of communication; his medium of exchange, and his means of testing, partly incorporating and partly mastering external realities.'

> (1982, p. 33)

Children are comfortable with play long before they speak; adult nuances of language are lost on them. They play to show how they feel when words so often fail them.

Child psychotherapy

Child psychotherapy offers long-term help to the most damaged children. The child attends hour-long sessions, often three or more times a week, for a year or more. The therapist observes the child's play, offering interpretations which enable the child to understand unconscious processes.

A detailed discussion of the theories and techniques employed by child psychotherapists is beyond the scope of this book. However, play therapists have drawn extensively from the understanding that psychoanalytic thought has brought to our comprehension of a child's inner world, and its impact on his or her emotional functioning.

Until recently, most child psychotherapists considered play, not as a therapeutic activity in itself, but the context in which transference (see Chapter 2: *Theoretical Contributions*) can be interpreted and understood (Esman, 1983). The therapist joined the play as little as possible, and regarded him- or herself as a participant observer rather than playmate.

Lately, child psychotherapists have re-evaluated the role of play, and are more willing to recognise it as a means of communication that is valid in itself:

'In psychoanalysis, play is basically seen as a symbolic expression of unconscious conflicts which need to be interpreted in terms of psychoanalytic theory. In humanistic and existential therapies, on the other hand, play is seen as an expression of self and current experiencing which call for therapeutic understanding.'

(Mook, 1994: p. 43)

Mook suggests that child psychotherapists should involve themselves more directly in the child's play, and advocates

'timely interpretations [to] help the child ... explore and work through his/her personal and relational problems in an imaginative way.'

(p. 52)

This work is highly skilled, and applied to severely disturbed and needy children. It requires a long and arduous training based on the theories of Klein (1937) and Anna Freud (1946), and includes a period of analysis designed to help the therapist disentangle his or her own childish feelings. Other writers suggest that psychotherapeutic techniques are accessible to anyone willing to consider the child's inner world, and understand its influence on current behaviour and relationships. Reismann's (1973) approach to child psychotherapy is easily understood and his principles underlie much of the work undertaken by less intensive practitioners. He accepts the role of a child's current environment, and regards manipulation of that environment (for instance, facilitating a change of school) as a valid part of treatment; an approach echoed by O'Connor (1994).

Some American literature appears to blur the boundary between psychotherapy and play therapy. Webb defines play therapy as:

'a psychotherapeutic method, based on psychodynamic and developmental principles, intended to help relieve the emotional distress of young children through a variety of imaginative and expressive play materials.'

(1991: p. 27)

In Britain, play therapists agree with Winnicott, who promoted play as a healing activity in itself (Davis & Wallbridge, 1983); followers of Klein and Anna Freud emphasise play as the context in which understanding and insight into defence mechanisms is achieved.

Non-directive play therapy

The role of the non-directive play therapist is to provide the space in which healing through play is possible:

'In this method of therapy, play itself is the therapeutic invention; play is not used as a stimulation for other forms of therapy. The focus of the theory is on the process of play which heals the child.'

(Cattanach, 1992: pp. 39–40. See also Schaefer, 1993)

Axline (1964, 1969) first described her approach to therapy with children in 1947. Her book *Play Therapy* has become essential reading for anyone trying to help troubled children. She emphasised the role of the adult as offering the containment and security in which the child discovers for him- or herself, through play, a personal road to recovery. Axline described non-directive play therapy as:

'an opportunity that is offered to the child to experience growth under the most favourable conditions. Since play is his natural medium for self-expression, the child is given the opportunity to play out his accumulated feelings of tension, frustration, insecurity, aggression, fear, bewilderment, confusion.'

(1969: p. 16)

It is essential that the therapist respects totally the wishes and feelings of the child: it is the child who dictates the process of therapy, and the therapist who enables him or her to do so. Axline's ideas are still valid today, and are reflected in the work of Pinney (1983), with her *Children's Hours* technique, and Bray (1991), who has adapted this approach and uses it in the investigation of child sexual abuse. West (1992), and Wilson *et al.* (1992) base their practice almost entirely on her theories. Cattanach (1992) applies them initially with every child she sees. Most of Gil's work (1991) with abused children is based on non-directive techniques, as is Webb's (1991) with children with a range of disorders and difficulties. It should be stressed from the outset that practitioners interested in pursuing this approach should seek appropriate training and on-going supervision.

Focused interventions

For many practitioners, a non-directive approach seems either too long-winded or the results too vague; they have developed a range of focused techniques with more clearly defined goals. Perhaps the best known is Oaklander (1969), who uses structured play to encourage the child to illustrate his or her problems. Many of her ideas are creative (and fun), and allow plenty of free, imaginative use of materials. James (1989) acknowledges the value of non-directive play, but believes that focused techniques are essential if the child is to make progress.

In Britain much of the literature on directive techniques focuses on the plight of children parted from their natural families, and considers methods to help them with the grief of separation, coming to terms with past abuse, and the formation of new relationships (Jewett, 1984; Redgrave, 1987; Fahlberg, 1988c; Doyle, 1990; Cipolla *et al.*, 1992).

One of the most popular approaches is the use of life story work (Connor *et al.*, 1985; Harrison, 1988; Ryan & Walker, 1993). This seeks to provide children who have moved away from their natural families with a book in which their early history is described in a way that makes sense to the child, and gives him or her pictures and mementoes which will promote recall of good as well as bad things about the past.

In Chapter 6 life story work is discussed in more detail, alongside many other practical techniques. While the reader may be tempted to turn to this chapter first, hoping that it will provide the answer to a particularly pressing problem, I would urge you to consider first the importance of assessment. Many of these techniques look instantly inviting: they are designed to be fun. However, unless the purpose of a specific method reflects accurately the needs of the particular child, little will be achieved.

Non-directive play therapists view play as the primary medium of healing. Practitioners employing more focused techniques also play; however, they regard play as a tool for enabling the child to gain insight into his or her circumstances and relief from distressing feelings. In addition, they advocate the adult taking responsibility for providing materials that will meet the needs of each child:

'It is up to me [the therapist] to provide the means by which we will open doors and windows to their [the children's] inner worlds.'

(Oaklander, 1969: pp. 192–3)

In my opinion, all approaches to working with children are equally valid. Not all authors agree; Axline is committed to a non-directive play therapy approach; James is equally certain that, while non-directive methods can engage a child in the therapeutic process, he or she will not resolve painful issues without the additional application of directive techniques. Some children require the intensive help of child psychotherapy, while less traumatised children will respond happily to focused techniques without an introductory period of non-directive play. The task of the worker is to select that approach which best meets the needs of this child, with this problem, at this time.

The aims of therapy

Axline (1982b) describes the fundamental aim of all therapies quite succinctly:

'The overall objective is probably basic to all procedures: namely, to provide a relationship with the client that will enable him to utilise the capacities that are within him for a more constructive and happier life as an individual and as a member of society.'

(p. 121)

Such a global objective is not specific enough for many agencies. Children present with a variety of difficulties, and, for each child, a clear set of goals should be outlined at the onset of treatment. These may be short- or long-term, and depend on both current and previous circumstances.

Many children who are referred for therapeutic play have experienced disruption and abuse during the early years of their lives. In these circumstances the aim of therapy is:

> *to enable the child to understand and leave behind the emotional luggage associated with destructive early life experiences.*

Such referrals are common, and non-directive play therapy is often an appropriate response. The process of play empowers the child, offers him or her mastery over inexplicable events, and promotes exploration of feeling and self-awareness.

For children who are grossly understimulated as infants or toddlers the aim may be:

> *to 'make up for' some early lost experiences, especially missed opportunities to play.*

Some children take one look at sand and water and regress willingly. These children are particularly rewarding to work with. Their over-eagerness may lead to extremely messy play, but their overt pleasure more than compensates for the time spent clearing up.

Sadly, many children are unable to approach the materials with such abandon. Age-appropriate toys may be offered, but lack of imaginative capacity impedes the child's ability to illustrate fantasies in play. For these children a gentle and sensitive approach to regressive activities is essential if they are to play without self-consciousness. Wilson *et al.* (1992) successfully apply non-directive techniques to adolescents, and find that a tactful approach, with the young person offered the choice between age-appropriate counselling or regressive activities at each session, is empowering for him or her, as well as making up for lack of opportunities to play in early childhood.

When a child is first referred one of my earliest questions is whether s/he can laugh. Too many children are unable to relax completely, and lose control of themselves giggling. For these children, I aim:

> *to enable them to experience fully a range of emotions, pleasurable as well as painful.*

For such children non-directive play therapy is ideal. More focused methods assume the child has a basic understanding of his or her emotional life. Non-directive play therapy enables the child to master feelings gradually without being overwhelmed. It provides the context in which children needing help to identify and express appropriate feelings can learn to do so. Children who resist feeling pain are often unable to enjoy pleasure; their responses to situations that should be fun are wooden. They take their cues of expected behaviour from the facial expressions of those around them, but remain disconnected from their emotional reactions. I knew that Carol, a 7 year old rejected by her natural parents and abused in her foster home, was beginning to heal when her adoptive mother told me that she suddenly realised that Carol could laugh: she had been watching television, and, for the first time in her life, sank to the floor with giggles.

Many children are brought to a therapist because their behaviour causes concern to others. Generally, this behaviour is anti-social in some way: aggression, defiance, soiling, bullying, destructive behaviour, etc. Adults who refer these children hope that therapeutic play will:

enable children to modify anti-social behaviour.

It is adults who want these children to change – with good reason. They are difficult to live with, making impossible demands on those who care for them. They are often unhappy and confused beneath the bravado, but will rarely recognise their own need for help. The practitioner has to decide whether the help s/he can offer meets the needs of this particular child, and at the same time offer support to those struggling to manage such challenging behaviour.

Schools, playgroups, and foster families are now beginning to recognise the distress of the withdrawn, over-compliant child. These children do not draw attention to their plight in the dramatic way that anti-social children do. Many abused children have learned that, in order to protect themselves, they must perform whatever task is demanded of them. They cannot say no. Others rebuff social contact because all it has ever brought them is pain. Others cannot believe themselves worthy of attention or love, and reject all signs of affection.

Although these children are relatively easy to live with, they are still in urgent need of help. They are unlikely to recognise the value of therapeutic play; indeed, the prospect of anyone offering a relationship may be terrifying. They are dependent on an adult deciding that help is needed, and supporting them through the initial anxious stages.

Referrers are becoming increasingly aware of the connection between the child's self-esteem and other behavioural or emotional difficulties s/he may have. The therapist is asked to address this issue and:

to improve the child's self-esteem.

Axline (1969), and other proponents of non-directive techniques, show how the non-judgemental acceptance of the child in the context of therapy is sufficient to enable him or her to experience being valued. James (1989) and Oaklander (1969) suggest exercises that directly address issues of self-esteem. Practitioners who undertake life story work with children find that the process of making the book confirms his or her own worth to the child. Cook & Sinker (1993) illustrate the value of play in promoting mastery in disabled children. There are now an increasing number of books for children which address this issue (Waterhouse, 1987; Carlson, 1990; Palmer, 1992).

Some children exhibit pronounced developmental delay. Although delayed emotional progress may be tolerated within a foster home, marked discrepancies between the child's chronological age and emotional development can have extensive impact at school.

Both Wilson *et al.* (1992) and O'Connor (1991) believe that:

'The primary goal of play therapy is to bring the child to a level of functional development consistent with biological development.'

(O'Connor, 1991: p. 93)

They suggest that all children who experience trauma will have developmental difficulties. It is certainly true that many struggle to maintain progress; however, the child whose development is arrested by trauma poses special difficulties for the therapist. His or her teachers and carers may seek maturity, whilst the therapist understands that s/he cannot learn until the feelings that belong to the past are unlocked and understood. Some regressive children deny or repress feelings, making them even more difficult for the therapist to reach.

These children need the opportunity to re-examine feelings aroused by the trauma. Without understanding these feelings they cannot master them. They remained locked in pre-trauma behaviours, which become less and less commensurate with their chronological age. Non-directive play therapy, which permits children to express themselves symbolically, offers a constructive approach.

Children need specific help adjusting to separations from birth families and the move to a permanent home. Social workers are familiar with the needs of these children. It is hoped that treatment will enable the child:

to make sense of confusing events in the past, understand and come to terms with feelings about those who may have abused him or her, and prepare for life in a new family.

It is not uncommon for children who cannot live with their birth families to have several changes of foster placement before a permanent home is identified. Small children may become increasingly bewildered by alterations in circumstances that they cannot understand. They carry this chaos with them into a permanent home.

Many social workers are familiar with the techniques of life story work, which is aimed to address this issue. However, practitioners need to look to other interventions for children unable to utilise this method. Jewett (1984), Redgrave (1987), Fahlberg (1988c), Cipolla *et al.* (1992) and Ryan & Walker (1993) are among those with imaginative suggestions for practitioners struggling to meet the needs of these children.

The context of therapeutic play

Practitioners rarely have more than one hour a week to spend with each child. It is easy to over-estimate the impact of that hour, and to forget that those who care for these children or try to teach them are also an essential part of their worlds. Good communication between all those concerned with the child is essential if the goals of therapeutic intervention are to be achieved. Therapy alone is not enough.

Adults who refer such children are not always ready for the changes therapy will bring: during treatment the worker hopes to enable the child to become more assertive, to be aware of his or her own needs and to ensure, within reason, that they are met. Such assertion can too readily be translated by parents or foster carers as naughtiness. Other children regress, or resort to acting out behaviour, as they struggle to control reawakened feelings. Those who care for these children must feel part of the process of change, and not simply onlookers who have to manage challenging behaviour whilst excluded from the therapeutic experience.

It is essential to respond sensitively to each child and family's cultural expectations; families from parts of the world where a child's labour is needed for economic reasons may continue to regard play as unimportant (Moyles, 1989). Clear explanations of the role of the practitioner and objectives of therapeutic play promote involvement of these families in the process of therapy.

In addition, there may be other important events in the child's life: for example, is s/he about to move to a new school? It is too easy to assume that everything a child does in a therapy session is related to past experiences, or to misinterpret play on the basis of knowledge of his or her history. One 8-year-old girl spent an entire session making small cakes and handing them round to pretend friends to eat. Had I not known that she was going to a birthday party that afternoon, only the second she had ever attended, I might have been tempted to consider this play a meaningful attempt to feed and nurture herself. Knowing the circumstances, I could understand and reflect her excitement and anxiety about current events.

Another 11-year-old boy drew me a picture of a monster, and alongside it a small boy. I tried to understand whether he needed me to empathise with his monstrous feelings or the vulnerability of the small boy: his subsequent play gave me no clues. He finally became so upset that he climbed into a cupboard and stayed for the remainder of the session. A phone call to his foster carer revealed that he had been very frightened by the behaviour of another child in her home the previous weekend: without this knowledge my ability to help this child was severely restricted.

Summary

The various approaches to therapeutic play with children have a common aim: the alleviation of distress and promotion of emotional health. Other, more precise goals should be selected carefully before the onset of therapy. The techniques available to practitioners range from non-directive to focused methods, and the needs and circumstances of the child as well as the defined goals will assist in the selection of an appropriate intervention. All those who care for the child must be part of the therapeutic process if goals are to be achieved.

However, all the knowledge and expertise in the world is futile if the therapist is unable to put his or her adult wisdom to one side and try to understand the child's view of the world. Each child teaches me something new about children, and about therapeutic play. I must be as receptive to the lessons s/he is teaching me as I hope he or she will be to the opportunities that I am offering.

Chapter 2
Theoretical Contributions

Introduction

As well as familiarity with therapeutic play techniques and principles, practitioners can draw on the theoretical contributions of psychologists, psychoanalysts and child psychotherapists. These include an understanding of the nature of attachment and consequences of separation, the impact this may have on all subsequent relationships including that with a therapist, and the role of defence mechanisms in promoting a healthy response to feelings. In addition, Erikson's concepts of development, recent understanding of post traumatic stress disorder, and studies of the role of play in human development all contribute to the theoretical foundation of therapeutic play.

Many of these ideas were first explored before recent societal changes in the role of women. It was assumed that infants and children were cared for by their mothers, and paternal roles were peripheral. Although I refer to mothers as the primary carers in this chapter, reflecting the views of those first enquiring into child development, it can no longer be assumed that the female parent is the main carer of babies and small children, or that childminders are in any way 'second best'.

A thorough understanding of normal physical and psychosocial development is also essential, but beyond the scope of this book (Fahlberg, 1988b; Davenport, 1991; Smith & Cowie, 1991). A useful developmental checklist can be found in Jennings (1993: Appendix 1). Practitioners will find Piaget's understanding of the role of cognitive development invaluable (1952), as well as subsequent critics of Piaget's work (Donovan & McIntyre, 1990). Therapists working with abused children must be familiar with the common sequelae of abuse (Beitchman *et al.*, 1992).

Attachment and the effects of separation

The days and months following birth are crucial in the life of every child. Early attachments and experiences provide the foundation for subsequent expectations and understanding. Bowlby (1959, 1969) explored the development and importance of attachment. His work coincided with early studies of the impact of separations lasting several days on infants and young children (Robertson, 1952). Subsequent research (Ainsworth *et al.*, 1979; Ainsworth, 1989) has confirmed the vital role that mothers play in infant development, but allows for additional supportive relationships.

Bowlby proposes that attachment behaviour reflects a basic human need to form a close relationship with another.

> 'Attachment behaviour is any form of behaviour that results in a person attaining or maintaining proximity to some other clearly identified individual who is conceived as better able to cope with the world.... [It is] a fundamental form of behaviour with its own internal motivation distinct from feeding and sex, and of no less importance for survival.'

> (Bowlby, 1980b: pp. 26–7)

It is normal for children who are healthily attached to their parents and siblings to experience anxiety at separations. As infants, they feel abandoned if mother is away; they cannot yet believe that she will return. Intense distress is common, with the child gradually settling into quiescence. Separations lasting more than a few hours can lead to more prolonged difficulties for the child, and anger towards mother on her return. As the child develops, s/he learns that these separations come to an end, but each parting is difficult. Separation anxiety is common.

Many children cope with the pain of separation by developing an attachment to a soft blanket or toy, used to comfort themselves during the absence of mother. The child generally holds the blanket to his or her face, and enjoys auto-erotic comforts such as thumb-sucking and mumbling gently. Winnicott (1971) describes these as transitional objects; they are not mother, and not child, but the repeated use of the object during separations offers a representation of the reality of mother when she is not physically present. This is the child's first use of symbolism: this object is a representation of an external reality which brings inner comfort to the child (Schafer, 1994).

Subsequent research (Ainsworth *et al.*, 1979; Ainsworth, 1989) has developed our understanding of the varied attachment patterns of infants and children, and some of the difficulties that can develop. Ainsworth undertook structured laboratory observations of parents and infants; she concluded that the majority of infants (62% in Ainsworth's sample) formed secure attachments which were rewarding to both partners. Thus 38% presented with disordered attachments of escalating severity, caused mainly by inconsistent or inappropriate parenting. Children whose mothers rejected their attachment behaviours, or ignored attempts at physical contact or emotional access, developed insecure-avoidant attachments in which the parent was actively avoided. Others, whose mothers were unpredictable and insensitive to their children's signals, were assessed as having an insecure-ambivalent attachment, in which the child shows anger or resistance to the parent concurrent with a desire for proximity and contact (Cassidy & Berlin, 1994). Those children who had experienced unusual trauma, such as that associated with abuse, frequently developed insecure-disorganised/disorientated attachments, with strong avoidant behaviour followed by anxious clinging. These children generally exhibit contradictory behaviour in their primary and subsequent attachments, which leads to difficulties within foster homes (James, 1994).

Whilst these writers' concern is to highlight the importance of healthy attachments, psychoanalytic thought has concentrated on the internal meaning of this relationship for the individual child. Understanding of an inner world underpins all psychotherapeutic practice. Much of the activity in this world is carried on at an unconscious level, emerging only in dreams and fantasies. However, the characters and fantasies of this world have a profound influence on each individual's understanding of external reality.

The infant's first relationship with his or her mother is the initial contributor to this inner world. She is perceived as a fragmented being: one that feeds and another that abandons (Klein, 1937). The first task of the child is to bring together these fragments, and understand their connections with one mother. However, the separate parts are internalised, and each has a place in fantasy. They emerge later in fairy stories as wicked witches or fairy godmothers, each representing primitive images of good and evil, loss and recovery, that are experienced as an infant (Cattanach, 1994b).

There are references throughout this book to children's fantasies: the term is used to describe

> 'an imaginary scene in which the subject is protagonist and which is related to wish fulfilment and intrapsychic conflict.'
>
> (Donovan & McIntyre, 1990: p. 27)

However, there are times when children's fantasies are difficult to distinguish from beliefs. For instance, abused or traumatised children can redraw past events in fantasy, and come to believe that real events never happened (Terr, 1990).

The richness of the child's inner world is a vital consideration for any therapist. Later experiences will make inner sense in the light of past events and understandings. A child who experiences nothing but abuse, with no comforting relationships to help him or her, cannot recognise a non-abusive relationship when it is later offered (Waters *et al.*, 1994). The monsters that people the inner world prompt the child to redefine external reality to meet their view of the world (Copley & Forryan, 1987).

Psychoanalysts concentrate on understanding the inner world. Analytically trained art therapists and those qualified in sandplay may also interpret unconscious material. Play workers are rarely trained to interpret such fantasies; however, an understanding of the vitality of the unconscious is essential. In play, giants and monsters will emerge; they may represent the child's own feelings of power or ugliness, or they may symbolise others who have behaved monstrously towards the child. The practitioner can be certain that they have a meaning for this child, and their appearance in his or her play makes sense, if only at an unconscious level.

Occasionally children regress to memories that can only be contained within their inner worlds. I recall the first occasion that a child replayed a birth fantasy; a 3-year-old boy took off his clothes and climbed into the water tray (this occurred on a hot day, and pre-dates current concern about sexual abuse; I would no longer permit any child to remove clothes). He curled up in the water tray, and asked for the cover to be placed on it; having ascertained that he could still breathe I agreed. He then crawled slowly out, and continued to lie, curled up, looking at me. While I struggled to find something useful to say, the child repeated the exercise. When I eventually commented that it was a little like a baby being born he gave me a delighted flash of understanding, and went on to other, infantile, play.

Winnicott's concept of integration has extended our understanding of the psychological tasks of infancy (Winnicott, 1986). Infants experience the world as fragmented, and their primary task is to achieve cohesion of objects and experiences; when this is achieved the child is described as integrated. Until this is accomplished children remain unintegrated, with no coherent understanding of the world and their place in it.

> 'Ego-integration ... has as its basis the continuity of the line of life. The infant self cannot be said to have started until the ego has started, and the beginning and foundation of the self and of identity is this first organisation of the ego that results in going-on-being.'
>
> (Davis & Wallbridge, 1983: p. 33)

The task of the primary carer during this vital stage of development is to hold the baby together until s/he can achieve this for him- or herself. Bion (1962) extended Winnicott's concept of the maternal function of 'holding' the infant by proposing that the mother offers containment to her baby. The infant's confusion is projected onto the mother and understood by her in a process defined as maternal reverie. The mother contains the projections of the child, and the child experiences containment within the mother's emotional world. Healthy containment as an infant is an essential prerequisite to the ability to tolerate mental pain later in life, and the capacity to think about emotions.

These ideas are used extensively in later literature exploring psychotherapeutic work with children. Copley & Forryan (1987) understand the role of the therapist as providing emotional containment for the child, as mothers offer containment to the disjointed ego of the infant. In the safety of therapy, the child can 'fall apart', and bring together the fragments of experience in a way that enables him or her to understand them. By ensuring that the toys and materials are looked after, and that the child is kept safe, the therapist mirrors his or her care for the child. Safely contained, s/he can explore with impunity.

When undertaking an assessment it is often difficult to discover exactly what happened during the first few months of each child's life; the therapist may be dependent on fantasies that emerge during play to give clues as to the health of the child's early attachments and the vitality of relationships that sustained him or her.

Transference and counter-transference

Pivotal to all analytic psychotherapy is the concept of transference. Freud (1905) proposed that the infant's first attachment to his or her mother, and subsequent early experiences with his or her father, provided the basis on which all later relationships and interactions could be understood. All subsequent relationships contain elements of primary feelings and experiences, and difficulties in these relationships can be understood by consideration of the transference of these feelings (Rosenbluth, 1970). This naturally includes any therapeutic relationship, when transference issues are particularly pertinent due to the exclusive and concentrated nature of the interactions.

Most play workers lack the training to interpret transference. However, understanding that feelings the child brings into the playroom generally belong to past relationships and traumas enables the therapist to understand and contain those feelings. At its simplest level, the child who is angry with a mother who has abused him or her will shout at the therapist. At a more complex level, all the child's feelings and behaviours make sense if his or her past is understood:

'No-one can isolate herself from her past experience and ... every experience a person has in the present is intimately tied to everything that has gone before.'

(Cattanach, 1994b: p. 57)

The term counter-transference describes the response of worker to client material. Occasionally, this triggers feelings from the worker's own past. Supervision is essential to help therapists separate feelings that rightly belong to themselves from those projected by the child. Those working with abused children can expect to experience horror and revulsion as their stories unfold. This is a normal, human, reaction to the reality of child abuse, but the feelings have no place in therapy sessions and need to be explored in supervision (Reynolds-Mejia & Levitan, 1990).

The role of defence mechanisms

The term defence mechanisms is used to describe the range of behaviours used by everyone to protect themselves from psychic pain or intolerable anxiety. They are a valid, necessary, part of life. Feelings from childhood and infancy cannot be carried in our conscious minds throughout our lives; we need to repress them and find energy to meet with the challenges of every day.

There is a wide range of behaviours commonly used to cope with emotional demands and each child develops his or her personal means of survival. The worker who sets out to breach the child's defences seeks to leave him or her defenceless, with feelings raw and exposed. When s/he is strong enough to share intimate feelings s/he will do so, knowing that s/he can still cope with situations outside the sessions that may cause anxiety.

Splitting

Infants understand the world in fragments, and divide these into good and bad. Klein (1937) describes how this arrangement of the world enables the child to make sense of the confusion that greets him or her at birth:

> 'It is splitting which allows the ego to emerge out of chaos and to order its experiences. This ordering of experience which occurs with the process of splitting into a good and bad object, however excessive and extreme it may be to begin with, nevertheless orders the universe of the child's emotional and sensory impressions and is a pre-condition of later integration.'

> (Segal, 1986: p. 35)

It is the first step towards making order out of chaos.

With splitting comes the idealisation of the loved object, and rejection of the bad. Healthy infants resolve this in time, and understand that good and bad can co-exist. In a crisis, older children and adults may retreat into splitting, until more age-appropriate defence mechanisms are applied as the individual settles.

Children whose worlds remain chaotic can continue to use splitting to defend themselves from reality. They understand the world solely in terms of good and bad. The imperfect parts of themselves are projected outwards, and seen as threatening. This fragmentation of reality and inability to create a coherent world can eventually emerge as psychosis (Segal, 1986).

Projection and introjection

Projection and introjection are also evident from birth; they permit the child to avoid the impact of overwhelming emotions. Projection involves the passing of a feeling or problem onto another. It is common for mothers to experience the despair of their infants; as the child cries the mother struggles to contain her own panic. It is common for children in therapy to continue to use projection to express feelings that they cannot own themselves (Copley & Forryan, 1987). The therapist experiences waves of feelings that s/he cannot fully explain; the therapeutic role is to contain them without making them one's own. If the worker rejects these feelings too soon, the child may believe that they are so destructive that even an adult cannot tolerate them. If the worker can be patient, and allow the child to see that the feelings have not destroyed him or her, the child will eventually be strong enough to risk owning them for him- or herself.

Introjection is the acceptance of projected feelings, taking responsibility for others' emotions and problems onto oneself. The mother nursing a distressed child rightly introjects his or her unhappiness. If the child feels fully contained and understood as an infant, s/he will develop the ability to hold feelings for him- or herself. The mother who receives the child's projections and keeps them as her own helps neither of them. She is retaining feelings or beliefs that rightly belong to her child.

Many children who are abused introject blame for the abuse. In their immaturity, they do not understand that individuals must carry responsibility for themselves; telling children that abuse is their fault reinforces the process of early introjections and becomes part of the child's unconscious explanations for the mysteries of the world. Fantasies of omnipotence recur endlessly when the child enters therapy; it takes a long time for the reality of the child's helplessness to emerge.

Allied to the concepts of projection and introjection is the experience of projective identification. This is an extension of projection; the child passes his or her feelings and beliefs on to another, and believes that is where they belong. All unwanted pain is transferred to another, and then rejected. At its most extreme, the recipient is at risk of physical attack by the projecting child, who cannot tolerate the rejected aspects of him- or herself (Copley & Forryan, 1987). It is common for very young children to project unwanted aspects of themselves on to a parent or sibling; those who continue to believe these projections can become prey to paranoia as adults.

Repression

We all push painful thoughts and feelings out of consciousness. At times it is essential: if the house is on fire it is more constructive to respond to the emergency and panic later. However, if the feelings are never expressed appropriately, they will emerge in other ways. It takes psychic energy to keep emotions repressed, and they are likely to be triggered by later events that resemble earlier circumstances. For instance, a person made redundant may be surprised by feelings from earlier losses that are confused with the response to the loss of employment.

Whilst repression is a necessary part of individual functioning, its excessive use is problematic. Some people go to extraordinary lengths to avoid facing unwanted feelings, performing complex actions to escape one that is more simple. At its extreme, it becomes obsessional: those who spend hours washing their hands cannot face the reality that we all carry psychic 'dirt' around with us.

Denial

Denial, the refusal to accept that an event has happened, is surprisingly common. It can be impervious to reason and tangible evidence; at its most extreme it becomes negation: inner belief that events have not occurred. It is common for children to deny a wrongdoing in spite of clear indications to the contrary; to an adult their intransigence presents as lying, but the child comes to believe the untruth.

The mechanisms for denial are based in the infantile process of splitting: identifying and rejecting those aspects perceived as unwanted or bad. It is common for intra-familial sexual offenders to share their defence of denial with their victims. It is the basis for the distortions of thinking that are common in perpetrators and survivors of sexual abuse, such as a belief that the survivor actively encouraged his or her abuser.

Idealisation

Children and adults who idealise another have failed to absorb the reality that good and bad can co-exist. Idealisation is common in children: many will look to older children or celebrities and believe that they are flawless. Young adolescents worship distant pop stars or sports personalities. As fantasies, these figures do no harm; they provide the material for day-dreams and the fuel for aspirations.

The child or adult who continues to reject painful feelings is likely to seek perfection where it cannot exist. It is common for small children, separated from their natural parents, to idealise them and their memories of them. The reality of less happy aspects of life at home is denied.

Occasionally a child will idealise his or her therapist. These are not easy feelings to accept. Whilst it may make a pleasant change not to be the recipient of negative projections, the child who idealises the therapist will be unable to share painful feelings with him or her for fear of contaminating a perfect individual (Powell, 1991). The therapist should openly acknowledge that s/he is human and makes mistakes, and can also contain difficult emotions or behaviours without becoming damaged in him- or herself.

Reaction formation

Many children respond to difficult situations by substituting opposite feelings from those that are appropriate. The most common example is the child who laughs while being scolded: the pertinent response would be to hang his or her head, possibly cry, and certainly look remorseful. Unable to express guilt or regret, the child responds with giggles. This reaction tends to produce even greater fury in the adult, resulting in an escalation of the original confrontation.

On other occasions, children who have been severely abused and cannot reach their anger respond with apparent timidity and speak very quietly. It is important, when assessing a child's response to current or past events, to recognise that an overt reaction may mask opposite feelings.

Dissociation

All children dissociate at times (Donovan & McIntyre, 1990): they become engrossed in an activity or fantasy and are oblivious to all other stimuli. However, there has been increased attention in recent years to children who dissociate as a response to abuse (James, 1989; Wilson *et al.*, 1992; Sinason, 1994) or loss (Irwin, 1994). In order to avoid fully experiencing pain and degradation, these children are able to split their psychic from their physical reality, watching events from a distance but not being fully part of them. It becomes a

'fixed way to avoid the pain of psychological abuse.'

(McElroy, 1992: p. 839).

It is an effective response to extreme abuse, enabling the child to continue with family or school life alongside abusive episodes.

Dissociation in response to abuse, although adaptive at the time, is destructive to the individual's long-term psychic health.

'The cost to the victim is of psychological helplessness, being taken over by apparently spontaneous episodes of altered states, during which cognition, physiology and affect may all be adversely affected; all systems become state dependent in their function.'

(Conway, 1994: p. 257)

Unexpected events may cue a retreat into the altered state; the individual is unable to control or predict his or her responses. At its extreme, children separate from the abused part of themselves, and present with multiple personalities (Mollon, 1994).

The contribution of Erikson

Erikson (1977) proposed that each individual faces a succession of psychological tasks, and the successful outcome of these tasks leads to personal equilibrium and the ability to achieve emotional satisfaction. He defines these as the 'eight ages of man' (Erikson, 1977: pp. 222–46). Whilst this term is now unacceptably sexist, the concepts which underpin it remain valid.

Erikson defines eight stages for the individual to negotiate:

- Basic trust *v* basic mistrust
- Autonomy *v* shame and doubt
- Initiative *v* guilt
- Industry *v* inferiority
- Identity *v* role confusion
- Intimacy *v* isolation
- Generativity *v* stagnation
- Ego integrity *v* despair

Only the first five are discussed here, as these concern the child and adolescent.

Basic trust v *basic mistrust*

The primary task of the infant is to develop a sense of basic trust in his or her surroundings and caregivers:

'The infant's first social achievement ... is his willingness to let his mother out of his sight without undue anxiety or rage, because she has become an inner certainty as well as an outer predictability. Such consistency, continuity, and sameness of experience provide a rudimentary sense of ego identity which depends ... on the recognition that there is an inner population of remembered and anticipated sensations and images which are firmly correlated with the outer population of familiar and predictable things and people.'

(Erikson, 1977: p. 222)

Wilson *et al.* (1992) underpin their practice of non-directive play therapy with Erikson's ideas, using his understanding to help assess each child's struggle to achieve psychological comfort. Children who have not achieved basic trust attempt to destroy situations which they cannot understand; great tolerance and patience is required of the worker, who must continue to offer an experience which challenges the child's expectations, hoping that eventually the certainty of therapy will tempt the child to risk an element of trust.

Autonomy v shame and doubt

With physical maturity comes a need to climb over, under, into and behind everything. With the egocentricity of young children, prohibitions of adults are inexplicable; they cannot understand why this is the moment when they must put on a heavy coat and be strapped in a chair. Time, space and freedom are essential if young children are to achieve real autonomy. Independence is accomplished by repeated trial and error; too many restrictions and the child learns that exploration is dangerous or worthless. Similarly, the child whose exploits are ignored or devalued learns that achievements are insignificant. This does not imply that the family condones the anarchy of the toddler. The child must be kept safe; s/he needs certainty and containment as much as s/he did as an infant.

Chaotic households cannot contain the toddler in this way: limits change from day to day. The child's emotions escape in a comparably unpredictable way, and life has no certainty. These children have great difficulties when the drives of adolescence emerge. Without the experience of external limits restricting their behaviour as toddlers, they develop no internal controls on their behaviours. They are at the mercy of unexpected impulses and drives.

In therapy many children return to the messy exploration of the toddler. They need the space and freedom to make discoveries for themselves, and have their explorations validated. The worker provides materials, and consistent limits; s/he may also reflect pride in the child's achievements until s/he can discover this for him- or herself.

Initiative v guilt

As the child grows, s/he begins to gain control of the bewildering feelings that beset him or her during toddlerhood, and presents as more settled. S/he is more realistic about his or her abilities and ambitions, and can begin to role play: simple games of cooking tea develop into more complex roles derived from television programmes and from fantasy.

This stage also marks the time when children reach an understanding of gender-related roles. Both genders may experience shame and guilt as a result of destructive fantasies, which is resolved when the child settles into his or her appropriate, childish, roles. Well-maintained intra-familial boundaries and a strong marital bond help the child to readjust these fantasies. In families where adult relationships are conflictual, or there is overt abuse, children struggle to realise a same-sex identification and remain confused and unhappy in their relationships with adults.

Children who carry guilt and shame from this stage tend to continue to see themselves as responsible for everything during the ensuing years. This will heighten if the child feels responsible for embodying the wishes of his or her parents. Some parents limit the child's behaviour as they believe it reflects badly on themselves. Some need the child to increase their own self-esteem; others ask their children to parent them (Covitz, 1986). A child with parents who cannot permit free expression will experience guilt about his or her feelings; in fantasy s/he will see these feelings as potentially harmful.

Industry v *inferiority*

This stage lasts from 7 until 11 years old. If the child has completed previous stages successfully s/he will be ready for the rigours of school.

This developmental change is recognised in all cultures; it is the stage where children are expected to receive instruction as to the workings of the world. In western society this involves going to school, becoming part of a system and sub-culture that is separated from the family. In this context children increase in competence, grow in intellectual and physical skills, and develop a social identity. Close friendships are formed with other children; organised games bring notions of rules and fair play.

Children who do not develop an inner satisfaction when mastering intellectual, physical or social tasks will flounder at this stage (Wilson *et al.*, 1992). Children judge themselves in relation to each other; those who are different may be bullied and become miserable at school. Race, gender, home circumstances, disability, appearance: any unusual feature can result in bullying from other children (Lane, 1992; Tattum, 1993). Those who do not enter school with self-esteem built during their early years, will find the rough-and-tumble of school life extremely difficult.

Identity v *role confusion*

It is impossible to overestimate the turmoil of the adolescent (Smith & Cowie, 1991). After several peaceful years sudden physical maturation, hormonal imbalance, familial and societal expectations of greater personal responsibility, and increased academic pressure combine to make this a time of great upheaval.

During the early stages of adolescence young people commonly feel out of control; some worry that they might be mad. Inner turmoil is reflected in unpredictable behaviour; they become easily upset or angry, and are inconsistent in their willingness to accept comfort. A secure base (Hipgrave, 1985), in the form of stability within a family or residential home, provides a safe context for this upheaval; adolescents without this solidity find the process all the more stressful.

Few young people who have reached this stage are referred for therapeutic play. However, those whose early years were full of abuse and confusion struggle to cope with the upheaval of adolescence. Those who care for them may seek help, possibly hoping that attention to the deficits of their early years will help with current crises. Practitioners who work with older children must adopt a flexible approach, adapting their interventions to meet the fluctuating needs of the young person.

The importance of play

'Child's play is often described as the territory between the real world and the child's inner world.'

(Sjolund & Schaefer, 1994)

Winnicott (1971) considered play as part of the world of both the mother and child, and yet disconnected from them. As the child becomes aware of him- or herself as a separate individual, play becomes an external symbol of the fantasies in his or her inner world. It reflects both events in the real world, and the interpretation of the real world by the child's unconscious processes (Schafer, 1994). The play of the older child bridges the self and environment, mirroring its original manifestation in the space between the mother and infant.

Lowenfeld (1935) first studied the content of children's play, and analysed its facets and importance to normal child development. She emphasised how essential the play experience is to every child:

'Play in childhood is the expression of the child's relation to the whole of life, and no theory of play is possible which is not also a theory which will cover the whole of the child's relation to life.'

(p. 36)

Lowenfeld understood play to include every spontaneous or self-generated activity in which the child participates.

She divides the different aspects of child's play into:

- Play as a bodily activity,
- Play as a repetition of experience,
- Play as a demonstration of fantasy,
- Play as preparation for life.

The play worker hopes that play brought to a therapy session will be a repetition of past experience. Lowenfeld understood this activity as part of a basic human need, first identified by Freud (1920), to recreate compulsively any disturbing event in activity, either physically or verbally, until the individual has mastered the complex feelings associated with it:

'There seems to be a strong inner drive in all human minds to externalize themselves, or to re-create their experiences in order to be able to assimilate them, and the small child in relation to its early experiences is no exception.'

(p.107)

The mechanism whereby events and feelings are brought into conscious thought, considered, mastered and returned to memory, is an important process. Children who are unable to play cannot externalise experience in this way. Child's play, when it involves the externalisation and assimilation of events into the child's reality, is the prelude to adult thought and problem-solving. Adults no longer need toys to express themselves, but those materials are the foundation for later thinking and understanding (Singer, 1994).

Lowenfeld understands play to be a demonstration of fantasy, which she describes as:

'the name given to that kind of mental functioning which was earlier called day-dreaming or reverie, and which stands in opposition to imagination and controlled thought.'

(Lowenfeld, 1935: p. 149)

Thus fantasy reflects the contents of the child's inner world; its expression in play allows the child to bring unconscious material to the fore, and compare it with external reality. Lowenfeld invited children in therapy to create a succession of different Worlds in sand, which she understood as reflecting the child's inner world. Using this method she enabled children to express fantasies, explore the reality of past events, and resolve anxieties (see Chapter 7).

Both Winnicott and Lowenfeld have contributed much to our understanding of why children enjoy play, and its unique place in their natural development. McMahon (1992) describes it succinctly:

'The pleasure and excitement of playing, the intensity and concentration, the freedom to experiment, to explore and to create, to find out how things and people work and what you can do with them, to give imagination free rein, and to fill the gap between reality and desire, all these derive from the fact that in play the child is in charge.'

(McMahon, 1992: p. 1)

Jennings (1993) has added to our understanding of children's play by showing how it changes as the child grows and develops. She describes the first stage as embodiment play: the child uses his or her physical resources alone to explore the world. This play occurs during the first year of life, when each physical achievement – sitting, rolling, standing – is greeted with delight.

Children explore every nook and cranny of their bodies, seeking to understand its abilities and sensations. During this stage children need freedom to enjoy this play, in the context of sufficient physical and emotional containment to ensure feelings of safety and trust. Children who are not contained adequately fail to develop an understanding of a body-self: the essential preliminary to an understanding of body-image. Children who are over-protected may become fearful of exploring, and have difficulties achieving autonomy.

During the second and third years of life the child gradually extends into projective play, in which he or she begins to use symbols to express feelings and describe an inner world. S/he is introduced to small toys and materials, and slowly develops the ability to use them symbolically. First activities are likely to involve sorting and arranging; gradually toys assume representative significance and play is imbued with meaning. There are many reasons why this play may fail to develop: serious illness or hospitalization may restrict the child's mobility; abuse or neglect within the family may limit his or her freedom; parents who emphasise educational activities may fail to appreciate the importance of this stage.

As children grow and develop they come to enjoy dramatic and role play. In this stage they revel in performing plays and recreating the world around them in drama. This does not have to occur in groups: teddies and dolls can be pupils to a stern teacher, or patients to the young doctor. This play begins with impersonations of people or roles with which the child is familiar. It extends to genuine role play: in his or her head the child is not pretending to be mummy; s/he *is* mummy. S/he may need time to adjust to being a child before returning to family life.

The play of children with few or inconsistent role models is impoverished. They cannot build on the real world in their drive to understand its reality. Some will look to television or fictional characters to provide roles to play. For some children, these roles can assume exceptional importance in the child's life: those whose lives are characterised by neglect or abuse may find more excitement if they see the world as Superman or Peter Pan. Therapists should never underestimate the strength or significance of such fantasy roles; it may even be necessary to discover whether the child is him- or herself or another when s/he arrives for a session.

Cattanach (1994b) agrees with Jennings' description of the stages of children's play. She adds her observation that imaginative play can be divided into object-independent fantasy play, in which children evoke imaginary worlds, and object-dependent fantasies, in which existing objects become part of the fantasy. Object-dependent children often construct arrangements and patterns of existing toys, rearranging them as they tell a story. Object-independent children can incorporate real objects into fantasies, but their creative play is not reliant on external materials. Children tend to favour one form of play over another, and both provide opportunities for healthy expression of feelings.

Landreth (1991) points out that the play of disturbed children rarely follows the predictable pattern of their healthy contemporaries. Practitioners can anticipate erratic development of play skills, and unexpected use of materials.

Post traumatic stress disorder (PTSD)

Some practitioners find the concept of post traumatic stress disorder (PTSD) helps to evaluate and understand a child's difficulties and experiences. Post traumatic stress disorder is classified as an anxiety disorder by the American Psychiatric Association (1987). Onset is always associated with a psychologically traumatic event that is generally outside the range of normal human experience.

Diagnostic criteria include the following:

(1) Existence of a recognisable stressor that would evoke significant symptoms of distress in almost everyone.
(2) Re-experiencing of the trauma as evidenced by at least one of the following: recurrent and intrusive recollections of the event, recurrent distressing dreams of the event, sudden acting or feeling as if the traumatic event were recurring, intense psychological distress at exposure to events that symbolise or resemble the trauma, including anniversaries of the event.
(3) Persistent avoidance of stimuli associated with the trauma, or numbing of responsiveness to or reduced responsiveness with the external world, beginning some time after the trauma, as shown by at least three of the following – efforts to avoid thoughts or feelings associated with the trauma, efforts to avoid activities or situations that arouse memories of the trauma, inability to recall important aspects of the event, markedly diminished interest in one or more significant activities, feelings of detachment or estrangement from others, restricted range of effect, a foreshortened sense of future.
(4) Persistent symptoms, not present before the trauma, such as sleep difficulties, irritability or bursts of anger, difficulty concentrating, hypervigilance, exaggerated startle response, physiological reaction to events that resemble or symbolise the trauma.
(5) Disturbance that continues for at least a month (American Psychiatric Association, 1987: pp. 250–51).

Research has shown that there are differences in children's and adults' responses to trauma (Terr, 1990); children are especially affected by recurrent and intrusive memories of the event, often emerging in repetitive play, and a marked diminished interest in significant activities. Terr also suggests that children who perceive that they have some control over the situation in which they find themselves find recovery easier than those who experience extreme helplessness.

Many of those children who have survived major disasters such as the fire at the Bradford football stadium or the capsize and sinking of the *Herald of Free Enterprise* showed clear evidence of PTSD (Yule & Williams, 1992). Research suggests that children who survive prolonged sexual or physical abuse (Johnson, 1991), or who witness marital violence (Mullender & Morley, 1994) exhibit similar symptoms. Road traffic accidents and serious illness are also interpreted by a child as traumatic.

Victims do not experience a traumatic event as a coherent whole, but as a series of fragmented incidents. Normal reactions include a flight/fight response, followed by emotional numbing. They struggle to tolerate memories of the event, and their reaction to it (Hartman & Burgess, 1993). During this process victims can be beset with repetitive and intrusive memories, whilst defence mechanisms try to block these recollections (Carroll, 1994).

This is a normal reaction to an abnormal event, and many children – and adults – need help to assimilate trauma before they can carry on with their lives. If this help is unavailable, either because no-one recognises the victim's distress, or the victim cannot acknowledge his or her need for help, the severe disorientation consequent to the trauma may lead to prolonged and entrenched behavioural and emotional disturbance.

Children who are repeatedly abused cannot recover from one incident before they are forced to face another. Some children witness domestic aggression as often as twice a week (Cooper, 1992), while survivors of sexual abuse testify to the terror of frequent abusive episodes (Ben, 1991; Sandford, 1991). Thus they may remain permanently in a state of post-traumatic shock, numbed by feelings of helplessness, vulnerability, and loss of control.

James (1989) evaluates the process of trauma resolution by considering nine traumagenic states. Consideration of these states provides guidelines for evaluating the impact of trauma, and can lead to the formulation of treatment plans. If some or all of the traumagenic states exist in a child, the practitioner can look for possible behavioural manifestations. She lists her nine traumagenic states as:

(1) *Self-blame.* Close exploration exposes the child's deep-rooted belief that s/he is responsible for everything bad that happens to and around him or her.

(2) *Powerlessness.* Helpless children cannot believe that they can ever recover from past experiences. Their feelings of powerlessness are exhibited in behaviour which seems designed to maintain their role as victims, or bullying aimed at warding off potential threats.

(3) *Loss and betrayal.* Betrayed children have lost the childish fantasy that their world is safe. This may be through abuse, a life-threatening illness, or the death of a parent. There is often intense denial of the traumatic event.

(4) *Fragmentation of bodily experiences.* These children feel that they have lost mastery of their own bodies, its functions and feelings, through the trauma. They need help to reintegrate the experience as a cohesive episode.

(5) *Stigmatisation.* Stigmatised children feel a profound sense of shame and separation from other children because of their experiences. No achievement can compensate for the total loss of self-worth.

(6) *Eroticisation.* Children who have learned that they can use sex to attract adults, or were rewarded for inappropriate sexual behaviour, are often preoccupied with, and confused about, sexual matters.

(7) *Destructiveness.* These children often seek retribution for past abuse. They perceive the destruction of all around them as essential for their own survival. They may identify with an aggressor, and seek punishment on his or her behalf.

(8) *Dissociative states/multiple personality disorder.* It is common for severely abused children to dissociate from the experience. Many of these children continue to dissociate whenever anything unpleasant happens. Extremes of this manifest as multiple personality disorder: the individual assumes a number of different persona, only one of which acknowledges and experiences the abuse.

(9) *Attachment disorder.* Children with disordered attachments are unable to utilise supportive and loving care when it is offered to them. The most common complaint of those who care for them is their inability to respond emotionally.

Many of these symptoms, or traumagenic states, are familiar to those who work with survivors of sexual abuse. James's point is that they are aspects of endurance of abuse that may emerge in survivors of any trauma, and should therefore be considered when any child is brought for therapy, and their significance for this child thoroughly assessed:

'By considering possible traumagenic states when evaluating a child, the therapist may determine, for example, that the child has a significant attachment impairment, no dissociative disorder or destructive behaviour but some degree of feeling powerless, feelings of loss/betrayal, and a significant amount of self-blame. This profile then becomes the framework that the clinician can use to develop a specific, detailed treatment plan.'

(James, 1989: p. 38)

Doyle & Stoop (1991) illustrate the application of James's concepts in their work with Randy, a multiply abused 10-year-old boy. His mother was addicted to heroin, and sold him into prostitution to pay for drugs when he was 3. He witnessed his mother having intercourse and, on one occasion, saw her shoot a client who was abusing her. He was present when his beloved aunt died of a heart attack. At 7, he was enticed into ritual abuse. He set fire to an aunt's home, leading to the death of four members of the family. Not surprisingly, the symptoms he presented were extensive: he continued to set fires, displayed a range of self-destructive behaviours such as playing on railway lines and attempting suicide, had nightmares, was sexually provocative and aggressive, abused drugs and alcohol, and was unable to identify or express his feelings verbally. Any practitioner faced with such a child would need a framework to help analyse the difficulties, and assess the work that needed to be done. Using James's concept of traumagenic states, Doyle & Stoop considered the issues which would need to be addressed during therapy, and included powerlessness, destructiveness, eroticisation, self-blame, stigmatisation, fragmentation of bodily experience, betrayal and loss, as well as possible dissociative states (1991: p. 117). This gave a framework to the worker, who might otherwise have been overwhelmed by the extent of Randy's difficulties.

Practitioners vary in the extent to which they utilise the concept of PTSD. It must be stressed that it is a condition that can only be diagnosed with any certainty by a qualified medical practitioner. Nevertheless, workers without medical training will recognise many of these symptoms. My own view is that it is helpful to understand how individuals experience trauma, and the process that is necessary for healthy recovery. I find it valuable to understand common reactions of children who have struggled to survive trauma, and the behavioural and emotional difficulties which might ensue. I am less sure that I need a label of PTSD for a child who has survived years of abuse, and is exhibiting symptoms of sleep disturbance, numbing of feelings, lack of self-worth, intrusive thoughts, flashbacks, etc., although I acknowledge that children with severe symptoms may need psychiatric oversight. My main concern is to understand what this experience means to this child, rather than attach labels.

Summary

The contribution made by psychologists and psychoanalysts to our understanding of human development and behaviour is extensive.

Comprehension that many current feelings, beliefs and behaviours have their roots in infant experience is essential for practitioners offering therapeutic play to children. Much of the material that emerges during sessions is drawn from an inner world, brought into reality and expressed symbolically, and returned to the unconscious mastered and understood.

The psychoanalytic concept of transference has made a valuable contribution to our comprehension of interactions that occur during therapy. The therapist can expect the child to bring feelings from past attachments and circumstances, which colour the therapeutic relationship. Untrained practitioners should not attempt to explore unconscious material, but comprehension of this process promotes tolerance of the projections of children.

Everyone has complex defence mechanisms which they use for protection from pain and anxiety. Some are present in infancy, others develop during childhood. These defences should not be breached; they have offered protection to the child until now and s/he will share hidden feelings when s/he is ready. S/he should not be left defenceless.

Erikson's (1977) 'eight ages of man' has offered an alternative view of human development, although there are many overlaps with psychoanalytic thought. His description of psychological tasks that are concurrent with each stage of development forms a valuable foundation on which an accurate assessment of a child's difficulties can be made.

Psychoanalysts and psychologists have also considered the meaning of children's play. A belief in the importance of play is the cornerstone of therapeutic play: play is not a peripheral activity, to be indulged in when there is nothing better to do. It is an essential component of normal child development; it is a means of communication and mastery; it is the bridge between the child's inner world and external reality; it provides the medium for healing hurt and damaged children; and it is fun.

Some practitioners find the concept of PTSD valuable, as it explains the disorientation and emotional numbing that is common following trauma. Some survivors cannot resolve these feelings and resume normal life: in these circumstances entrenched difficulties may ensue which require therapeutic intervention.

Chapter 3

The Essential Assessment

Introduction

Every child referred for therapeutic play needs a thorough initial assessment leading to a provisional diagnosis and consideration of appropriate techniques. The strengths, weaknesses and difficulties of each child are examined in depth. A suitable intervention can then be selected for this child.

On other occasions practitioners are asked to undertake an assessment of a child's needs and difficulties, and to share these with other professionals who are involved in care planning for the child. Social workers, residential workers, foster carers and resource centre workers, as well as play therapists, are familiar with assessments of this nature. Many areas of concern raised in this chapter are familiar to social workers undertaking *Orange Book* assessments (Department of Health, 1988). In addition, Guardians *ad litem* undertake comparable evaluations of children, and are directed to put the wishes and feelings of the child before the court (DHSS, 1984).

Much of the same information is needed for both assessments. However, the latter is time-limited. The practitioner's relationship with child, family and referring agency must acknowledge the short-term nature of the relationship.

The task of the worker is to understand the child's view of the world, to make sense of the context in which s/he lives, and to share this with those who care for him or her.

Assessment as a preparation for therapeutic play

The components of an assessment preparatory to therapy are:

(1) Consideration of reasons for the referral and current symptoms of distress.
(2) A family history.
(3) A history of the child, including his or her education and health.
(4) An assessment of social, ethnic and cultural background.

(5)   Details of other people who may be, or have been, important to the child.
(6)   A preliminary consideration of the child's defence mechanisms.

This framework includes material which may be impossible to collect. Social workers, health visitors, nursery or playgroup workers, teachers or other community workers may provide some of this information; parents may contribute a substantial amount. Assessment of the child's play can provide clues to individual functioning and difficulties. In my experience, the information most difficult to obtain is details of the child's early development and attachment. The child's response to the playroom may provide clues, but my conclusions remain tentative: I might be wrong.

Consideration of reasons for the referral and current symptoms of distress

There are many behaviours which prompt a request for help. Attention should be given to the meaning of behaviours to this child, their impact on his or her social, intellectual or emotional functioning, and the professional response to evidence of the child's distress.

Some symptoms are indicative of turmoil, and an inability to regulate emotional effect. Children are subject to disconcerting emotional responses, and cannot be expected to control themselves all the time. However, the child whose moods swing unpredictably will be bewildered by such feelings. Other children have a limited range of emotional responses: they appear perpetually angry; closer questioning reveals a child who cannot differentiate grief, jealousy, envy, greed, sorrow or other difficult feelings from anger (Wilkes, 1987).

Symptoms such as aggressive behaviour or encopresis can have a profound impact on the child's daily life (Sluckin, 1981). Children with anti-social behaviours are able to draw attention to their distress easily. Others, who suffer with symptoms such as eating disorders or extreme withdrawal, may bring little opprobrium, and the child continues to experience discomfort for many months before professional help is sought.

Children whose symptoms are unusual, or who present with obsessively repetitive behaviours, may benefit from psychiatric intervention. There is a possibility that extreme withdrawal, or sleep disturbance, may be indicative of depression (Aylward, 1985; Black, 1987). Similarly, physical difficulties such as soiling require medical assessment before it can be assumed that the origin is entirely emotional.

Consideration of the child's history can often provide an explanation of apparently bizarre behaviours. Eight-year-old Adam's foster mother was perplexed by continual bedwetting. Medical examinations found no physical problem; medication was largely unsuccessful, and a 'pad and bell' were inappropriate as he shared the bedroom with his foster brother. After four months of play therapy he disclosed that his elder brother, who had abused him, was repelled by a wet bed: thus he tried to protect himself. Rearrangement of the sleeping facilities within the family, so that Adam could sleep alone, led to a marked improvement in his bedwetting.

The impact on those who care for the child, whether birth or foster parent, teacher or nursery nurse, is often the factor that prompts an assessment for therapeutic play. The context of the referral, the effect of the child's behaviour on those around him or her, and the reason for seeking help at this time are important indicators of the adult response to this child's symptoms.

A family history

'The history is the most important part of the evaluation, because without the context it defines and its priming effect on the clinical encounter with the child the risks of blind clinical interview rise dramatically.'

(Donovan & McIntyre, 1990: pp. 76–7)

Some practitioners suggest seeing the child with no prior knowledge of his or her difficulties. I try to gather as much information as possible before that first meeting: thus any embarrassment or ridiculous questioning is avoided (such as asking the bereaved child if he or she lives with mummy and daddy). Much of this information should be available in social work records. Many children come from extremely complex families, and disentangling this can be a challenge. If the worker finds it confusing, it is likely that the child will too!

Donovan & McIntyre (1990) advocate that all aspects of family life should be explored at this initial meeting, including any problem behaviours the child may exhibit or adult 'secrets' which the child is meant not to know. If adult material needs more detailed discussion it can be done separately, but the introductory interview should establish a norm of openness and honesty about difficulties and challenges facing each family. Whilst this approach may be valid for birth families, it is less applicable for children in foster care. These children will have difficulties connected with separation from their natural families, and may or may not have additional problems relating to their current carers.

Stresses on parents may have serious consequences for the child. Children of parents who abuse alcohol or drugs live with unpredictable parental behaviour, for which many feel responsible (Priest, 1985; Robinson, 1989). Harriet, aged 4, was removed from the care of her single mother following her repeated admissions to psychiatric hospital. It was important to understand the florid nature of her mother's symptoms in order to comprehend the difficulties Harriet had forming attachments.

Family relationships are often extremely complex. Family therapists are familiar with situations in which children carry the symptoms of parents' conflicts: children cannot be relieved of these symptoms without their parents also receiving help (Barker, 1981; Covitz, 1986). Roles become distorted or enmeshed; children cannot be disentangled from these relationships without help for the whole family. Consultation with a family therapist (where these are available) can assist in the appraisal of children whose distress or behaviour appears to stem from family difficulties.

Families who experience sudden trauma will be disorganised and confused. It may be difficult to assess the strengths of a family prior to the trauma, but these will re-emerge as the crisis begins to resolve. It is wise to be alert to fantasies of family life prior to the traumatic event, as individuals may embellish reality.

Many children replay scenes from family life during play sessions. However, caution should be exercised when interpreting domestic play; it will include fantasy as well as day-to-day material. For instance, the child who plays at being shut in a cupboard may indeed have been locked away; s/he may also feel excluded from important events that are absorbing his or her caregivers.

Therapists cannot ignore the impact of television on family life. Some families permit their children to watch television and videos freely; others censor programmes rigorously. Whilst research is not complete on the impact of television violence on young children, Gill (1996) confirms the view of many professionals who are appalled by the material some young children are permitted to watch. The problem is even more acute for children who have witnessed or survived violence, as the images on film may mirror their own reality, thus blurring the distinction between internal and external experience (Mapp, 1994).

It is helpful to know family attitudes to nudity and sexual matters. Some families encourage discussion of these issues; others refuse to speak of them. Many insist that they answer children's questions, but admit an embarrassment with the subject. Other families are unable to maintain appropriate sexual boundaries between adults and children.

Relationships and attachments within the child's immediate family need a thorough appraisal. Fahlberg (1988a) offers guidelines for assessing the strength of attachments between children of different ages and their parents or foster carers. Observations of the ease of interactions between adult and child, and the existence of appropriate boundaries, all give clues to the nature of familial attachments. I seek to identify anyone likely to offer support to the child during the difficult times of therapy, and consider whether individuals within the family will be jealous of the attention given to this child. The rivalry of a sibling (or parent) can undermine the most constructive therapy.

A *history of the child, including his or her education and health*

This personal history should begin with an assessment of the child's birth and infancy. It may be difficult to obtain details of an older child's experiences during his or her pre-school years: health visitors see these children less frequently, and, unless the family is known to a statutory agency, there may be few objective records. Not all parents are honest about difficulties they experience with their children; they may blame themselves or feel ashamed that they cannot manage difficult behaviour.

The impact of sudden trauma during these years may go unrecognised. The significance of events such as a house fire or serious road accident is rarely acknowledged: it is not until the practitioner is faced with picture after picture of car crashes that the impact on the child is acknowledged. Eight-year-old Terry had been cared for by foster parents for some years before efforts were made to help her understand why she did not live at home. When she repeatedly painted pictures of a house fire, her worker made further investigations of Terry's history: she had, indeed, been rescued from a fire when she was 3 years old. Shortly after this Terry left the care of her mother. She now believed that she could not live at home because the house burnt down; she had no understanding of the physical abuse she also experienced.

It is helpful to know about the child's early educational experiences, his or her attendance at playgroup or nursery, and how s/he fared when first attending school. Evidence of separation anxiety or any difficulties relating to other children is also valuable. Some indication of his or her intellectual capacity is helpful, as is an assessment of the contribution emotional difficulties may have made to any educational delay: this information can best be supplied by an educational psychologist. Teachers are in an excellent position to observe the consequences of stressful situations at home: children unable to contain their distress or anxiety about difficulties at home often respond with altered behaviour at school (Kurtz *et al.*, 1993).

Health visitors or social workers may have details of the child's physical development, and the ages at which milestones were reached. They should be able to provide information about any physical disability or past illnesses, especially those which involved a hospital admission. Prolonged separations from home, or invasive medical procedures which caused distress and fear, may emerge later in play (Crompton, 1991). A disability may inhibit efforts to play, or lead to rejection at home. Even relatively minor difficulties, such as a hearing loss in one ear, are relevant: the therapist should always sit on the child's hearing side.

Practitioners should be alert to the possibility that the child is being abused or neglected (Kempe & Kempe, 1978). Child Protection Services are always willing to discuss any concerns that may arise.

The child's contribution is the most important component to this assessment (Sjolund & Schaefer, 1994; Ryan & Wilson, 1996). Children communicate more readily through play than with words. Such symbolic messages are not always easy to comprehend, and may be particularly difficult to unravel during a few introductory sessions; persistent efforts to understand the child's experience may be rewarded in time (Garbarino & Scott, 1989; Bannister *et al.*, 1990). Distressed children need the opportunity to have their voices heard, to be believed and allowed to express their feelings safely, by someone who makes the effort to understand both verbal and symbolic communications.

Accurate assessment of the significance of a child's play is extremely difficult. Perry & Landreth (1991) have formulated a play therapy observational instrument: a scale on which behaviours are measured. They assess the child's social skills, his or her emotional effect and use of fantasy; manifestations of these three aspects are measured, and tentative conclusions made. However, the authors recognise that further research is needed into children's play and measurements of its significance.

I undertake a minimum of four, with a preference for six, assessment play sessions. For children under 12, I always begin by using non-directive play therapy techniques. In my experience, observation of a child's free play gives the clearest preliminary idea of his or her difficulties. For instance, Jenny emptied the contents of my toybag onto the floor, explored each item for about 30 seconds, and then scattered them around the room in a haphazard fashion. She frequently made to leave the room, and needed company during visits to the toilet to ensure that colleagues were not disturbed. At no time did she seek my company, nor look for a response. I concluded, from this play alone, that Jenny lacked personal boundaries, and it was likely that her inner world was chaotic.

For many children, it is a combination of observation of the child's play together with an understanding of his or her history that provides essential clues. Alan came from a large and complex family, in which the living space was generally full of adults drinking and watching television. He explored my toys methodically, selecting the small animals to take into a corner to play. He enacted scenes of animals repeatedly eating each other, and indulging in vicious fights. At the end of the session, everything was tidied away. Alan was playing in corners with me, as I suspected he played in corners at home. The content of his play included some violent fantasies, and I considered that he was likely to be extremely angry with those adults who could not give him the emotional and physical space that he needed.

With early adolescents, or articulate and worldly wise younger children, I select a range of focused techniques. Like every practitioner, I have my favourites: *squiggles* will engage all but the most reluctant, and help to establish a relationship. *King or queen of the island* provides a view of factors that are important, and those that are abhorrent, to the child or young person. I embark on direct discussion of the child's feelings only when the relationship is established, and generally use the *list of feelings* and *emotional barometer* to help children to begin to consider their emotions (see Chapter 6).

The projections of children during these initial sessions are valid indicators, both of defence mechanisms and past attachments. Some attachment disordered children are over-friendly; they exhibit no preliminary caution and seek physical closeness from the moment of introduction. Others are superficially polite, but unable to make emotional contact. Some become so anxious when meeting someone new that they cannot enter the playroom without the reassuring presence of a parent or foster carer.

Projections are a vital diagnostic aid as they give clues as to how the child may be feeling even when his or her verbal communications are non-committal. Children who project during assessment sessions are likely to do so indiscriminately; they will feel chaotic and uncontained, and are likely to produce highly disturbed behaviour.

An assessment of social, ethnic and cultural background

Great importance should be attached to this issue, and family practices of children from other cultures or social backgrounds fully understood (Ryan & Walker, 1993). Practitioners must take care that they refrain from judging child-rearing practices which they do not understand and with which they cannot empathise. Some cultures feel that open expression of emotion, including anger, is a virtue. Others teach children to repress all outward expression of feeling (O'Hagan, 1993). In addition, research into emotional development has largely taken place among healthy, and relatively wealthy, children. Those whose families live in grinding poverty, who struggle in the decay of inner cities, cannot realistically be compared with their more fortunate contemporaries. Practitioners must be vigilant in their efforts to understand the contexts in which all children live.

Therapists working with black children not only need an understanding of the child's cultural background but should also be attentive to the child's experience of living in a white-dominated culture. Black children whose families keep their cultural history alive cannot avoid the reality that the society they live in seeks to marginalise their heritage.

'Most black children in white dominated societies are reinforced positively when they show signs of adjustment and acceptance to society and its values, even when the said society is so often hostile and rejecting to them as black people.'

(Maxime, 1993: p. 98)

Mixed race children may have extensive difficulties resolving conflicting societal messages (Tizard & Phoenix, 1994). White therapists should also be in touch with their own response as a white adult offering help to a black child (Stubbs, 1989).

Islamic children may feel particularly misunderstood in a political climate and social culture which challenges many of their customs and beliefs. Many Asian children come from families with a strong work ethic, derived from an economic need for all members of the family, including the children, to work (Moyles, 1989). Practitioners assessing these children should take account of cultural attitudes to play, and the difficulty some parents may have in recognising its therapeutic value.

Therapists may also be asked to consider the therapeutic needs of refugees. Some of these children are separated from their families as well as displaced culturally (Cervi, 1995). Some will have little or no spoken English. They may have witnessed atrocities within their own countries. Many have experienced sudden separation from all that is familiar. They are bewildered and frightened, and require an extremely sensitive response.

Details of other people who may be, or have been, important to the child

A therapeutic alliance with those caring for the child is an essential component of therapy. The foundations for this alliance can be built during the assessment stage, ensuring that all the adults concerned for the child are working together for his or her recovery.

All significant relationships and events need consideration. The child may have found someone to trust, but been moved away. This relationship was important: it implies that s/he is capable of feeling safe enough to expose vulnerability and neediness. Those with whom the child now lives are essential allies for practitioners working with these children; it is helpful to understand the strengths and weaknesses of these families to enable them to offer support and security to the child in therapy. The worker should be aware of any difficulties within this family: for instance, if the presence of a foster child is causing difficulty for natural children.

For those in residential care, it is helpful to understand the milieu in which the child is living. The experience of residential workers is often invaluable: they may find it easier than foster parents to take an objective view. Many will be familiar with the child's projections, which can give the therapist an idea of the feelings which may arise during the course of therapy.

A preliminary consideration of the child's defence mechanisms

Consideration should be given to how this child has coped with life so far. Families and foster carers are in a good position to offer suggestions about coping strategies, although careful questioning may be needed to elicit helpful information. For instance, I ask how a child responds to being told off, as this is likely to lead to anxiety. The child who giggles may use reaction formation; a child who appears to daydream may be dissociating; denial is common, especially in young children, and may not indicate disturbance. I ask if a child understands that the world is not neatly divided into good and bad: children who use splitting will divide those who care for them into friends or foe, and classify experiences similarly. Children in a tantrum who make adults feel irrationally angry may be using projection.

The worker should never seek to wear down a child's defences, nor to threaten them in any way. They have allowed the child to survive until now, and s/he needs them. However, understanding how this child has functioned in the circumstances that have faced him or her provides suggestions as to appropriate interventions. For instance, children who respond with denial or negation cannot acknowledge the presence of stressful stimuli; direct techniques are likely to be met with insistence that events have not occurred, or have not involved personal distress. Alternatively, children who repress feelings may warm to anxiety-reducing stimuli, such as drawing or kneading playdough, which help them to relax sufficiently to consider feelings that would otherwise remain hidden.

Using the assessment to select a therapeutic play approach

Having gathered this information, the next task is to make it meaningful. Clear evidence of abuse or other trauma can be highlighted as sources of difficulty for the child. However, the milieu in which a child has lived often has a more profound effect on his or her functioning than separate incidents of abuse. I recall working with Mary, an adult survivor of sexual abuse: she told me that the hours of anticipation were worse than the actual abuse. Other survivors testify to the extent to which abuse invades every area of their lives (Hall & Lloyd, 1989; Wyatt & Powell, 1988).

Given that everyone brings the vitality of early experiences into later relationships and situations, it is unlikely that a child who has lived in chaos, with no opportunities to experience warmth and care, will recognise such opportunities when faced with them. If, however, s/he had just one person who offered security and love amid the confusion, s/he will seek, and often find, opportunities to repeat that experience.

Jack, the youngest of a sibling group of six, was removed from the care of his natural family at the age of 5, and referred to me for therapeutic play when he was in his first foster home. Following his removal from home the extent of intra-familial abuse and profound neglect became clear. He ate voraciously, and did not recognise when he was full (evidence that he was ill fed by his natural mother). He soiled himself, and smeared faeces. His language was severely delayed; he could not use a knife and fork; he had no response to pain (bumping his head on the table). In his foster home he was withdrawn and watchful. He projected feelings of great loneliness and need, but could not recognise, nor accept, comfort. He had protected himself from abuse, as far as was possible, by drifting into the background of family life: thus the price he paid for his survival was the abandonment of his emotional needs.

One of his sisters, Nicola, was also referred for assessment. Her behaviour was overtly disturbed, with severe temper tantrums and aggressive outbursts. However, she sought comfort from male members of the foster household. It became clear that, in spite of extensive chaos and abuse within this family, someone had made an attempt to offer care and affection to Nicola, and she could seek this in subsequent relationships.

The task of organising this information and making a tentative diagnosis is a complex, and ongoing, process. Decisions taken now are not a final solution, but a signpost to future interventions. They may need revision at any time during the therapeutic process.

During the assessment, the worker should bear in mind the goals of therapeutic play. The first consideration is the nature of the referral, and whether s/he can fulfil the aspirations of the referring agency. Therapeutic play is not a panacea; it cannot offer protection to a child at risk; it cannot be the complete solution for the child manifesting severe behaviour problems whilst in a short-term placement; it cannot meet all the needs of the disabled child.

The common goals of therapy, as discussed in Chapter 1, are:

(1) To enable the child to understand and leave behind the emotional luggage associated with destructive early life experiences.
(2) To 'make up for' some early lost experiences, especially missed opportunities to play.
(3) To enable the child to experience fully a range of emotions, pleasurable as well as painful.
(4) To enable the child to modify anti-social behaviour.
(5) To improve the child's self-esteem, and sense of his or her own intrinsic worth.
(6) 'To bring the child to a level of functional development consistent with biological development.' (O'Connor, 1991: p. 93)
(7) To make sense of confusing events in his or her past, understand and come to terms with feelings about those who may have abused him or her, and prepare for life in a new family.

It may be that several goals are applicable to this child; it may be that none are. Nevertheless, the practitioner should be clear, before agreeing to engage a child in therapeutic play, what s/he hopes to achieve. These aspirations are shared with the referring agency, who need to agree with the practitioner's recommendations and not be left with false hopes about the potential outcome (West, 1992).

It may be appropriate to share these aims with the child. Children vary in their ability to understand the words spoken in play sessions. Some continue to deny that they have problems whilst attending eagerly; others are too young to understand a verbal discussion but are able to communicate on a symbolic level. However, the worker should attempt to share his or her understanding of the purpose of their meeting with the child by acknowledging that the child has difficulties and declare a willingness to help, suggesting that, by playing together, they may be able to solve some of those difficulties (Cattanach, 1994b).

Guerney (1983) suggests that clarity over goals is unnecessary for the non-directive play therapist. She writes that:

'The concept of the child mapping out the most appropriate route to personal maturity at his or her own pace eliminates the need to set specific behavioural goals for each child's therapy.'

(Guerney, 1983: p. 30)

I disagree. Lack of clear goals can lead to aimlessness in therapy.

Having reached a decision as to the purpose of therapy, the task is to select those interventions most likely to achieve these goals. The strengths, weaknesses and circumstances of the child should assist in the selection of relevant techniques. Practical issues, such as lack of appropriate facilities, may dictate which approach is selected. It may be that short-term interventions are needed to address a defined issue, prior to the child moving to a new family. There may be restrictions over funding for therapy; unless the worker is reasonably assured that money is likely to remain available for lengthy treatment, s/he should be cautious about working non-directively.

Many non-directive play therapists recommend its application to all children in trouble. Guerney (1983) suggests that only two categories of children cannot be reached by this technique: those who are severely autistic or out-of-contact and schizophrenic. Axline (1969), Moustakas (1973) and Wilson *et al.* (1992) agree that very few children cannot be helped by this approach.

James (1989) believes strongly that non-directive play therapy alone is never enough. In her experience, a non-directive approach cannot enable children to confront the pain of the past. A worker who does not introduce the topic of past trauma, confirms the message that the event is too dreadful to talk about. With the worker firmly in control of events in the playroom, and a warm relationship to support a child in pain, directive techniques enable damaged children to face and recover from the consequences of the past.

Rigid adherence to a theoretical approach cannot meet the needs of every child. Practitioners able to take an eclectic approach offer the widest possible help to children; each child will have individual needs understood and met, personal goals defined, and techniques selected that reach his or her private pain. Webb (1991) illustrates the application of this principle; each of her contributors outline case examples in which they describe the child's circumstances in depth, and explain their reason for selecting a particular therapeutic technique. Practitioners who follow an eclectic approach can learn much from careful reading of Webb's book.

The most difficult assessments are those in which the distress of the child is only too evident, but circumstances do not permit him or her to join in therapy at that time. The practitioner has to be honest with the child and the referring agency: if s/he does not have the skills or the time to work with this child, s/he must say so. No practitioner can meet the needs of all children (Cattanach, 1994b). S/he must also be clear that therapeutic play is no substitute for child protection: if a child is perceived as being at risk of abuse that risk must be addressed (Nicol *et al.*, 1988).

Assessment in practice

The task of assessment is so complex that a single case study does not fully do it justice. However, the process of Kelly's assessment illustrates many of its challenges and pitfalls, and is an example of the need to compromise when information is not available.

Kelly, aged 6

Kelly was referred by her social worker, whose main concern was her aggressive behaviour. The social worker hoped that therapeutic play would enable Kelly to address feelings derived from past experiences, and promote age-appropriate behaviour at school.

Kelly's mother was just 14 when Kelly was born. Both parents lived in a depressed rural area in southern England. Reluctantly, her mother agreed to part with the baby, and Kelly was placed in a short-term foster home whilst social workers looked for a family to adopt her. Kelly never saw her mother again. She was a lively baby, and formed a healthy attachment to her foster mother, who described her as delightful.

The process of finding an adoptive family for Kelly was delayed by her father, then only 17, belatedly admitting his responsibility and asking for contact. This led to a full assessment of him and his extended family. They had been known to Social Services for a number of years; Kelly's father and uncles were involved in petty crime; the relationship between her paternal grandparents was often stormy. However, their commitment to Kelly appeared unequivocal, and, with support from the social worker, Kelly left her foster parents and went to stay with her father and his family when she was just a year old. The transition from one home to another was difficult for everyone, with her grandparents failing to understand her attachment to her foster mother, who, in turn, had grave misgivings about this placement.

Kelly's father left most of her care to his parents, and continued to flirt with delinquency. He formed numerous transitory relationships with women. In spite of careful preparation by the social worker, her grandparents were unable to adapt to meet the needs of such a young child, and Kelly was often inadequately supervised. On one such occasion she pulled a saucepan full of boiling water and potatoes on top of her. On another she pulled linen off a clothes-horse onto an electric fire, causing considerable damage. Her grandparents never sat and played with her; the toys she was given were rarely age-appropriate; her toilet-training was haphazard and punitive.

By the time she attended playgroup, Kelly was sullen and withdrawn. Playgroup leaders were alerted by her sexualised behaviour with other children. When she was 4, she inadvertently disclosed sexual abuse by a friend of her father's; the family responded with anger and rejection, unable to believe her. They insisted she was removed from home on the day of her disclosure, and they consistently refused further contact with her.

Kelly found herself in a short-term foster home, with two other children, both slightly older than Kelly. Although she was given clear boundaries, appropriate attention, stimulation and affection, she was expected to be able to share. Her foster parents showed endless patience and understanding, making every effort to help Kelly adjust to her suddenly changed circumstances; however, she remained withdrawn and distant, responding aggressively if other children tried to play with her. This placement lasted just over a year, as social workers struggled to clarify her legal status, and to find a long-term home for her. However, when Kelly pushed another child down the stairs it was agreed that she must move again, this time to a single parent who could offer undivided attention.

In this placement, Kelly gradually began to 'thaw'. With her foster mother she could ask for, and accept, affection. However, at school she remained unresponsive and prone to unexpected outbursts of aggression. She was unable to concentrate for longer than a few minutes, and she seemed constantly anxious.

Kelly's father and grandparents refused to meet with me; I was therefore reliant on the social worker's records and opinions for details of Kelly's early life. I hoped that her early attachment to her first foster mother had provided the foundation she needed to be able to recognise trusting relationships in the future.

I was impressed by the commitment of her current foster mother: she had tolerated extreme temper tantrums from Kelly, but had consistently, and patiently, maintained appropriate boundaries and she was clearly fond of her. This was important: her foster mother's unwavering affection for her helped sustain Kelly during the difficult times of her therapy. On occasions Kelly projected extreme anger onto her foster mother, who had managed such children before and coped with these projections well. However, they indicated that Kelly defended herself by projecting all that she could not tolerate onto those around her, and denied any grief at the losses she had sustained. This visit confirmed my initial impression from the social worker that Kelly had a core of integration and ability to trust, which had remained intact since her first foster placement.

Kelly was most difficult to manage at school; her only response to incidents that upset her or caused anxiety was aggression. In a large, open plan classroom, her frequent outbursts led to complaints from parents and increasing concern among her teachers. However, the headteacher was anxious that Kelly should receive help now; the future looked bleak for such a young child presenting with extreme behaviour.

I undertook only four play sessions with Kelly: although not ideal, this enabled me to complete the assessment before the long summer holiday. In view of her response to anxiety, I arranged to see her at school with an agreement that the headteacher would be available for her if she found the sessions stressful. The social worker had warned me that any mention of past events would be likely to result in heightened anxiety, with consequent challenging behaviour. I was not concerned about the behaviour, but saw no need to promote more anxiety than was inevitable in meeting a new person. I felt non-directive play therapy techniques would be less stressful for her, and offer the best picture of her current functioning and difficulties.

I explained to Kelly that her social worker had asked me to come to see her a few times, to see if we could help her with her worries. I said that I knew lots of children who lived in foster homes, and had helped them with all sorts of problems, and I hoped I could find a way to help her. I assured her that I wasn't going to ask her questions, we were just going to play together, and I would think about her and try to find a way to help.

All four assessment sessions were chaotic: the room was left in turmoil, and I felt bewildered by her play. Efforts to record the sessions thoroughly gave me few clues as to any coherent theme or issue. However, Kelly always came willingly, and was extremely reluctant to leave. After much discussion with my supervisor, I surmised that Kelly's inner world was totally confused, and this emerged clearly in non-directive play. The most hopeful aspect of these sessions was her willingness to attend; I felt she had some understanding of the therapeutic nature of these sessions, and was hopeful that a long-term therapeutic relationship could provide the context for her to unravel the myriad difficulties from her past.

Her foster mother, social worker and I agreed that all seven aims of therapeutic play were valid for Kelly; however, I felt the emphasis of my work should lie in her need to consider the emotional impact of past experiences, and to enable her to fully experience a wide range of emotions. I emphasised that a child with such extreme difficulties was likely to need an extended period of therapy; her social worker negotiated funding for up to a year. I continued using non-directive play therapy techniques for two reasons: Kelly found talking about her difficulties almost impossible, and she had demonstrated that she was able to use play to illustrate the chaos of her inner world.

The process of Kelly's play therapy is described in Chapter 5.

Therapeutic play as part of a comprehensive assessment

There are many circumstances which prompt this type of assessment. Guardians *ad litem* are expected to represent (but not necessarily agree with) the wishes and feelings of the child in their reports for the court (Kerr *et al.*, 1990). Increasingly, play therapists are asked for an expert assessment of children's emotional health (Ryan & Wilson, 1995b). From time to time social workers are required to make complex assessments of a child's or a family's needs (Department of Health, 1988). Practitioners helping children prepare for adoption also undertake a preliminary evaluation of the child (Cipolla *et al.*, 1992). Residential workers, resource centre workers, nursery nurses, foster parents – all seek to understand the child's view of the world; to do that, they need to know where the child has come from and how s/he perceives his or her situation.

A worker asked to contribute to a comprehensive assessment needs much of the same initial information as one preparing for therapy. Often the different members of a therapeutic team appraise one aspect of the child's functioning and difficulties, and consider these different approaches collectively. Thus the team identifies and prioritises the child's needs and how these are to be met. The therapist is not looking for solutions for the child in play, but is seeking understanding of the child and his or her world, and trying to put this in context for a therapeutic team. Recommendations may include therapeutic play, or they may not.

The major difference in this form of assessment is that it almost always includes a few, focused, sessions with the child. These should never be seen as a preliminary to on-going therapy, and honesty with the child is essential. I tell children that I have been asked by their social worker, or by the court, to assist in finding the best help possible, and to do this I would like to spend some time getting to know him or her. I am clear how many sessions will be involved, and what the process will be. I am also honest that information gleaned in these sessions will be shared openly with others caring for the child. I rarely undertake this assessment in fewer than four sessions, and have found that six can be more productive, a view shared by Ryan & Wilson (1996). This allows space for the child to settle into the relationship and feel comfortable talking about intimate matters, and gives time to ensure that the child is not rushed. I can also bring the sessions to a satisfactory end.

I bring a range of materials with me to each session, much as I would in non-directive play therapy. I begin with a non-directive approach: this gives the child the opportunity to experiment with the situation, and to discover all s/he needs to know about me.

Some children illustrate their difficulties graphically in the context of non-directive play therapy, and there is no need to introduce more focused techniques. Leroy, aged 12, had moved from foster family to foster family, excluded from school after school, until a home could be found to tolerate his tantrums and regressive behaviour. During his assessment, he rearranged the playroom totally, creating a physical barrier consisting of chairs, beanbags and cushions between us, before settling to play in his corner of the room. I was allowed occasional glimpses of scenes of graphic violence, but he could not show me any cohesive sequence of play. There were other occasions when he offered me a few toys, which he tried to destroy by throwing his toys at them. I did not need directive techniques to tell me that this boy was highly defended, that his inner world was full of fragmented violence, and that he perceived anyone who came near him as hostile.

Ryan & Wilson (1995b) advocate the application of non-directive play when undertaking an assessment which will form the basis of expert evidence to a court. They point out that it's non-coercive nature and lack of interpretation or suggestion make it easier for children to express themselves honestly. Reports should offer straightforward opinions based on clear evidence from the child's play, and practitioners should not omit material which may not support their views (Roberts, 1994).

I agree that, within the constraints that are an essential component of working with courts, non-directive play therapy offers the most appropriate technique for young children. However it is important to have other methods for adolescents, or children with a limited ability to express themselves symbolically. Some children respond to a guided fantasy (see Chapter 6). When the child is sitting quietly, I tell a story, describing an imaginary journey ending with a secret door with his or her name on. Gently s/he is encouraged to open the door, and draws what s/he sees. This provides a glimpse of the child's inner world, and an assessment of the richness of his or her fantasies (Oaklander, 1969).

Other children, particularly those who think more concretely, I ask to draw an island where they would like to live, where they can be queen or king (see Chapter 6). They choose who and what lives with them on this island; across a shark-infested sea is another island where they put everyone and everything they never wish to see again. This is an illuminating exercise for some children: Robert, aged 12, asked for a car park full of Lamborghinis, a million *Game Boy* computers, a swimming pool with slides and wave machines, Arsenal football team, and then thought of his mother!

The 'World technique', originated by Lowenfeld (1979) and extended by Kalff (1980) and Newson (1983, 1992), also prompts children to illustrate their inner worlds through small figures placed in sand (see Chapter 6). Few children need encouragement to play with sand: its tactile qualities make it an ideal medium for children who regress easily. There is little need for direction, and the practitioner's role is purely facilitative. Peripatetic therapists rarely have the opportunity to use sand; however, a large lump of playdough can also provide tactile experience and the scenery for a world.

Irwin (1983) underlines the value of pretend play, and uses symbolic material to help her consider the child's customary way of looking at the world. Pretend play represents the child's fantasies and dreams; it is a mirror of his or her inner world, and unqualified practitioners should interpret this play with extreme care.

Waterhouse (1987) has developed an imaginative collection of games, books and other techniques which she uses in her role as guardian *ad litem*. She uses sticky labels on her fingers with different 'feeling faces' drawn on them, to help children discuss their emotions. She makes board games similar to snakes and ladders, in which children talk of something they have enjoyed when they climb a 'happy ladder', and something that upset them when they fall down a 'sad snake'. She uses strong envelopes to make paper houses and figures to represent a child's family, to facilitate understanding of the child's perception of events.

It is rarely helpful to interpret the play of children when undertaking an assessment. Unless the worker is convinced that an insightful comment will enable a child to make sense of an event or feeling that would otherwise elude him or her, s/he should keep these thoughts to him- or herself. This is a brief relationship; the worker is not in a position to help the child build on the experience. It is dishonest to indicate that this association can be anything other than transitory: although a good rapport and unambiguous regard for the child is important, a close relationship can only cause pain on ending, and many children have experienced more than enough pain in their lives already. A child's fantasy of a longer term relationship needs honest acknowledgement and discussion.

The sole purpose of gathering this information is to enable the worker to understand, and to share with the court or with colleagues and others who care for the child, his or her view of the world and needs. The professional team should respond to this information by making every effort to ensure these needs are met. This is not the responsibility of the therapist alone (although s/he may have strong feelings about it), but of the team who must attend to the child's educational, social, attachment, emotional and behavioural, as well as therapeutic, needs.

Summary

There are two reasons why a practitioner might undertake an assessment of a child: preparatory to therapeutic play, and as a contribution to a comprehensive assessment of needs.

The information needed in both instances is similar, however the focus of the work is very different. When contributing to a comprehensive assessment, sessions with the child are short-term and focused, with little or no overt interpretation of the child's play. When considering the needs and difficulties of a child prior to therapeutic play sessions, practitioners need to reach a provisional diagnosis which will lead to a thorough appraisal of the techniques needed to help the child. Both processes require the worker to collate as much information as possible.

Full and honest communication with the child, with his or her parents or foster carers, and with other professionals, facilitates this assessment. Everyone should be aware of the nature of the appraisal, and the enquiries that are being made. Conclusions should also be made available for everyone, and the worker prepared for a full and open discussion of any recommendations.

Chapter 4

The Organisation of Therapeutic Play

Introduction

Thorough preparation consists not only of a full assessment of the child's difficulties, but also paying adequate attention to practical arrangements, including the time, space and the provision of toys and other material. A child beginning treatment is often chaotic: his or her therapy should offer a haven from that chaos and not mirror it. Careful preparation assists in alleviating the anxiety of both practitioner and child before the initial session; this includes attention to issues of confidentiality and recording.

Consideration must be given to the race and gender of the worker. On-going consultation from someone of the same racial background as the child will assist practitioners working with a child from an environment different from his or her own (Brummer, 1988; Owusu-Bempah, 1994). Families from an Islamic culture may have strong feelings about the gender of the worker, which should also be respected. Children from urban or rural environments, or from different social groups, will have divergent cultural expectations. All organisations offering therapy to children must adhere to anti-discriminatory practice (Thompson, 1993).

Research indicates that both men and women can make successful play workers (Doyle, 1990). However, the needs of each child must be the primary consideration. An abused child may find it impossible to share intimate feelings with a therapist who is the same gender as his or her abuser (Hall & Lloyd, 1989). Bereaved children may produce strong transference feelings with a practitioner who is the same sex as a surviving parent (Carroll, 1995b). Careful assessment of the child's needs should indicate if the gender of a particular worker is likely to help or hinder the process of therapy.

Reliability

Practitioners wishing to help children must be totally reliable. S/he should be prepared to insist that s/he is never available for meetings when sessions with children have been arranged. Breaks in therapy (apart from illness, when cards sent from home show that children are not forgotten) should be planned and prepared for.

It is not easy to maintain predictability in the day-to-day turmoil in which many practitioners work. However, if one can take a minute to look through the child's eyes, it is clear how essential this is. Traumatised children experience major disruptions in their lives. In such circumstances, certainty of the therapist will provide the child something to 'cling to'. For children who have been abused, neglected or deprived of their natural families, therapeutic certainty is even more vital: it offers the reparative relationship which provides an alternative to the insecurity of the past. A worker who cannot offer this only proves to the child that adults are untrustworthy, and the chance to experience otherwise is lost.

Time and space

Child psychotherapists may try to see children several times a week. There is some evidence (quoted in Reismann, 1973: p. 170) that more frequent sessions bring about more enduring change. Some children are assessed as needing intensive intervention. However, this level of frequency is often impractical.

Non-directive play therapists generally agree that most children need to be seen weekly: few can contain the content of a session for longer than a week. Wilson *et al.* (1992) advocate twice-weekly sessions for children under 4 or 5. In my experience it is not the age of the child that influences his or her ability to wait a week between sessions, but his or her level of integration. Unintegrated children, who may be as old as 12 or 13, find it impossible to contain the therapeutic experience, and each session can feel like beginning again.

Play workers may also offer a succession of planned weekly sessions. Others arrange less frequent sessions, depending on the techniques employed and the needs and circumstances of each child. Directive workers vary in the length of sessions they offer. Some have regular, time-limited sessions, as the non-directive therapist does. Other techniques, such as life story work, dictate that arrangements for sessions are more flexible.

Play therapists offer each child the same time, and the same space, for each session. I try to see children as early in the day as is practical: many are tired after school and need recuperative time in front of the television before they can function. In addition, if the child explores troublesome material towards the end of the day, feelings that emerge may linger beyond bedtime, thus making additional difficulties for both child and those who care for him or her. In my experience, schools are eager to release children regularly, if they are assured that the child is receiving help.

Most child psychotherapists and play therapists undertake sessions lasting from 50 minutes to an hour. Few children (and few therapists) can concentrate for longer than that. Occasionally, with highly anxious children, whose personal boundaries are few and diffuse, I reduce the length of sessions to half an hour. Sessions shorter than that are rarely constructive.

Many practitioners do not have access to a fully equipped playroom. However, there are few rooms that are totally unsuitable for sessions with children: with imagination and a willingness to compromise, children can be seen almost anywhere. Children need a 'therapeutic space' (Donovan & McIntyre, 1990: p. 110), and within that space everything will have personal meaning for each child. A private corner in a school, a colleague's office, family rooms in a resource centre: all can become a playroom if necessary.

Occasionally it is impossible to find an alternative location, and children have to be seen at home. For small children, I cover the living room floor with a 'magic carpet' (an old blue sheet), transforming the room into a playroom. At the end of the session, the magic carpet is ritually returned to the toybag, and the child has his or her living room back again. I find this technique less effective with children over about 7, who are unimpressed by the appearance of an old sheet! For these children I make strenuous efforts to ensure that sessions have a clearly defined beginning and ending, thus maintaining a boundary around the therapy. Cattanach (1992) carries round a blue mat, with which she indicates the boundaries of the play area, and implies that older children find it as useful as younger ones.

Whilst almost any room can become a playroom if necessary, a well-equipped, purpose-built room is a luxury that makes therapy significantly easier for both therapist and child. Ideally, it should include an area that can be easily cleaned (for messy play), small tables and chairs, and a cosy corner with bean bags to curl up in, or to beat up. It should be light and airy, with comfortable furnishings which are easy to clean. There should be no telephone point. Although it is important that the child does not feel overheard, it is unwise to site a playroom too far from other offices. There are rare occasions when a therapist may need help with a distressed or angry child. In addition, children who have been asked to keep secrets may find a playroom without external sounds too reminiscent of past experiences. (This meets the needs of the child, but not those of colleagues who do not welcome the various noises of children.)

I find the floor area of the room to be important. If the room is too small, the child may feel swamped by the therapist, and unable to separate enough to find space to play. Children who are reluctant to attend, or who cannot tolerate anxiety, may respond to a small room with aggressive or destructive behaviour, indicating a wish to be free from an environment which they perceive as too oppressive or intimate.

Alternatively, a room that is too large may allow the child to stay so far from his or her worker that s/he can never fully experience having feelings safely contained.

Some techniques are best undertaken elsewhere. Children being prepared for a move, either through life story work or other direct methods, may best be helped at home (see Jewett, 1984; Cipolla *et al.*, 1992). Life story work may also involve visits to places where the child has previously lived or attended school: on these occasions the work takes place not only during the visit itself but also on the journey.

The importance of clean toilet facilities should not be overlooked. Children need the toilet more frequently than adults, and anxious children need the toilet all the time. It is impossible to undertake therapy if there are frequent interruptions to accompany the child along several corridors to the loo!

The choice of toys

The choice of materials may depend on the theoretical bias of the practitioner. The toys offered by child psychotherapists and non-directive play therapists are often similar. Reismann writes that:

> 'Toys that are provided for the child's use are intended to serve as a media of communication... The purpose of play therapy is not to provide amusement for the child, not to see that he is entertained by the latest gadgets advertised on television, not to demonstrate that the therapist is a better provider than the child's parents, not to keep him busy building models, not to offer training in checkers, chess or some less popular game, not to furnish decorations for the therapist's office, and not to prove that the therapist can win. The play materials and toys are there to help the child communicate or express his feelings and thoughts.'

(Reismann, 1973: pp. 89–90; see also Landreth, 1991)

Lowenfeld (1979) supplies a sand tray and numerous small figures, creatures, vehicles and houses with which the child can illustrate his or her world in the sand, but excludes items such as paints and puppets which might distract the child from the sand. Newson (1983, 1992) adds dressing-up clothes and hats which encourage children to parti-cipate in role play (see Chapter 6).

Klein (1955), along with many child psychotherapists, provides a separate drawer of toys for each child, including numerous small figures. She also feels that running water is essential. When working with unintegrated children Dockar-Drysdale (1968) makes a point of providing large boxes which can contain the child, with materials to encourage regressive play.

Ginott, a non-directive play therapist, has five criteria which he uses for assessing appropriate material:

'A treatment toy should (a) facilitate the establishment of contact with the child; (b) evoke and encourage catharsis; (c) aid in developing insight; (d) furnish opportunities for reality testing; (e) provide media for sublimation.'

(1982a: p. 146)

Thus the therapist is encouraged to consider the function of the materials offered, and ensure that it meets the needs of this child.

Non-directive play therapists regard play itself as the medium of healing, and materials are selected with this in mind. Axline found the following list of toys most successful:

'Nursing bottles; a doll family, a doll house with furniture; toy soldiers and army equipment, toy animals; playhouse materials, including table, chairs, cot, doll bed, stove, tin dishes, pans, spoons, doll clothes, clothesline, clothespins and clothes basket; a didee doll; a large rag doll; puppets; a puppet screen; crayons; clay; finger paints; sand; water; toy guns; peg-pounding sets; wooden mallet; paper dolls; little cars; airplanes; a table; an easel; an enamel-top table for finger painting and clay work; toy telephone; shelves; basin; small broom; mop; rags; drawing paper; finger-painting paper; old newspapers; inexpensive cutting paper; pictures of people, houses, animals and other objects; and empty berry baskets to smash.'

(1969: p. 54)

Small figures and dolls should reflect the racial mix of our society, and give children from every ethnic group figures with which they can identify. Toys commonly thought of as appropriate for boys or girls should be made available to both genders.

Like Reismann, Axline avoids construction toys such as *Lego* and *Meccano*, and board games and cards. Other non-directive therapists find them useful. Donovan & McIntyre (1990) do not have theme toys from television or films, thus excluding *Star Wars* or *Power Rangers* figures, since they wish to explore the fantasy life of the child, not the television programmes. They do not permit children who smear faeces to use clay or finger paint, since this reinforces the behaviour; a view challenged by Arlow & Kadis (1946) and Woltman (1950). West (1992) notes that, if left to direct the play themselves, children will invent new rules for board games, or cheat; Donovan & McIntyre (1990) feel it is essential to enforce the rules of games if children elect to play them. Gardner (1986b), although commenting on the relatively low therapeutic value of games, uses them to assess a child's self-esteem and degree of egocentricity. He also stresses that the games selected should be enjoyed by both partners: children rapidly recognise when an adult is bored. Wilson *et al.* (1992) include items such as colouring books and puzzles, which they find useful if a child is particularly anxious or unwell. There is an increasing range of picture and story books to help distressed children: some workers have these available as a matter of course, while others find the appropriate book for each child.

Some practitioners, myself included, are unhappy working with guns. Although research does not suggest that playing with war toys makes children more violent (Sutton-Smith, 1994), my concern is that modern toys mirror real weapons, and children can find all manner of objects with which to pretend to shoot me without the provision of guns. I don't go as far as Donovan & McIntyre (1990), who do not permit any toys of harm or violence, including toy soldiers. They feel that children can find means of expressing anger without these toys. However, West (1992) and Wilson *et al.* (1992) are comfortable with guns. My only exception is when working with children who have witnessed serious violence; these children have quite specific difficulties, and need appropriate materials to enable them to gain mastery over their experiences (Pynoos & Eth, 1984; Harris-Hendricks *et al.*, 1993). Practitioners working in Northern Ireland may need materials to help children explain their view of the world. Similarly refugees and survivors of wars have special needs, and practitioners wishing to help such children need further training and consultation (Garbarino, 1993; Miljevic-Ridjicki & Lugomer-Armano, 1994).

Most current practitioners are cautious about including anatomically correct dolls: they have their place prompting disclosure of sexual abuse, but their routine use in the playroom is not appropriate. Children find other ways to express feelings about sexual abuse without these dolls. I have only used them therapeutically with a small, pre-verbal boy, who needed to describe what had happened and could find no other way (Carroll, 1993b).

Many therapists have small items which they find invaluable. Gil finds sunglasses:

'give children anonymity that can disinhibit their communications, particularly when they have been feeling embarrassed or reticent.'

(1991: p. 65)

Similarly, Bray (1991) finds 'rainbow glasses' are a particularly poignant way for children to illustrate that they can see rainbows as well as monsters in their worlds. Sloss (1978) provides a dressing-up box big enough to climb in. I always include a doctor's set, as it can be used to explore both the nature of healing, and the experience of pain.

Moustakas (1973) writes that the range of toys made available is less important than the opportunity for each child to use materials as he or she chooses. However, he feels it essential that the same toys are offered every session, to ensure predictability. I agree that the provision of the same materials is important for young children, or those who are particularly anxious and need a high level of containment. However, as I have no playroom, I am unable to carry enough choice to satisfy older children who attend for several months, and alter materials from time to time to prevent the process of therapy stagnating. In addition, older children may shy away from anything they consider 'babyish'. Although they may need to indulge in regressive play once engaged in therapy, they need age-appropriate materials at first. Many 10 to 12 year olds are highly competitive, and target games are popular. Technical equipment, such as a stethoscope, and electrical items such as a tape recorder, are generally welcome (Guerney, 1983).

Before seeing any child I discuss his or her interests and normal play with parents or foster carers, assuring that I bring something that is generally popular at home. Like Reismann, I give priority to toys which encourage imaginative play, within the developmental level of the child. I include pens, paper, glue and scissors unless the child has severe problems at school and I could be seen as another teacher if I introduce such materials. I bring toys that enable children to play regressively. Although some are insulted by any suggestion that they might be interested in anything babyish, a small baby bottle, included for the benefit of a doll, provides the opportunity for children to indulge in a little nurturing of themselves. Whilst not wishing to reinforce gender stereotyping, I cannot carry everything, and may exclude gender-specific items. Toys which are accepted as 'part of the furniture' in a playroom tend to be rejected scornfully when discovered in my toybag!

Practitioners working with survivors of ritual or sadistic abuse must be particularly careful about the selection of toys. Some of these children have witnessed fetish dolls cut or pierced, prior to the same actions being applied to themselves or others. Apparently innocent objects take on symbolic meaning, and provoke extreme reactions (Hale & Sinason, 1994).

Directive play workers may not provide the wide range of materials found in the child-centred therapist's playroom. Although s/he may have many of the same toys in the cupboards, they are selected individually for each session and for each child. The choice of materials, and how they are used, rests not with the child but with his or her worker. Nevertheless, the range of materials used by practitioners such as James (1989), Redgrave (1987) and Oaklander (1969) are as imaginative and varied as those provided by the non-directive therapist.

The provision of a narrow range of materials can be a facilitative intervention, designed to focus the attention of both child and therapist on the issues that concern them. Extraneous distractions are reduced to a minimum. Thus there is no confusion as to the purpose of the session.

Some practitioners automatically offer children a snack during therapy (Haworth & Keller, 1964; West, 1983, 1992), recognising the importance of providing children with a reparative feeding experience. Haworth & Keller acknowledge the emotional importance attached to food:

> 'In providing food for the child the therapist is, in effect, presenting herself as the all-giving, good, and nurturant parent. But the child may experience such a situation as very threatening, since it may dramatise his conflict between wanting to receive such nurturance and his feeling that this food is somehow forbidden or potentially dangerous.'
>
> (1964: pp. 132–3)

Others regard the provision of food as a diversion.

Similarly, there is no agreement as to whether children should help to clear the playroom. Practitioners concur that the room should look welcoming at the beginning of each session: thus, each worker must ensure that the playroom is left reasonably clean. Some practitioners encourage children to clear up after themselves. Others are happy for the child to use every minute of the sessions for playing, and are content to tidy up alone. Donovan & McIntyre (1990) insist that the child stays in the playroom until all the materials have been put away, with or without the help of the child, to illustrate the adult's capacity to 'put things back where they belong' (p. 120). Ginott (1982c) advocates that agencies should employ someone to clean the playroom!

My own compromise is to assure a child that s/he does not have to tidy up if s/he does not wish to: this is the place where 'the mess can be left behind'. The response of the child is often interesting: some clear away so thoroughly that it looks as if they have never been there, while others leave their 'mess' symbolically behind. (One 9 year old spent most of one session making as much clutter as possible: I learned later that she had recently had an argument at home about the state of her bedroom and announced that Jo doesn't mind if she makes a mess!)

Recording

The literature on direct work with children contains many imaginative ideas, but few concrete suggestions for recording the process of therapy. However, Doyle (1990) acknowledges the importance of accurate and comprehensive recording, and discusses the value of video equipment to aid evaluation of sessions. Accurate recording is particularly essential for practitioners undertaking court reports, who must record sessions immediately to ensure accurate recall (Ryan & Wilson, 1995b).

Wilson *et al.* (1992) assess the value of audio and video recording of sessions. As a learning tool video recording is invaluable; however, it is time-consuming, as it may take twice as long to view and discuss the recording as was spent with the child. However, it is retraumatising to video children who have been filmed for pornographic purposes. As a second choice, audio recordings can be extremely valuable (although I recall one session which I audiotaped in which very little was said and I was left with a mysterious series of splashes to identify!).

There are occasions when photographs can make a valuable record of a session. Cattanach (1994b) records the Worlds that children create in this way. Occasionally I have a camera available, and encourage children to record the session themselves (Berman, 1993).

Many play therapists have evolved their own method of recording. West (1992) outlines her useful system (pp. 174–80): each account begins with a history of the child. The first session, and occasionally subsequent sessions, are process recorded. The purpose of writing at such length is to identify specific issues which may recur, or to analyse sessions which had been particularly stressful. Other sessions are recorded in note form, and may include a chronological account of the session, the development of themes, verbal and non-verbal interventions, new or relevant material, and the feelings of both play therapist and child. Records should include regular summaries, which enable the therapist to stand back from weekly events and to overview the process of therapy.

My records begin with a comprehensive assessment of the child's history and difficulties. Each session is then process recorded, in note form. I write over two-thirds of the page only: alongside these notes I use a different coloured pen to comment on what has occurred, including my own feelings and impressions of the significance of the play. Reviewing the process of therapy is simplified, as I look through my coloured notes rather than the details of each session. I add notes on other events in his or her life (beginning a new school, visiting his or her mother at the weekend, falling off his or her bike and spending an afternoon in casualty, etc.) which may influence the therapy. Each child is reviewed monthly, with the themes of his or her play and difficulties s/he is experiencing clearly included.

Some practitioners take notes during the course of a session. Axline took notes through every session with Dibs (1964). Cattanach (1994b) writes children's stories as they are enacted, offering to read her notes back to the child to ensure that she has captured the child's meaning accurately. Other workers are uncomfortable taking notes during a session. Having tried both ways, I have found that children adapt to either method, provided the therapist is consistent, and does not rush to his or her notebook if it is not routinely available.

Recently, I have undertaken therapy with violent children. In order to ensure everyone's safety, a colleague has stayed in the playroom, and recorded the session as it occurs. The result: verbatim records taken at the time, which are illuminating for me and form an ideal training opportunity.

There are occasions when the worker's notes may be required in court. In these circumstances practitioners are recommended to consult a solicitor, as the legislation has become increasingly complex.

The importance of thorough recording must not be underestimated. Time taken to consider each session in depth is time for the worker to digest the contents of that session, and to consider his or her own feelings alongside those of the child. Some sessions are so stressful that only the support of a supervisor will enable the therapist to survive, but many feelings can be resolved in the action of recording with care.

Confidentiality

It is unavoidable that information about children is shared with others who care for them. Children are, and must be, dependent on adults. All have a legal guardian who gives permission before therapy begins. Some are brought by parents; others are referred by welfare agencies, seeking help on behalf of the child. Before the child is seen, the worker should discuss his or her history and difficulties with the referring agency. It is not unreasonable that they will also seek feedback about the progress of therapy, and guidance on how they can best contribute.

It is important to distinguish between secrecy and privacy. Children have the right to have intimate details of their lives kept private; it is reasonable for him or her to object to the details of play sessions being shared. S/he may say what s/he wishes to the therapist, and should feel confident that only the outline of the session will be disclosed and not the contents. However, the child should not be asked to keep contents of the session secret: s/he may discuss them with everyone if s/he chooses to do so. Many abused children have been asked to keep secrets: therapy is private; it is not a secret.

Practitioners should guard against becoming part of a child's secret. If a child discloses abuse, this must be shared with child protection agencies to ensure his or her safety and that of others. A worker should feel able to share details of the child's play in supervision; collusion with the child's suggestion that such difficulties remain only between them is to confirm the child's belief that the telling of such secrets is potentially harmful (Sinason & Svensson, 1994).

Most practitioners have a professional obligation to disclose allegations of abuse. However, there are occasions when the issue of the confidentiality of sessions may be questioned. For instance, a child's play may include sexually explicit material indicating that he or she has been exposed to inappropriate experiences, but even gentle questioning offers no indication of the origin of this play. It is relevant to share an opinion that the child is inappropriately aware of sexual matters, but disclosing details of the child's play is not necessary at this stage. Only if the child later makes direct allegations of abuse, and the details coincide with his or her play and could therefore constitute evidence to support the allegation, should practitioners consider sharing the intimate content of a play session. In these circumstances the child may need additional help to understand why it is necessary to disclose the particulars of his or her play.

Some agencies have clear expectations that details of play sessions will be shared within the therapeutic team. Others maintain that the minutiae of a child's play should only be discussed in supervision, and an overview of his or her progress shared with the rest of the team.

Practitioners will be asked to share information at conferences and reviews. It is not easy to strike the balance between disclosing material that is confidential, and membership of a professional team concerned with the welfare of the child. If participants keep too much to themselves, the team is unable to function adequately to ensure the protection and welfare of the child. The sharing of ideas and feelings about a child with others who care for him or her promotes consistency and professional trust. It is possible to discuss the fact that a child makes one feel sexually uncomfortable without describing precisely what has happened. Similarly, it is helpful to discuss the child's growing ability to express his or her feelings, as this may be misinterpreted by parents or foster carers as increasingly challenging behaviour.

Occasionally children are removed from treatment prematurely; an understanding of the views held by the parents or foster carers can help to pre-empt this (James, 1989). For some, the child's therapy can revive memories from their own childhoods that they cannot face, and the child is withdrawn to ease the adult's pain. Others are jealous of attention given to the child, or the relationship that develops between child and worker. Others believe treatment is ineffective, seeking instant solutions to challenging behaviours. If practitioners can understand these feelings, it may be possible to meet the needs of adults and keep the child in therapy.

Foster or adoptive parents, struggling to cope with bewildering behaviour, may need additional explanations to help manage the child, and to understand the meaning of the behaviour. Hunter (1994) points out that adoptive and foster parents often believe that they are making constant mistakes in their management of these children, blaming themselves for failing to tolerate extreme behaviours. She discusses details of the child's difficulties in depth, to help caregivers understand that they are shouldering the child's pain.

Some children, especially those in care, believe that everyone knows all about them, and can see no point in offering confidential sessions. Others, especially older children and adolescents, may test out a promise not to share personal information. One 10 year old asked me not to disclose that he had deliberately scratched his arms that morning: I looked at them and, although they were sore, they were not bleeding and were clean. I elected to keep this information to myself, knowing that his foster carers would notice the injuries later. On another occasion he told me he was thinking of running away: I shared this information immediately after the session, in order to ensure his safety.

Every practitioner chooses his or her own words to tell children how much of their sessions can be confidential. Mine are: 'I shall not tell anyone the details of what we do together in here, unless you tell me that a child is being hurt. Then I must tell someone, because I can't stop children being hurt on my own. Apart from that, it is just between you and me. But I shall be talking to your foster mum and your social worker from time to time, to tell them how you are getting on, and to hear how things are at home. I shall also make a point of telling your foster mum how you feel after your sessions, because if I think you might need an extra hug, I shall try to make sure you get one. You can tell who you like about our time together; it is not a secret. But I shall not tell anyone the details; I shall keep those to myself.'

Beginning therapy

Many authors offer advice on how to manage the first session. It is a situation which provokes anxiety in worker and child alike. However well-rehearsed the worker's introduction, it may need to be repeated several times before the child's anxiety lowers and s/he can hear what is said.

Ginott (1982b) raises the issue of the choice children are given at the onset of therapeutic play. He feels strongly that children cannot make this decision; it must be made for them. Donovan & McIntyre (1990) agree; enabling children to attend play sessions is an appropriate application of adult authority. It is difficult for many therapists, devoted to empowering children, to acknowledge the lack of choice that children have when entering therapy. Some children can express their displeasure by open rejection of both therapist and toys; others indulge in verbal abuse. Most accept the dictates of adults and 'do as they are told'. It is for the worker to illustrate, by his or her acceptance of the child's anxiety and reluctance, that such feelings are permitted.

With most children, the initial task is to effect a separation from their parents or foster carers. Some therapists (Oaklander, 1969; Reismann, 1973) include carers in the first session, and regard the initial meeting with adult and child as part of the process of therapy. Others (Ginott, 1982b; Cattanach, 1992; West, 1992), undertake an initial assessment with carer and child away from the playroom, and make efforts to separate them in the waiting room before the first therapy session. Lowenfeld (1935) always separated children from their carers from the outset, unless the child was extremely shy. However, all are sensitive to the attachment needs of children, and make great efforts to lower the child's anxiety sufficiently to allow him or her to separate comfortably.

Each practitioner decides for him- or herself how to welcome each child into therapy. Up to a point, this is dictated by his or her theoretical orientation, and the aims of treatment. A worker embarking on life story work would be irresponsible to promise that the child could choose what to play with each week; nevertheless, some element of freedom to choose will help children settle more readily. The purpose of their time together, and the structure of the sessions, needs to be made explicit.

Some workers employ games or techniques to help children relax and engage in therapy. Oaklander (1969) often asks children to draw a picture of their families, a technique also employed by many Guardians *ad litem* or social workers (Waterhouse, 1987). Winnicott (1971) invited children to play 'squiggles' with him (see Chapter 6).

Non-directive play therapists, devoted to the child's right to choose, have no such introductory technique to help 'break the ice'. They rely on patient acceptance of the child, and clear directions that the child may play as s/he wishes. Some children are overwhelmed by anxiety in such circumstances. They have never had choices before, and cannot begin to exercise them now – especially with a stranger. The therapist acknowledges the child's anxiety, and some will wait quietly for several sessions while a highly anxious child struggles to select an activity. Others may introduce a non-threatening material such as playdough. Gentle kneading of the dough helps to reduce tension, and the child may find him- or herself playing.

All practitioners acknowledge that the first session is crucial for both adult and child. Good preparation, in terms of a thorough preliminary assessment, is essential. Supervision, in which this first session can be discussed in depth, and the anxiety of the worker disentangled from that of the child, is also imperative.

Summary

All practitioners who work with children must offer total reliability. Sessions should be frequent and predictable if they are to be effective.

Materials should be selected carefully, with the aims of therapy borne in mind. Practitioners who work in a fully-equipped playroom can offer a wider choice than those who travel to the child; however, with imagination, therapy can occur almost anywhere.

Effective recording practices are important, if the worker is to understand the process of therapy and adapt his or her responses as the child progresses. Similarly, the therapist should be honest with him- or herself and with the child as to the extent to which sessions can remain confidential.

Both therapist and child are likely to be anxious at the outset of therapy, and measures taken to ease the child into the therapeutic relationship will help them both. The first session is the opportunity for the child to be introduced to the structure of therapy, and told what to expect from subsequent sessions.

Chapter 5

Non-Directive Play Therapy

Introduction

Axline defines non-directive play therapy as:

'a play experience that is therapeutic because it provides a secure relationship between the child and the adult, so that the child has the freedom and room to state himself in his own terms, exactly as he is at that moment in his own way and in his own time.'

(Axline, 1982a: p. 47)

Axline's work with *Dibs* (1964) and prescriptive work on *Play Therapy* (1969) developed Rogers' work with adults (1951) and applied it to children. Rogers emphasises the importance of the therapist developing an empathic relationship with the client, believing that s/he would use the context of this relationship to discover an innate capacity for growth.

All play therapists echo this emphasis on the importance of the relationship between adult and child providing the milieu in which therapy can take place. O'Connor (1991) describes it as a 'holding relationship':

'one in which the child is sure of your ability to contain his most frightening and destructive thoughts and feelings in such a way that neither of you is harmed.'

(p. 214)

Therapy cannot occur in an emotional vacuum; the relationship that grows between child and therapist is the vital component for the therapeutic experience (Landreth, 1991).

Axline's eight principles of non-directive play therapy

Although Axline first wrote her book on *Play Therapy* in 1947, her eight principles of non-directive play therapy still form the cornerstone of current practice.

(1)   The therapist must develop a warm, friendly relationship with the child, in which good rapport is established as soon as possible.
(2)   The therapist accepts the child exactly as s/he is.
(3)   The therapist establishes a feeling of permissiveness in the relationship so that the child feels free to express his or her feelings completely.
(4)   The therapist is alert to recognise the feelings that the child is expressing and reflects those feelings back to him or her in such a manner that s/he gains insight into his or her behaviour.
(5)   The therapist maintains a deep respect for the child's ability to solve his or her own problems if given the opportunity to do so. The responsibility to make changes is the child's.
(6)   The therapist does not attempt to direct the child's actions or conversation in any manner. The child leads the way; the therapist follows.
(7)   The therapist does not attempt to hurry the therapy along. It is a gradual process and is recognised as such by the therapist.
(8)   The therapist establishes only those limits that are necessary to anchor the therapy in the world of reality and to make the child aware of his or her responsibility in the relationship. (Axline, 1969: pp. 73–4)

These principles are so fundamental to current practice that they merit discussion in detail.

(1)   *The therapist must develop a warm, friendly relationship with the child, in which good rapport is established as soon as possible.*

All play therapists stress that the formation of a constructive relationship is an essential preliminary to any therapeutic progress (Landreth, 1991). However, the non-directive play therapist will not use the customary introductory tactics to endear him- or herself to the child: s/he will make no comment on the pretty dress or new shoes. It is for the child to express such pleasure, when s/he is ready to do so. Much communication between therapist and child is non-verbal. Welcoming smiles, an open regard for the child and close attention to his or her play, as well as acknowledgement of feelings, all assist in the formation of this relationship.

Children who have not developed basic trust struggle to recognise the relationship offered to them. Unable to understand the behaviour of a play therapist who does not expect anything from him or her, nor judge behaviour in any way, children can become bewildered. The non-directive play therapist continues to offer attention and warmth, and looks for opportunities to articulate the child's feelings.

When David, aged 12, was referred to me I knew that his early years had been characterised by chaos and abuse. His foster mother described him as '12, going on 6!'. He spent the first few sessions rearranging the furniture to make himself a den. This was followed by a game of hide and seek. David was illustrating his difficulty in committing himself to the therapeutic relationship; I waited before making any comment or joining the game. He found a puppet to hide with him: at his instruction I enlisted the help of a second puppet, and we began to communicate. As David and his puppet hid, I kept mine quite still, suggesting that his puppet was finding it difficult making friends with mine, as it was scary being friends. His puppet peeped out, and retreated; and I carried on chatting about how difficult it is not knowing what to expect. When his puppet emerged to inspect mine, I said that trusting was really difficult when you don't know someone well. At this David was able to leave his hiding place and looked for the teaset, announcing that both puppets needed food. Thus I had reflected and accepted David's uncertainty; when he could see that such anxiety was understood he was prepared to risk reparative play. He could begin to make use of the relationship that was offered to him.

(2) *The therapist accepts the child exactly as s/he is.*

It is challenging for therapists to suspend adult judgement. We have grown accustomed to expressing praise or displeasure with children (Garbarino & Scott, 1989). We notice new clothes, or brushed hair, and find unattractive the child who does not clean his or her teeth or is ineffective with toilet paper. However, it is not for the play therapist to teach the child to use a toothbrush. The therapist pays no heed to the clothes, nor unpleasant smells, and understands how this child is experiencing him- or herself at this moment. (There is a danger for any therapist commenting on new clothes: they may have been bought by a loving grandmother, and the child made to wear them when s/he would rather be in jeans!)

This lack of judgement is confusing for children at first. Many are bewildered by a therapist whom they cannot please nor displease. However, once they have understood this aspect of therapy, the refusal on the part of the play therapist to offer approval or disapproval is liberating. Energy that was once spent defending the child from anxiety provoked by adult reactions is released, and the child can now use it to heal him- or herself.

Many troubled children consider themselves inferior and inadequate. Such self-doubt is fuelled by perceived criticism or punishment. The acceptance experienced in non-directive play therapy gives the child the opportunity to understand him- or herself as s/he is. Slowly these children internalise the worth that the therapist feels for them; without realising it they come to value themselves (Moustakas, 1973).

Abused children are particularly observant of adult behaviour and moods: they have learned to watch for signs of adult displeasure, in the struggle to protect themselves. James, aged 10, always noticed when I was tired, and would be very quiet throughout these sessions. It took a long time before I made the connection between his subdued play and my tiredness; then it became clear that his watchfulness related to a need to protect himself from physical abuse in the past: his mother had been prone to aggression when she was tired. When I commented on this behaviour to him, without suggesting that it was surprising in any way, he was able to tell me more about the violence he had experienced in the past.

Many sexually abused children have been taught that adults will not believe them, and it may be necessary for the non-directive play therapist to challenge this in a very direct way. However, s/he can make it clear that s/he understands the child's perspective, whilst still disagreeing with it, with comments such as: 'I know you think that nobody will listen to you, nor believe you, and that you feel really alone at the moment. But I don't agree. I think there are people who will listen, and people who can believe. And I shall try to understand if you want to talk to me about anything that has happened to you.'

(3) *The therapist establishes a feeling of permissiveness in the relationship so that the child feels free to express his or her feelings completely.*

This milieu of permissiveness does not imply a lack of limits (see below), but the creation of an atmosphere in which the child's most intimate and frightening fantasies and impulses are tolerable. Children are often bewildered by the vivid turns their imaginations may take; the task of the play therapist is to follow where the fantasy leads, and to understand the feelings that are being expressed.

For many children, these fantasies are best explored symbolically, through play. The play therapist creates an environment in which the child has the freedom to choose what s/he wishes to do, and to express him- or herself in a medium that is meaningful. S/he may not always use the materials as they were intended, and play therapists need to decide whether they can tolerate (or afford) small figures to be covered with paint, or cars to be buried in clay. On other occasions, the child may struggle to decide what to do, fingering a succession of toys indecisively. The play therapist stays with the indecision, commenting that the child is having difficulty choosing what to play today, and resists the temptation to suggest an activity.

As Guerney writes:

'Since the therapist never challenges the validity of what the child expresses ... the child is free as nowhere else in his (or her) experience to look at him or herself as he or she really is, would like to be, or not like to be in relation to others and physical reality.'

(1983: p. 43)

This permissiveness underlines the acceptance of the child, and provides the context for symbolic expression of feeling that is the core of play therapy. Events and circumstances that were once filled with shame and guilt lose their terror, as these feelings are explored in the safety of therapy (Moustakas, 1973).

A wide range of emotions may emerge during therapy sessions. For instance, abused children have a plethora of feelings which need disentangling: fear, mistrust, shame, guilt, despair, helplessness and rage (Doyle, 1990). It is common for children to have murderous feelings towards siblings from time to time: if they discuss these at home they are likely to be told that they don't really feel like that! In play therapy, these fantasies can be played out, with a clear distinction maintained between fantasy and reality, and the sibling remains unharmed. Children whose sibling subsequently dies are particularly distressed by past death wishes, and need skilled help to understand that their fantasies had no power (Davies, 1991).

Small children cannot understand ambivalence (Harris, 1989). Play therapists working with these children have to remember that their feelings may swing drastically, leaving the child bewildered. It is not for the therapist to offer explanations of the child's confusion, simply to contain and reflect it. Eventually, s/he will make sense of these feelings for him- or herself.

(4) *The therapist is alert to recognise the feelings that the child is expressing and reflects those feelings back to him or her in such a manner that s/he gains insight into his or her behaviour.*

This expression of feeling, through the medium of play, is the core of the therapeutic experience:

'Through exploration of the various levels of his feelings and attitudes in an extended personal relationship such as that offered by play therapy, the disturbed child gains a sense of emotional insight and inner comfort, relaxation, and a sense of personal adequacy and worthiness, thereby decreasing the damaging effects of intense attitudes of hostility and anxiety.'

(Moustakas, 1982: p. 221)

Children rarely show their feelings directly: they emerge symbolically in their play. The task for the therapist is to help each child to make sense of them, and utilise this understanding to help him- or herself. Occasionally, it is possible to make direct connections between the child's actions and feelings: it is reasonable to suggest to a child who is beating at cushions that s/he is full of rage, or that one who bleakly rocks him- or herself in a corner is sad. Positive as well as negative feelings may need identification: it is appropriate to comment that the child giggling with delight with some regressive water play is happy.

Other children express feelings through figures in their play; the therapist can comment on the emotions of the participants in the game. However, it is not always easy to assess which figure more closely represents the feelings of the child: as the dinosaur is brought closer to the doll, the therapist can comment on the doll's fear and helplessness, or the powerful feelings of the dinosaur. Some children cannot tolerate interpretation of the symbolism of their play, but respond well to comments indicating acceptance and understanding of the significance of their activities (Donovan & McIntyre, 1990) Abused children often need to experience power in the playroom, and have their wish for total mastery recognised by the therapist, before they can consider their vulnerability.

It is common for children to project feelings during the early stages of therapy, seeing that the play therapist can survive them, before the child can take the risk of experiencing them for him- or herself. Therapists need to be prepared to tolerate waves of unexpected feelings without flinching.

Many abused children develop a distorted way of thinking, and confused belief systems. Children use such distortions to justify abusive situations to themselves (Jehu *et al.*, 1985–6). It is not for the non-directive play therapist to challenge these views directly, but to offer an alternative that the child can accept or reject as s/he wishes. Comments such as 'I know you think that it was all your fault, but I don't agree' are more constructive than 'I think it was Daddy's fault and not yours'. Gradually, each child may learn to see matters differently, and this fresh understanding will be all the more significant for having discovered it for him- or herself.

Children may express positive as well as negative feelings about adults who have abused them (Ellis *et al.*, 1990). For some children, the acknowledgement that they can continue to have good memories as well as bad can be a pivotal point in therapy.

(5) *The therapist maintains a deep respect for the child's ability to solve his or her own problems if given the opportunity to do so. The responsibility to make changes is the child's.*

This belief is fundamental to non-directive play therapy. Moustakas describes:

'[The therapist] approaches the child with a sincere feeling of belief in the child as a person who has capacities for working out his diffi-culties.'

(1973: p. 60)

It is difficult for the inexperienced play therapist to continue to believe that the child who creates chaos in the playroom week after week is engaged in constructive efforts to solve his or her own problems.

'Her play may be full of monsters or mayhem, and her feelings of personal self-loathing projected on to her therapist. But one day, she will find a heroine among the monsters, and her scenes of chaos may be resolved and those who have died may rise again and be allowed to live (until next week at least). She has found some hope for herself.'

(Carroll, 1995a)

It is stressful for therapists, faced with troubled children, not to seek solutions for them. As adults we expect to care for, nurture, and teach children until they are ready to make decisions for themselves. When a child falls we are quick to kiss the bruises better and provide elastoplast if necessary. Accepting the acute distress of abused or traumatised children is far from easy. Many adults would rather turn away.

(6) *The therapist does not attempt to direct the child's actions or conversation in any manner. The child leads the way; the therapist follows.*

Non-directive play therapists offer each child the freedom to select an activity (or inactivity) for him- or herself. The role of the therapist is to try to understand the significance of the child's choices, and to find ways to share this understanding.

Some children find the task of selection almost impossible. They turn frantically from one toy to another, unable to complete one activity before embarking on another. Others stand helplessly, seeking guidance. Conditioned to pleasing adults, they find selecting for themselves alarming. The play therapist does not attempt to alleviate the anxiety of either child by guiding him or her in any way. With a highly active child a comment such as 'You are finding it really difficult to decide what to do today, and are rushing from one toy to another' reflects the child's feelings in a non-judgemental way. The silent, frozen child can respond to gentle comments about how different it is in here, where s/he can choose what to do, from other places where adults make the decisions. Thus the child's view is validated by the therapist, and permission given to behave differently in the playroom.

Therapists like myself and Cattanach, who carry our materials with us, cannot adhere strictly to the principle that the child has a free choice of activity: that choice is limited by the selection that we have already made. When working non-directively I include as wide a range of materials as possible, and maintain a non-directive approach when I am with the child. Such arrangements make the practice of non-directive play therapy possible in circumstances when it would otherwise be limited.

(7) *The therapist does not attempt to hurry the therapy along. It is a gradual process and is recognised as such by the therapist.*

No child responds predictably to the challenge of play therapy:

'When a child is ready to express his feelings in the presence of the therapist, he will do so. He cannot be hurried into it. An attempt to force him to do so causes him to retreat.'

(Axline, 1969: p. 125)

In every other sphere of their lives children are hurried, and expected to conform to the times dictated by adults. From climbing out of bed in the morning to falling into it at night, much of their time is controlled. They must eat, leave for school, do lessons, go out to play – all at the direction of adults. Only in therapy can they relax, and take the time they need. It is a new experience; some children linger deliberately and savour the delight of really free time. Others hurry to the toys, and relish the chance to rush without being told to slow down. In time, each child finds the right pace for him- or herself.

Hellendoorn (1988) describes a case reported by Donker-Raymaker (1982). A therapist was trying to help Gerald, aged 10, come to terms with his feelings of grief following the death of his mother. He repeatedly denied the reality of his mother's death, enacting scenes with the small figures in which she was a constant presence. His therapist attempted to hurry his therapy and confront his denial by building a small cemetery in the corner of the sand tray; Gerald responded by building large walls round the small figures in the dollshouse. Wisely, the therapist helped him build the walls, and permitted Gerald to explore his grief in his own time.

This principle applies equally to individual sessions. Some sessions are full of emotional content, whilst others are free of it. Children rapidly become accustomed to the regular length of sessions, and are able to judge their play accordingly. Some 'wind down' during the last few minutes, whilst others try to cram as much in as possible. There are numerous occasions when children select the most significant play at the end of the session: generally they are well aware of the time, and are dependent on the practitioner to contain the anxiety engendered by this play by terminating the session on time. Practitioners should refrain from trying to rush the child to complete this play: the child knows what he or she is doing, and has selected these final minutes deliber- ately. However, a gentle reminder of the play at the beginning of the next session ('Do you remember, last week, you finished off by playing with the puppet? Well, maybe you'd like to play with that again this week, or perhaps you would like to choose something else.') assures the child that the importance of this play has been recognised.

Committed non-directive therapists adhere rigidly to this principle, and many embark on open-ended work, bringing the relationship to a close when they feel that the child has resolved those issues that brought him or her into therapy, and has adjusted to current circumstances. It is often impossible at the outset to suggest a time limit for this work, as some children respond more quickly to the opportunities of therapy, while others struggle to overcome anxiety and express themselves symbolically. Whilst it is generally true that more disturbed children take longer to unburden themselves, and that younger children respond more quickly than older, there are always exceptions. Such uncertainty makes it difficult for therapists to manage a heavy workload, and impossible for managers trying to assess the cost of treatment.

(8) *The therapist establishes only those limits that are necessary to anchor the therapy in the world of reality and to make the child aware of his or her responsibility in the relationship.*

Non-directive therapy is not a free-for-all. Whilst anger is understood, violence is not tolerated. Destructive urges are acceptable; acting on them is not. However, such actions are forbidden because they are dangerous, not because the play therapist disapproves of them or will be cross. Hitting people is wrong because it hurts, not because of the consequences it brings to the aggressor (Haworth, 1982a).

Many non-directive play therapists have struggled with the necessity of imposing limits. However, the provision of a set time and place in which therapy occurs naturally limits the opportunities that children have for total freedom. They provide a boundary around the therapeutic experience. Children rapidly learn to judge the length of therapy sessions, and some become anxious if they do not end on time. They need the containment offered by the predictable boundary of therapy (Bixler, 1982; Ginott, 1982b; Guerney, 1983).

Similarly, children need to know that destructive impulses will be understood and contained. It does not help the child to hurt his or her therapist, nor to damage the materials. It is the task of the therapist to keep him- or herself and the child safe, and to prevent deliberate damage to the playroom. Occasionally, this may require assistance: I am small and slight, and, when working with large aggressive children, I always ensure that someone is within earshot. Thus the child can see that I will not allow harm to come to either of us.

There has been more controversy about the imposition of limits in non-directive play therapy than any other principle of this technique. The need for limits appears to contradict the permissiveness that pervades all other aspects of the work. However, the concept of appropriate boundaries coincides with Winnicott's notions (1974) of productive play occurring in the safe space between the mother and child, mirrored in the experience of therapy.

Although they may disagree as to which limits are essential, few therapists fail to impose any. Even Pinney (1990), who permitted children to leave the playroom and even knock on neighbouring doors, kept a strict time limit. Wilson *et al.* advocate that:

'The guiding principles for the use of limits in non-directive therapy are that they should both reflect the practical reality of the constraints imposed by the physical context in which the therapy is conducted, and should also address the therapeutic needs of the child. In relation to the latter, the skill needed is to establish a level of permissiveness which is sufficient to allow the child to express and explore feelings freely, and at the same time to set boundaries to the child's behaviour which will both offer a sense of security and the potential for certain therapeutic experiences.'

(1992: p. 205)

Thus the therapist may be flexible. No child should inflict injury to him- or herself or the therapist, but some children may make more mess than others. The therapist who clears up after him- or herself may impose a limit on the muddle s/he can accept, but relax this with an inhibited child who has been able to regress into gloriously messy toddlerhood. This meets the therapeutic needs of this child, but does not need to be tolerated from all children.

I have found the issue which causes most distress to children is my refusal to allow them to take toys home, in spite of protests that they will bring them back next week. I cannot allow every child to keep a favourite toy; my budget does not permit it and the same toys must be available for all children in therapy. In addition, it may blur the boundaries of therapy if toys enjoyed in the playroom are shared elsewhere; and it is too great a responsibility for a child to care for an item from the playroom.

In my experience, direct confrontation is rare. Since I am not asking children to behave in a certain way, there are few opportunities to challenge me. There is no such thing as misbehaviour in the playroom as there is nothing that I disapprove of; but there are angry feelings that we can shout and stamp about without resorting to aggression.

Current interpretations of Axline's principles

Many of Axline's ideas are mirrored in the work of Moustakas, who defined his approach as 'child-centred play therapy'. Like Axline, he advocates the reflection of the child's feelings, which should:

'convey through empathy the values or attitudes that the therapist believes an integral part of therapy, in the hope that it will lead to clarification.'

(Moustakas, 1973: p. 2)

These values are: an unwavering faith in the child's ability to reach his or her own solutions, active acceptance of the child's feelings, and respect for the child as s/he is now, not who s/he might become.

The ideas of Axline and Moustakas underpin much current practice. Pinney (1990), influenced by Lowenfeld (1979) as well as Axline, founded the Children's Hours Trust which offers children unconditional acceptance and 'creative listening', a recapping technique in which the adult comments constantly on the child's actions, wishes and feelings, ensuring that the child recognises that the adult is totally committed to hearing and understanding the communications of the child.

'During the Hour the child plays freely within safe boundaries, at the same time as having the experience of being totally "listened to" without the intervention of adult views, values and judgements. This experience is rarely had by any child; when it happens it is a source of growth, of tension removal and the restoration of happiness.'

(Pinney, 1990: p.12).

With *Bobby* (Pinney, 1983) Pinney applied this approach to an autistic boy, following him through the streets of New York, in the firm belief that reflection of his reality back to him would enable him to make sense of his fragmented existence. Few current therapists would be so brave!

Play therapists in America have absorbed the ideas of Axline, along with the theories of psychoanalysts such as Adler (Kottman, 1994) and Jung (De Dominico, 1994), and promote a wide variety of practice. Oaklander (1994) has extended her earlier work which concentrated on focused interventions to embrace an eclectic approach which she entitles *Gestalt play therapy*. She promotes a strong therapeutic relationship, and enables each child to strengthen self-awareness through the use of all five senses, promoting expression of feelings, and encouraging the child to nurture him- or herself. In the latter stages of therapy, she draws the child's attention to inappropriate behaviours, believing that sufficient skills and ego strength have been developed to enable the child to choose to change. Although Oaklander uses games and focused techniques, the emphasis she gives to valuing each child as an individual and promoting unconditional regard on the part of the therapist will be familiar to all practitioners.

Wilson *et al.* have added an awareness of the stages of emotional development as defined by Erikson (1977), and show how this can assist comprehension of the child's difficulties and the process of therapy (see Chapter 2):

'Erikson's framework gives a coherence and added meaning to our clinical experience with children in non-directive play therapy, as well as to our understanding of less troubled children. In particular, Erikson's stages in the life cycle organise the child's development of emotions based on social interactions, as well as on maturational processes within the child, into a general overview of normal emotional development.'

(1992: p. 136)

By linking play therapy principles to the ideas of Erikson, Wilson *et al.* (1992) have suggested a way of understanding the process of therapy. The progress that children make as they proceed through the stages of development can be clearly defined; termination is indicated when the child's development is commensurate with his or her chronological age.

This process was illustrated by Sally: she was just $4\frac{1}{2}$ when she was first referred by her playgroup leader, who was concerned by her daytime wetting and some sexually explicit play. After her initial uncertainty, and testing of the limits in the playroom, Sally retreated into infancy, climbing into the dolls' pram, crying like a baby (with a tiny cry, not the wail of an older child trying to be a baby), and demanding constant comfort and attention, which I gave her. During the ensuing few months she slowly 'grew up'. We had weeks of messy toddlerhood, with water and paint everywhere. This re-experiencing was clearly reparative for her, and she enjoyed every minute of it. Looking back, I can see that she was postponing 'being 4'. One day, her play suddenly changed; she took the doll which she had used to represent herself and painted it: the legs and genitals were red, the hands orange and the breasts black. I abandoned Axline briefly and asked her gentle questions, but she offered no explanation; she simply asked me to look after the doll for her. Two weeks later she wanted the doll washed clean again, and asked me to paint 'I am 5' for her; following this she invited me to draw round her on a large piece of paper, and was very proud of how big she looked. Thus Sally used the opportunity of non-directive play therapy to regress completely, to re-experience her unhappy infancy and toddlerhood in a more satisfying way, to reconsider her feelings about herself at 4, and grow into a normal, happy 5 year old (Carroll, 1993a; this child is also described in McMahon, 1992: pp. 105–6).

Copley & Forryan also describe practice familiar to the non-directive play therapist, with the additional understanding of unconscious mechanisms and processes. They contend that:

'Play ... has meaning, and is a vehicle for the expression of a child's phantasies, that is to say unconscious thoughts and feelings that underlie actions.'

(1987: p. 231–2)

They value the concepts of integration and unintegration (Winnicott, 1974), of transference (Klein, 1937; Rosenbluth, 1970), and of containment (Bion, 1962). Recognition of the importance of the child's inner world brings an understanding of the challenge that current circumstances may bring. Jack (see Chapter 3) showed through his play that his inner world was peopled solely by monsters; anyone who tried to care for him was instantly equated with his terrifying internal objects and became instantly monstrous.

West (1992) advocates a child-centred approach, in which the basic technique is non-directive, with more focused interventions contributing to play therapy when appropriate. She highlights four stages of therapy, drawing on her own experience and the available literature (pp. 81–3). Awareness of the process of therapy, through identifiable stages, enables therapists to assess each child's progress:

- *Stage 1*. Children often present as chaotic when first referred for therapy. Diffuse behaviours have become the immediate difficulty, masking their emotional origins. Frequently the child cannot make connections between these behaviours and feelings.

- *Stage 2*. Gradually, as trust develops, children begin to focus strong negative feelings on definite events or people. Initially, these feelings may be experienced strongly by the therapist (projected by the child); cautiously the child begins to recognise and accept them for him- or herself.

- *Stage 3*. In time, more positive feelings appear amongst the anger, sadness and fear. Ambivalence towards past abusers may appear, which the child may find difficult to understand and tolerate. Children may be bewildered by more positive feelings: these emotions are new and difficult to understand. However, with them comes hope: for him- or herself and for the future.

- *Stage 4*. Children begin to adjust to reality and to accept its shortcomings. They look outside therapy for emotional satisfaction and support, and show that they are ready to put the past behind them. It is time to bring play therapy to a close.

Subsequent writers have also described the process of play therapy in four stages (Kottman, 1994; De Domenico, 1994; Goetze, 1994). Whilst the focus and methods of therapy may differ slightly (Kottman follows an Adlerian approach and De Domenico a Jungian), each approach follows a comparable path.

Whilst forming an ideal foundation to practice, not all practitioners adhere strictly to Axline's principles at all times. For instance, occasionally, children become very 'stuck', repeating an activity week after week, comparable to the post-trauma play described by Terr (1990). Supervision can help to consider the meaning of such play, but appropriate comments do not always assist in promoting a change of game. The committed non-directive play therapist will continue with the activity until the child eventually finds a resolution for him- or herself. However, occasionally, I will gently suggest an alternative, in order to relieve my own frustration! Tony, aged 11, was living in a residential home whilst his future placement was considered. His insecurity was expressed in endless games of hide and seek, a common symbolic expression of uncertainty in children whose placements are not secure (West, 1990; Bergman, 1993). I continually reflected his feelings of being lost, and fear that no home would be found for him, but still spent week after week playing the same game and wondering how to help him. Eventually, I introduced him to *Where's Wally?* (Handford, 1988); we talked together about Wally being lost and found, and I could sit on chairs instead of hiding behind them!

Strict non-directive play therapists, committed to working at the child's pace and continuing until problems are resolved, offer open-ended contracts to children and their parents or foster carers. Others work within an agreed time limit. Wilson *et al.* (1992) believe that time limits enable both child and play therapist to remain focused, whilst open-ended agreements can heighten the anxiety of a child who may believe s/he will be attending therapy for ever. They generally offer 10 sessions to begin with, extending this with a further agreed number of sessions when it is appropriate. Sloves & Peterlin (1994) also advocate a time-limited approach, setting contracts for work to be undertaken within 12 weeks.

There is no agreement about the extent to which play therapists should involve themselves in the child's play. When she wrote *Dibs* (1964) Axline sat quietly in the corner of the room, making notes whilst Dibs played. Ginott states a firm belief in the value of therapists staying apart from the child's play:

> 'The writer believes that therapy is retarded when the therapist participates whether as "parent" or "playmate". The unique therapeutic role can best be carried out when the play therapist maintains a non-playing relationship with the child, thus assuring that the session is strictly the child's hour ... Effective therapy must be based on mutual respect between the child and the therapist without the therapist ever abdicating his adult therapeutic role.'

> (1961: pp. 92–3; quoted in Guerney, 1983: p. 43)

Other play therapists involve themselves actively in the child's activities, happily adopting roles at the direction of the child. Guerney advocates that therapists should become full participants in the child's play, and insists that it is possible to maintain appropriate adult control and boundaries whilst playing alongside children in therapy:

> 'It is this kind of personal, noncontingent attention to the child which characterises the unique experience.'

> (1983: p. 43)

None of these authors attend to the difficulties an older or disabled therapist may have playing with small children. No practitioner should be prevented from undertaking play therapy with children by reason of age or disability. An understanding of the child's world, and an ability to face his or her pain, are more important than the willingness to participate in a vigorous game. Ideally, the play therapist should sit on the floor alongside the child; however, no practitioner should feel prohibited from working with children if, once sat on the floor, s/he has difficulty getting up again. S/he can be just as effective sitting in a chair.

I believe each child brings his or her own individual needs and difficulties to the playroom, and it is unwise to apply principles as rigidly as either Ginott or Guerney. Some children need active participation by their therapists, whilst others require therapeutic distance. Danny needed to involve me fully in a game in which he nurtured me before he could consider asking for such care for himself. John, aged 8, built himself a den, hiding himself totally from me, and asked me to build another den for myself. I refused, saying I thought I could help him better by sitting still and thinking about him hiding. In my opinion, such flexibility meets the needs of children more effectively than strict adherence to principles.

The theoretical base of non-directive play therapy

Guerney (1983: pp. 53–7) offers a comprehensive overview of outcome research into non-directive play therapy prior to 1983; it is beyond the scope of this book to repeat that here. Much of the literature has concentrated on case studies, which illustrate the efficacy of a non-directive approach (Gil, 1991; Webb, 1991; Carroll, 1993b, 1995a; Ryan & Wilson, 1996). Research into the efficacy of therapeutic play techniques is scanty, and inconclusive. Faust & Burns review the research in this area, and comment that:

> 'There is a conspicuous void in the psychological research literature designed to measure child psychotherapy outcome, and sadly, child therapy outcome research has lagged significantly behind adult work in this area.'

> (1991: p. 663).

They go on to propose a scale on which outcomes can be measured, and apply this to only two children, one of whom received non-directive play therapy and the other directive techniques. They acknowledge the need for further research.

Many practitioners have long considered non-directive play therapy a valid technique for helping troubled children. Wilson *et al.* (1992) developed a theoretical base to explain its success. They set non-directive play therapy within a Piagetian framework, suggesting that the effectiveness of the technique makes sense in the context of an understanding of the personal, objective and motor development in young children. The child learns by relating every activity to past experience, organising them into structures known as schemas. These schemas are used to provide the context in which the child recognises and responds to current events, but are flexible and can accommodate change. They are divided into a number of separate but related components, with both personal and objective schemas having affective, cognitive and motor components. In addition, children develop coping strategies, which enable them to control anxiety and survive trauma. Children whose early attachments were distorted can find the reparative relationship offered by a non-directive play therapist recreates the infant relationship, and is a corrective experience (Ryan & Wilson, 1995a).

Children learn to represent unconscious material in their play:

'Symbolic capacity is used in two different ways: first, to transform an event into objective symbolic representation; and, second, to transform an inner or outer event into personal symbolic representation.'

(Wilson *et al.*, 1992: p. 40)

In non-directive play therapy, children express emotions symbolically, externalising them, thinking about them, then internalising their conclusions. These conclusions are used to adapt previously dysfunctional schemas, enabling the self-awareness and understanding to promote permanent change (Schmidtchen, 1994). Donovan & McIntyre (1990) caution that the schemas of abused children are particularly inflexible, but can respond to sensitive therapeutic approaches.

For instance, Jack's inner world (discussed above) was populated solely by monsters. During the course of his therapy, he began to draw small pictures of himself, surrounded by monsters, and describing the 'bogey men' who had lived in the house with his mother. For weeks Jack drew monster after monster, symbolising his inner experience, and gaining mastery over it. As I continued to accept his pictures without flinching, his mood gradually lightened. At the same time, he experienced unexpected waves of emotion, which had to be contained in his foster home as well as his play therapy sessions. However, he could now accept reparative cuddles. Gradually, his drawings changed, and he repeated pictures of his foster family, seeking to fill his inner world with comforting images. Finally he announced that his 'monsters had all gone', and it was time for our work to come to an end.

Jack's schemas were severely distorted and confused at the onset of therapy. He could illustrate them pictorially, thus enabling him to externalise past experience and think about it in a way that he could tolerate. Gradually, in the context of a therapeutic relationship, past beliefs that there was no-one who would not harm him were replaced by a willingness to accept and seek comfort. He could put the horrors of his early years behind him.

This view of play therapy is reflected by O'Connor (1991). In his opinion, the therapist joins the child's world on two levels. The child brings to this relationship feelings and behaviours from past experiences, which must be identified and dealt with in the transference between therapist and child. Thus the therapist takes a role in the child's fantasy life, and can be introjected as a good object to challenge past experience and relationships, in a similar way to the adaptation of schemas proposed by Wilson *et al.* (1992). Alongside this role in the child's fantasy life, children carry memories and feelings about their time in the playroom: the therapist exists as part of the child's real world. The child may go home and talk about his or her therapist, who is then part of the child's ecosystem in a way that s/he cannot fully control. The lessons learned in the playroom spill over into other situations, and colour other experiences.

> 'It is this hybrid relationship, one part reality and one part projection, that becomes the container for the child's negative feelings as they are played out.'

> (O'Connor, 1991: p. 216)

Therefore, both O'Connor (1991) and Wilson *et al.* (1992) have proposed mechanisms whereby the process of therapy is internalised by the child, who becomes able to leave behind maladaptive coping strategies and see him- or herself and the situation in a more realistic light.

Non-directive play therapy in practice

Only by describing numerous studies in depth is it possible to give the full flavour of non-directive play therapy in practice. That is beyond the scope of this book. However, I shall try to give some idea of the nature of this work by describing details of one play therapy session with one child, and outlining the process of therapy, lasting 9 months, for another. Thus the minutiae of non-directive play therapy can be seen in the context of the long-term process.

Richard, aged 10

Richard was removed from his mother's care to a place of safety when he was 2; prior to that his mother's nomadic lifestyle and haphazard parenting meant that Richard's care swung from gross neglect to loving mothering in an unpredictable way. After he had left the care of his mother the extent of his disturbance became clear; three attempts to adopt him failed, and with each breakdown his behaviour became more challenging. When he was referred to me Richard was living in a long-term foster home with a professional foster mother who had plenty of support and relief care. He was attending a school for children with emotional and behavioural difficulties.

After a full consultation with Richard's carers and teachers, and an assessment of his therapeutic needs, I considered that he had a fragmented inner world, and would be more likely to respond to a non-directive approach which he would perceive as less threatening. I was concerned that the lack of any stable figure in his life had left him unable to recognise a valuable relationship and find solace in it. Thus I knew that therapy would be a long, slow process. I arranged to see him weekly, in a small room in his school.

Initially, Richard was extremely hostile. Although I could sense the vulnerability beneath the chaos, he could not let me close enough to offer comfort. I was concerned by his inability to tolerate good experiences, and need to spoil any treats he was given. I considered that he was still employing the infantile defence mechanism of splitting, separating the world into good and bad, and failing to recognise circumstances in which the two can co-exist.

I sat still throughout my first few sessions with Richard, while he clambered around the room or crashed cars. I aimed to contain the chaos as quietly as I could. This was followed by some extremely violent play, much of which involved the symbolic murdering of me. Yet, in spite of this violence, he always joined me willingly from his classroom, and seemed reluctant to leave when it was time to return. Thus I knew that, in spite of the carnage, he was beginning to value his therapy.

His foster mother continued to find his behaviour challenging. Just as he was beginning to separate out his feelings in his sessions with me (entering the second stage of therapy as described by West, 1992), it was decided that he should spend some time with a sessional worker, away from the other children in his foster home. This would offer support to his foster mother, and relieve Richard from the stress of managing his peer relationships. His sessional worker would offer him normal, everyday experiences; this was not seen as something to envy by the other children. If they were taken out for the day, Richard was also taken somewhere special. Thus some positive experiences were offered to him in a non-threatening way, which he was able to tolerate and accept.

This is the content of the following session:

Case history 5.1

Event	Commentary
Richard arrived looking particularly pleased with himself. He told me that he had gone out the previous day, and had clearly enjoyed himself. I commented that he seemed happy: he'd enjoyed his day out. He showed me a small plane he had bought, which came with some stickers. He asked me if I could buy him some stickers, as he wanted to make a collection of the planes. I wrote down the details, and said I would try.	*Richard had contained a good experience.*
	This was the first time he had asked me for something. My response to this varies with each child: Richard so rarely asked me for anything that I agreed to try to find this for him, but told him we would keep it in the playroom.
Richard looked in my toybag, lifted it up and emptied everything out, sending some of the toys flying through the air in an uncontrolled way. I commented that things seemed to be flying around a lot today, but made no attempt to stop him as I knew nothing would break.	*This confusion was familiar. I just accepted it.*
Richard turned to the cars, asking me to choose one. Previously, he had always insisted that we take turns choosing cars, but on this occasion he selected all his favourites for himself, and gave me the rest. I smiled, but made no comment.	*Richard was able to take good things for himself, mirroring his ability to enjoy his recent outing.*
He asked me to make up a story about the cars. I replied that he really wanted me to decide what we were going to do today, and he nodded. However, he turned instantly to the farm animals, again dividing them between the two of us. He selected the pigs, horses and cows for himself, putting the bulls well away from the cows, telling me with a grin that: 'We won't have any of *that* going on!' I repeated what he had said, as he put his animals safely in the fields, protected by fences. He left me with a few sheep and chickens, and told me that he had been farming for years and years,	*Briefly, he asked me to take control of the play, but took it back very readily.*
	An age-appropriate sexual reference.
	He made sure his animals were safe, but is not yet ready for me to comment on his own need for safety.

Case history 5.1 (continued)

Event	Commentary
which was why he had a big farm, but I hadn't been there very long, and so mine was only small. We each had a dog. He turned to the playpeople, and again divided them between us.	*Richard wanted to experience the power of being big and ensure that I understood how he felt being small.*
We each arranged our farms and people, and he told me that my farmer had a birthday today, so everyone must sing 'Happy Birthday' to him. I arranged my people accordingly. He brought his farmer over to my farm, telling me that my dog should go and greet him. I took my dog across to greet his farmer, who took out a gun and shot the dog. I commented that the dog had died, and Richard told me it was a joke, the dog was really alive, and both dog and farmer were welcome into the house. His farmer told mine that he had a present for me, as it was my birthday, and it was necessary to come outside to see it. Both farmers were taken across the room, where mine was presented with a cow. This cow charged my farmer briefly, knocking him down; but this, too, was a joke, and my farmer took the cow back to his farm. Richard looked at it quickly, and then added a calf, telling me that I mustn't kill the calf for beef and could only use it for milk. I commented that it was important that the calf stayed alive.	*It is common for fantasies of death and dying to emerge in children's play. The therapist is wise to wait to discover which lost aspect of the child's experience is being expressed. By making the death of the dog a joke, Richard was showing his inability to consider past losses.* *If my farmer could survive having fun on his birthday, Richard's survival of his pleasure at his outing was reinforced.* *He almost destroyed the fun here, but allowed it to continue.* *Richard could not have tolerated me making the connection between my caring for the calf and his need to be cared for.*
I warned Richard that we had only 5 minutes left, and he went on to arrange a birthday party for my farmer. All the people were gathered together, with the children playing on the swings and the adults indoors. By now there were only 2 minutes left; Richard turned to the small plane that he had brought with him, flew it low over the party,	*He could not manage to leave this play without destroying it, but the survival of some of his animals suggested that possibility of hope.*

Case history 5.1 (continued)

Event	Commentary
knocking all the people over. However, his farm animals remained untouched. He stood up to leave, telling me that he had really enjoyed himself. I reflected that he had had fun today, but now all the people had died. He grinned at me, told me that next week he would help me to clear up (he didn't), and returned to his classroom.	*I reflected his enjoyment.* *This week he needed to leave the mess with me; another time he might own it for himself.*

By the end of this session the room was littered with toys. However, I felt quite elated, and recognised quickly that this pleasure rightly belonged to Richard. Enjoying himself and not destroying it completely was a new experience for him, and the fun he had had the previous day was still with him when he joined me. He was able to extend this within our session, and bring good (the giving of presents) together with the bad (the farmer being knocked down by the cow) together in one session. Thus he had moved from his infantile splitting, and was beginning to tolerate the existence of both good and bad. In addition, there were hints that he might begin to believe in his own survival: he had given a present, and both farmer and cow survived the giving. At the end, although he killed all the people, his farm was still intact, with the animals safely in their fields. I deliberately made no comment about this: had I done so, I felt he would have destroyed the farm, just to prove me wrong. It was too early for me to reflect the progress he was making: at the moment my task was to accept it.

Kelly, aged 6

My initial assessment of Kelly is outlined in Chapter 3.

It was not easy finding suitable premises for play therapy with Kelly. Although her foster mother would have willingly made arrangements for me to see her at home, I felt it important to try to take these difficult feelings from the past away from this newly formed attachment. Her headteacher agreed to offer me a room at school: although there were numerous distractions, I knew that we would not be disturbed. In addition, there was a doll's house with furniture in the room which I could use: an item I find difficult to carry with me. There was also a small sink in the corner, which gave the opportunity for limited water play. The major disadvantage was enforced breaks every school holiday; fortunately, this work began in the autumn, and came to a close before the long summer holiday.

After discussions with her foster mother, I filled my toybag with two telephones, to help her communicate with me; a little rabbit which shivers to reflect fear; a small doll in a little bed, with a baby bottle and change of clothes, all of which can be used in a nurturing or aggressive fashion; a doctor's set, which is a means of both inflicting and healing pain; a wooden snake, which might prompt sexual play; playpeople to live in the house and give her the opportunity to illustrate her experiences; three aggressive dinosaurs and other fantasy figures to help illustrate her inner world; face paints, to project feelings and fantasies on to me; and felt tips, crayons, scissors, Sellotape and glue, for 'artistic expression'.

Having made arrangements for therapy sessions to take place I explained that I would spend some time with her at school, as I felt that playing with me might help her with some of her worries. She was also told that I would meet with her foster mother monthly, and we would speak often on the telephone.

Nevertheless, this first session was difficult for us both. Although the headteacher had been extremely helpful during the assessment, I was uncertain how long-term arrangements would work. In fact, the teachers were welcoming throughout my work with Kelly; without their unquestioning support my task would have been significantly more difficult.

● *Stage 1:* Kelly's first few sessions were chaotic. She tipped all the toys on the floor in a heap, and made little effort to sort them. She returned constantly to the telephone, trying to make phone calls but unable to complete the play. The doctor's set was explored, but no effort made to examine a doll or me. She picked up the little rabbit, noticed its fright, but could offer neither empathy nor comfort. The baby dinosaur was repeatedly hurt by the snake, but left injured as Kelly turned to other toys. I was left bewildered by this play, with strong projected feelings of a confused and anxious child, overwhelmed by emotions that she could not disentangle. At the end of each session she struggled to leave; she seemed unable to believe that I would return, with the toys, next week.

During the fourth session she began to extend aspects of this play: the baby dinosaur was hurt by the snake, but deliberately abandoned as she sought another activity. After more chaotic play Kelly embarked on a brief sequence in which she used the doctor's set to examine and nurture a woolly doll. She told me that the doll was very sick, and it would take a long time to make her better. Although this scene lasted only a short time, reflecting her anxiety at the prospect of change, Kelly was beginning to recognise her need for help, and to use the toys to symbolise this need.

When I discussed her behaviour with her foster mother I learned that she was presenting with regressed behaviour following her sessions. Thankfully, her foster mother could permit her to express her need for more satisfactory early experiences at home, and respond to her as a much younger child.

● *Stage 2:* As Kelly settled into play therapy, her anger emerged most forcefully, and she spent many sessions exploring her need for control and omnipotence. She introduced more characters into her play, but the themes remained constant. This play was more violent than one would expect from a child of this age: the snake engaged in terrifying assaults which left the baby dinosaur dead or dying; the large dinosaur ate small children; the family living in the house were overcome by earthquakes or monsters. She was attempting to recreate the power of her abuser, and to control that power, before her own vulnerability could emerge.

This play seemed to go on for months. Half term and the Christmas holidays came and went; I generally buy children something small (that is no competition to parents or foster carers with little money, but acknowledges the importance of the season), and found a small dinosaur which could be perceived as both fierce and vulnerable.

When Kelly returned to this play following the holidays, seeming to ignore the break, I was concerned that she may be stuck in post-traumatic play for which she could find no resolution (Terr, 1990). Her teacher and foster mother both assured me that she looked forward to her sessions, and so I had to rely on a belief that this play was meaningful for her, and would stop when she no longer needed it. This was a long and difficult stage for me: week after week she repeated her play, and I tried to bring fresh insight into her activities and understand its significance. In supervision, I could admit that this became boring. However, Kelly was not going to end this play to suit me, only when she no longer needed it.

The change came very subtly. I gradually became aware that the feelings Kelly was projecting included empathy for the figure that was injured. Once I had commented on the fear and pain of the injured man in Kelly's play, her focus changed completely. She turned to the small doll, and engaged in nurturing play in which she began to repair the damage to her infant self. Most of the time this involved feeding and nursing the baby, recalling satisfactions from her own infancy. She began to bath the doll: again this play was repetitive, with the doll having numerous baths and hair washes in each session. After each bath she gave me the doll to dry; it was important that I did this gently, holding her carefully as Kelly needed to be held. It is common for children who have been sexually abused to feel dirty; washing is a familiar activity for these children in therapy.

At this point Easter intervened, and we had a two week break in therapy. This time Kelly made it quite clear how angry she was at the missed sessions: she spent most of the following session with her back to me, replaying the aggressive fantasies that she had left behind weeks before. I reflected these feelings, but it was not until the end of the session that she was able to face me. As she turned to leave she gave me a delightful grin and asked for a hug; she knew that I had not rejected her and our sessions would continue as usual.

Kelly returned to the doll play, but included brief scenes in which her own neglect was painfully apparent. She left the doll asleep, and settled to draw; as she was drawing she repeated baby cries, interspersed with angry insistence that the baby was naughty for crying. Eventually she turned to the doll and remonstrated with it for interrupting her when she really wanted to draw, angry that she couldn't be left alone for half an hour. The doll was thrown down, and Kelly returned to her drawing. Although it was clear that Kelly was illustrating life with her grandparents, I did not attempt to talk with her about events in her own life, but continued to comment on the feelings of the doll whose needs were so painfully ignored.

- *Stage 3*: Shortly after this I visited her foster mother, and learned that Kelly was beginning to talk about her past at home. Wisely, her foster mother asked no questions, but simply permitted Kelly to talk when she needed to. As Kelly learned that talking brought relief, she opened up more and more: the details of her past unhappiness came flooding out.

Gradually, Kelly's mood began to lift. As she brightened, it became clear how miserable she had been, and how much energy had been spent simply surviving. Her teacher described her as having a new approach to her peer relationships; no longer was she attempting to control other children, and she tried to co-operate. This was a difficult time for Kelly. She could see the other children enjoying themselves, and longed to join them, but she had had little practice in the give and take of children's games. Often her teacher found her in tears in the playground when another child had rejected her for spoiling a game. Following a discussion between her teacher and foster mother, children were invited home individually, to give Kelly the opportunity to succeed in her efforts to play with one child and give her guidelines to help with groups of children. It took some time for this to resolve, but with the support and understanding of her teacher and foster mother Kelly was able to persist in her efforts to make satisfactory relationships with her peers.

This anxiety about peer relationships extended into her play therapy sessions. Sometimes she would bring an imaginary friend; on other occasions she invited me to join the play. Although she needed me as a playmate to practise with, it was important that I did not lose sight of my role as an adult. I could role play 'shops' with her (a game often employed by children who are struggling to make sense of social norms and values); however, when asked to join her in climbing around the room without touching the floor I told her that this was a good game for children but not for grown-ups. I would think about her pleasure as she climbed round the room pretending the floor was full of sharks, but when you are older chairs are for sitting on!

It was often difficult to disentangle the significance of her play during these sessions. Some of the play mirrored games she sought to play with her peers; at other times it came from stories or her imagination. When she told me the floor was full of sharks I could have commented on the dangerous world she was living in; however, there was no fear in her projected feelings and her mastery over the sharks was clear when she slipped on to the floor and just sat and giggled. She knew the world is not a safe place, but she could create and master her own monsters; her inner world no longer frightened her.

• *Stage 4:* As we approached the end of the summer term I had to decide whether play therapy needed to continue into the autumn. Kelly still had difficulties relating to her peers; occasionally she returned to regressive behaviour in her foster home. She had never directly addressed the sexual abuse; but the associated feelings had emerged, and been resolved, very effectively during the process of her play therapy. However, compared with the difficulties she had presented when I first met her she was a different child. After long discussions with her foster mother I agreed to terminate her play therapy at the end of the summer term. We agreed that I would tell her 4 weeks before the end of term: I would see her three more times in school and have a final picnic with her in her garden at home.

Kelly responded by insisting that she did not want to stop seeing me. I explained again that she had changed since I had first met her, and she was so much happier that I thought she needed to spend the time in her classroom rather than with me. Kelly was not convinced. Her play returned to the aggressive play that had troubled me for so long: yet again figures were injured and left to die unattended. I commented on her anger and unhappiness that her therapy was going to end, but she did not reply. At home, her play was regressive and often defiant. She had her first tantrum for several months.

Although I was concerned by this response, I felt it was important to continue with my original plan to bring Kelly's therapy to a close. If she believed she could change my mind easily, there was a risk that the date of termination would become her decision and not mine. In addition, I knew that, in spite of her current behaviour, her progress had been impressive.

When Kelly came for her final play therapy session I greeted her as usual. She began by returning to the familiar aggressive fantasies, but moved on rapidly and managed to recap every sequence of her play in one session. She abandoned the baby dinosaur, then turned to the baby and nursed it, left it to cry while she drew me a final picture, then asked me to join her in a role-play of *The Little Mermaid* (which she had seen recently at another child's birthday party), and left with a reminder that next week I was coming to her house.

The picnic was a great success. Fortunately it was a hot day; we all sat under a tree and Kelly proudly offered me sandwiches and cakes that she had made herself. She sat still during the meal, but was then ready to run off and play. A child from a neighbouring garden was invited to join her, and the two of them enjoyed the delights of a paddling pool. Any doubts I had had about terminating Kelly's therapy disappeared as I watched her play. When it was time for me to leave she gave me a hug, then collapsed in giggles when she realised that she had forgotten to dry herself and made my skirt wet. She was still laughing when I left.

When I met her social worker, by chance, 2 years after this work was complete, I learned that Kelly had been adopted by a family in another part of the country, where she was settled and happy. I was extremely lucky to have this information: it is rare to hear how children fare once therapy is completed, unless there have been further problems.

Summary

Current ideas of non-directive play therapy are derived from the ideas of Moustakas (1973) and Axline (1969). They emphasise the importance of accepting each child as s/he is, and believing in his or her innate ability to resolve individual difficulties, if given the opportunity to do so; and in the therapeutic relationship between the adult and child being the essential context in which this resolution occurs.

Some practitioners have expanded Axline's original ideas, including the psychological theories of Erikson (Wilson *et al.*, 1992), or the psychoanalytic practice of Klein (Copley & Forryan, 1987). Others adopt broad non-directive principles, but are ready to be flexible to meet the needs of individual children.

There have been numerous case examples of non-directive play therapy in practice. I have included a detailed account of one session, and a discussion of the process of therapy with another, to illustrate this technique in practice.

Chapter 6
Focused Interventions

Introduction

This chapter includes a wide range of techniques whose common theme is the narrower range of materials than those employed by the non-directive play therapist. Some interventions will be familiar; others are new. It can be argued that techniques such as sand play and art therapy have more in common with non-directive play therapy than with many of the more active interventions outlined in this chapter. I agree that the training needed, and the awareness of the therapist on the importance of the child's inner world, mirrors the focus of the non-directive play therapist. In addition, many sand play and art therapists provide materials and make no subsequent suggestion as to how the child should use them. They are incorporated in this chapter only because they do not include the extensive range of materials used by the play therapist.

All practitioners who adopt a focused approach share the view of the play therapist that the relationship between worker and child provides the context within which change occurs. James defines this as a 'therapeutic bond' (1989: p. 18). Directive practitioners engage actively in techniques which encourage this relationship. Greeting the child warmly, they seek something to praise: a football jersey, a new tooth, the child's height. Such comments are designed to show that the worker is deeply interested in the child, and notices small personal details about him or her. It is important that each child regards the therapist as supportive and empathic, willing to listen and believe all communications.

However, practitioners who commonly employ active interventions place less emphasis on this relationship forming the basis for any reparative experience. The relationship itself is not a tool for healing; it provides the context within which child and therapist find resolution to this child's distress.

James cautions against therapists using relationships developed with children to correct distorted attachments:

'The primary treatment for attachment impaired children is to have them live in an environment in which they experience therapeutic parenting.'

(1989: p. 128)

She argues that attachment can best be promoted by interventions which concentrate on the dyad of parent (or foster carer) and child (Ammen, 1994), or focus on relationships within the family. These children need to be cared for with consistency and predictability, with non-punitive management of the child's behaviour. Non-directive therapists would argue that play therapy sessions which supplement attention given to attachment difficulties can be highly effective.

Practitioners who advocate a focused approach almost always engage actively in play from the outset, in contrast to the non-directive play therapist who takes the lead from the child. Those who advocate active intervention seek to understand each child's experience by being alongside him or her:

> 'The therapist must actually join the child in play until the young-
> ster has had sufficient actual experiences to realise that her feelings
> will not destroy her, that she will not be punished for them, and that
> a past aggressor will not harm her because of her wishes and
> fantasies.'
>
> (James, 1989: p. 164)

When practitioners actively engage in play with a child s/he learns that feelings and behaviour are containable. James argues that, left to play with minimal intervention from the therapist, children do not feel understood in such a profound and healing way.

The range of techniques that has been developed in recent years aimed at helping children understand and express their feelings, and make sense of past events, is impressive (including Oaklander, 1969; Schaefer & O'Connor, 1983; Jewett, 1984; Redgrave, 1987; Aldgate & Simmonds, 1988; Schaefer, 1988; James, 1989; Crompton, 1990; Doyle, 1990; Cipolla *et al.*, 1992; Fahlberg, 1988c, 1991; Newson, 1992; Jennings, 1993; Ryan & Walker, 1993; as well as numerous papers in professional journals). It is impossible to cover all these contributions in depth. I shall separate focused interventions into eight areas, and illustrate each with different games and exercises:

(1) Techniques that help the adult to get to know the child.
(2) Techniques that offer a glimpse of the child's inner world.
(3) Techniques aimed at improving the child's sense of him- or herself as a cohesive, unique and valued individual.
(4) Techniques to help the child make sense of his or her past and present.
(5) Techniques aimed to promote the expression of feelings.
(6) Special issues for survivors of sexual abuse.
(7) Practical aids.
(8) Contributions from art, drama and music therapists.

Techniques that help the adult get to know the child

Meeting and engaging children in the therapeutic experience is a challenge, and each practitioner has favourite ice breakers, which are designed to lower the child's anxiety and set the scene in which child and adult can communicate meaningfully.

Squiggles

This technique involves child and adult taking turns in closing their eyes, and drawing at random on a piece of paper. The other participant may turn the paper any way s/he wishes, and discover pictures in the 'squiggle' (Claman, 1980).

Winnicott (1971), a child psychotherapist, perfected this technique as a short-term intervention, and used the pictures seen by the child to reach an understanding of his or her inner world. He invited children to decipher his squiggle first, and used his contribution to complement the picture found by the child. His work is based on the premise that the images seen by the child reflect issues that unconsciously worry him or her; interpretation of the pictures will lead to insight and relief. Sometimes the squiggles formed the basis of a child's therapy; on other occasions they were the introduction. His book of case studies (1971) illustrates the successful application of this technique in the psychotherapy of a number of children.

Those without the training and understanding of the child psychotherapist should not attempt to interpret pictures drawn by the child. I use this game in two ways: to bring shy children into a session, when they are struggling to overcome anxiety at meeting me; and to fill in the last few minutes of a session if we have completed a chosen activity and still have a little time left. I have found it most successful with artistic and imaginative children: they can generally see many more pictures in the squiggle than I can and delight in my incompetence!

Oaklander (1969: pp. 37–40) also applies this technique, calling it a scribble. However, she encourages children to both draw the scribble themselves and to discover pictures in it. She finds that some children find several pictures in their scribble which they go on to use as characters in a story. She describes how one 8-year-old boy found a small figure of himself in the middle of a scribble; he went on to declare:

> 'I am laughing because this scribble is keeping everybody from getting at me. It's like a fence round me. I can see them, but they can't see me.'

> (1969: p. 41)

He had used his scribble to illustrate his private need to protect himself from close relationships.

King or queen of the island

The child is asked to imagine him- or herself as king or queen of an island, in the middle of a shark-infested ocean. S/he can select all those items, people, games and events that s/he wants with him or her, and banish all those s/he wishes never to see again. I begin by drawing both islands, and sharing a few of my own likes (my family and friends, cream cakes, hot days in the sun) and dislikes (the smell of Parmesan cheese, dead birds brought in by the cat) to give children the idea; generally they soon disregard my contribution and enjoy their own fantasies.

I have found this valuable with children who find talking about themselves almost impossible. If asked directly about a favourite food or toy, they struggle to think of anything. I have also found it useful with adolescents, who cannot express themselves directly. Sheila, aged 13, had been grossly abused by a number of men, and was feeling very fragile when she saw me but could not talk about it. I engaged her in this exercise, and she drew her mother and her foster family on her island. She looked thoughtfully at the other island, and suddenly wrote on it: 'dads, brothers, rapists, murderers, men who want sex for money'. With the prompt of this technique she was able to disclose details of what had happened to her.

Cattanach (1994b) enables children to create islands in the play-room, using small figures. Her descriptions of the islands created by children in play therapy bridge the technique described here and the Worlds created by Lowenfeld (1979), illustrating what can be achieved by a practitioner willing to approach the work imaginatively.

Shields

Redgrave (1987) and Cattanach (1994b) encourage children to design a shield for themselves. The *Anti-Colouring Book* (Striker & Kimmel, 1978) includes a shield shape, and invites children to design a crest to say something about themselves and their families. Redgrave divides the shape into four quarters, and proposes that the child use each segment to illustrate favourite pastimes or aspects of him- or herself (Fig. 6.1). He applies this technique flexibly, adapting the suggestions he makes to suit the circumstances of each child. He has also used it with families, inviting them to make a shield representing aspects of family life.

Cattanach encourages children to make shields during the course of an initial assessment. She divides the shape into six, and suggests that they illustrate each section under the following headings:

(1) What is the best thing that has ever happened to you?
(2) What is the best thing to have happened in your family – any family (some children in care have lived in several families)?

(3) What is the worst thing that has happened to you?
(4) What do you want most from other people?
(5) If you only had a year to live and all the money you wanted, what would you do?
(6) What three things would you like to be said about you after you have died? (Cattanach, 1994b: pp. 82–3.)

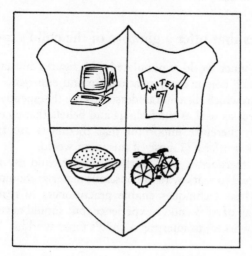

Fig. 6.1 A shield.

Cattanach is sensitive to the needs of bereaved children, and rephrases the final sections to avoid unnecessary distress. She is also understanding of children who prefer to write rather than draw, or with a limited imaginative capacity. Nevertheless, her results, some of which are illustrated in her book, show how illuminating this technique can be. It is most applicable to older children and young adolescents, who are able to think about the titles to each section, and draw with confidence.

Directed play with small people and animals

Many practitioners use small figures to represent a child's family, in order to help the child illustrate his or her circumstances. The child is offered a range of play people, and asked to use them to illustrate his or her family, or events that have happened in the past.

Children who struggle to describe their circumstances verbally may respond positively to this symbolic representation. If a doll's house and furniture are also provided, children can go further: creating scenes to illustrate a domestic environment and showing graphically how they perceive life at home. However, practitioners should be careful before believing that every scene is an accurate picture of home life: the drama created by each child will include fantasy material, and thus cannot mirror events at home exactly. A child who retains the view that his or her father is perfect in spite of repeated episodes of abuse will illustrate a fantasy in which he behaves impeccably. If the small child's thinking has been distorted to the extent that s/he blames his or her mother for the abuse, the female figure is likely to behave abusively. Practitioners must interpret this play with care.

Techniques that offer a glimpse of the child's inner world

Each child's inner world is populated with figures and fantasies from the past, which colour every relationship and experience. It provides the context in which the child understands the therapeutic relationship that is offered, as well as the feelings and beliefs that emerge in transference. It is therefore important that therapists are familiar with techniques that offer a glimpse of this inner world.

However, therapeutic play workers are not child psychotherapists: those untrained to work with unconscious material should not attempt to do so. These techniques enable practitioners to reach a greater understanding of each child's experience, but should never be used by unqualified workers to interpret a child's inner world.

Sand play and the World technique

Lowenfeld, a child psychotherapist, developed a technique which externalised each child's conscious processes and made them available for her to work with. She had a small metal tray, lined with blue to represent water, filled with sand and various objects: living creatures (men, women, children, domestic and wild animals), fantasy figures (including spacemen and dinosaurs), scenery (buildings, roads, trees, fences), transport (by road, rail, sea and air), equipment for fairs, playgrounds, hospitals, schools, etc., and miscellaneous objects which she added from time to time. Each child was given the opportunity to create his or her own World in the sand, using the figures available.

Thus children illustrate their worlds on both conscious and unconscious levels:

> 'The World apparatus, with the range of possibilities offered by its mouldable sand, amorphous objects and World cabinet, makes possible the simultaneous presentation, within a single framework, of processes and concepts going on at different levels in the psyche and consisting of differing elements.'

> (Lowenfeld, 1979: p. 14)

Lowenfeld gave children the opportunity to create World after World, with gentle interpretations enabling children to understand these representations of their fantasies and to build understanding and insight. She also believed strongly that playing was in itself a healing process.

Attempts have been made to research and evaluate the results of the World technique (Bowyer, 1970; Weinrib, 1983; Mitchell & Friedman, 1994). Kalff (1980) extended Lowenfeld's concepts, bringing a Jungian understanding of the psyche to her interpretation of the child's play. She regarded sand as symbolising 'Mother Earth', and physical engagement with it providing the opportunity for unconscious and irrational thoughts and feelings, generally submerged beneath material reality, to emerge symbolically. Her ideas and practices provide the foundation for the current practice of sand play.

Newson, a psychologist and play therapist, has successfully adapted this technique in a model of play therapy in Nottingham (1983, 1992). Her materials, and introduction to them, are similar to Lowenfeld's. She recognises the value of children symbolising themselves and their perceptions in the worlds that they create:

'In Make a World [the child] plays God, creating a world beneath hands and eyes in the sand-tray. He may choose or not, as he wishes, to have himself represented in this world; if he does put himself into it, it is at one remove in that he chooses a doll or animal of whom to say "This is me", or simply indicates a location (I'm in that bus).'

(Newson, 1992: p. 91)

Newson devotes the first part of each session to the child's creation of a World; she then introduces dressing-up clothes and props, which are designed for children to take roles and experience directly those aspects of themselves that had previously been represented symbolically. The child has responsibility for what happens in each part of the session, but the material offered enables the child to move from externalising his or her world to liberating role play.

Allan & Berry comment that:

'The crux of sand play therapy is not that it must be interpreted but that it must be witnessed respectfully.'

(1987: p. 123)

Sand is a common material in the playroom, and is often available for children to use alongside other toys. Practitioners wishing to concentrate on this as an intervention should seek further training.

When Sarah, aged 8, was first referred to me she was living in her third foster home, which was breaking down, after leaving the care of her family following physical abuse and extensive marital violence. I offered Sarah a small sand tray and figures similar to those suggested by Lowenfeld. She selected wild and farm animals, separating them carefully at each end of the tray. She spread the sand from the middle of the tray, telling me that it was a lake full of crocodiles. She selected one pig, who moved from one corner of the tray to another, trying to find a home, but was not accepted in safety anywhere. Thus Sarah gave a symbolic view of her own world: moving from place to place and unwanted everywhere.

Guided fantasy

Guided fantasies are designed to take children on an imaginary journey, at the end of which they find a place which is all their own (Oaklander, 1969: pp. 3–10). Children are helped to sit quietly, and listen to a story; the worker describes an imaginary journey through woodland and mountain, using fantasy transport as well as real (children can fly in stories), ending with a door with the child's name through which s/he is invited to look, and to draw a picture of what s/he sees. I find out as much as I can about a child before using this technique, and create a story which reflects his or her interests and ambitions.

Some children find this process easier than others. Children unable to sit for more than a few minutes cannot complete the final picture. Others have a limited imaginative capacity and cannot fantasise about climbing mountains or flying over lakes. Some therapists find making up stories easier than others, and may need practice with colleagues before they feel comfortable narrating to children.

With imaginative children this technique can produce surprising results, giving startling insight into their inner worlds and fantasies. Practitioners can note whether the child's drawing is cohesive, or whether it includes a number of disconnected components. Some children draw a place full of explicit violence, indicating an inner world full of conflict and lacking comfort objects. Other children cover the picture with sunshine, and deny the reality of any unpleasantness. Each picture is a unique, symbolic representation of this child's view of the world.

Once completed, children can be encouraged to talk about their pictures, and maybe tell stories about them. However, no child should ever be pressed to talk about a picture if s/he does not wish to do so.

Rosie (aged 8) was living in a secure foster home when she drew this picture (Fig. 6.2), but the pain of past neglect is held within the image of the castle in the corner, which is 'too scary to visit'. She insisted that the troll by the bridge is friendly (in spite of its malevolence in the *Billy Goats Gruff*), and her image of the Cheshire Cat in the tree (which disappears to leave only a smile) suggests uncertainty. The picture is quartered by a river crossed by a road, with a large bridge, which was an accurate illustration of Rosie's struggle to form a cohesive understanding of past experiences.

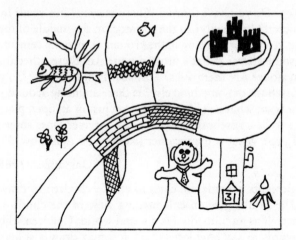

Fig. 6.2 Rosie's picture.

It is essential to remember that these pictures represent a fantasy, and not reality.

'Through fantasy we can have fun with the child, and we can also find out what the child's process is. Usually her fantasy process (how she does things and moves around in her fantasy world) is the same as her life process. We can look into the inner realms of the child's being through fantasy. We can bring out what is kept hidden or avoided and we can also find out what's going on in the child's life from her perspective.'

(Oaklander, 1969: p. 11).

Such imagery can also be used to help relax and desensitise fearful children (Singer, 1994). Suggestions are made which enable children to tolerate and then control the feared object in fantasy, which is followed by mastery of reality.

Rosebush fantasy

The rosebush fantasy is also more effective with imaginative children. The therapist asks the child to think of him- or herself as a rosebush, and makes suggestions to enable the child to create a picture:

'What kind of rosebush are you? Are you very small? Are you large? Are you fat? Are you tall? Do you have flowers? If so, what kind? (They don't have to be roses.) What colour are your flowers? Do you have many or just a few? Are you in full bloom or do you only have buds? Do you have any leaves? What kind? What are your stems and branches like? What are your roots like? ... Or maybe you don't have any. If you do, are they long and straight? Are they twisted? Are they deep? Do you have thorns? Where are you? In a yard? In a park? In the desert? In the city? In the country? In the middle of the ocean? Are you in a pot or growing in the ground or through cement, or even inside somewhere? What's around you? Are there other flowers or are you alone? Are there trees? Animals? People? Birds? Do you look like a rosebush or something else? Is there anything around you, like a fence? If so, what is it like? Or are you just in an open place? What is it like to be a rosebush? How do you survive? Does someone take care of you? What is the weather like for you right now?.'

(Oaklander, 1969: p. 33)

These prompts provide the clues to enable children to draw a clear picture. The results give an enlightening view of the child's image of him- or herself as an individual in a social world. Children who cannot find the words to say how lonely they feel may draw a solitary plant. Others swamped by well-meaning adults produce a crowded garden. Few unhappy children can see themselves in full bloom.

Michelle's roses (Fig. 6.3) were cut from the roots, and isolated in a bowl at the bottom of the paper. Aged 6, she had left the care of her mother only weeks before, and knew that her current placement was short-term. After 6 months of therapy, and certainty about her future placement, her view of herself had grown (Fig. 6.4).

Like the guided fantasy, this technique needs confidence on the part of the therapist. Not everyone feels comfortable suggesting to a child that s/he thinks of him- or herself as a rosebush! It is essential that practitioners feel confident with techniques such as this, or both worker and child will simply feel foolish.

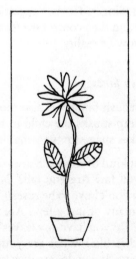

Figs. 6.3 and 6.4 Michelle's rosebushes.

Techniques aimed at improving the child's sense of him- or herself as a cohesive, unique and valued individual

The self-esteem of many referred children is extremely low. Practitioners cannot address this issue alone: those who care for troubled children on a daily basis should be vigilant and seek occasions when they can offer praise and approval (Roberts, 1993). Situations need to be created in which they cannot fail.

Some children have a fragile sense of themselves, and their emotional and physical boundaries. Many have been grossly abused, and lived in families without appropriate limits between adults and children. When, as toddlers, they should have been reaching a sense of selfhood, separate from their mothers, their autonomy has been threatened by adult behaviour. These children need help to reach an understanding of their rights to an emotional and physical boundary.

Using a box file

Redgrave (1987: p. 27) recognises that many children cannot respond to the greetings that adults normally use to begin relationships; the worker needs a 'third object' which both therapist and child can talk about. This object becomes an extension of both worker and child, and is the tool used to express feelings and achieve understanding.

Redgrave (pp. 30–31) often begins his work with a child by using a box file, which the child decorates with his or her name and other pictures and patterns. This file is gradually filled with memorabilia and bric-a-brac; ordinary items such as audio tapes, books, or dice games can be used initially; gradually more personal items are added as the child warms to the relationship and is able to talk about his or her interests, likes and dislikes, and private feelings.

This technique may precede life story work for children who lack understanding of past events, but become highly anxious when asked to engage in more structured work. The attention given to the child assures him or her that s/he is valued and important, and the opportunity to focus on him- or herself will be new and surprising. These children cannot adapt quickly; many are entrenched in their own chaos, which may be reflected in the muddle that grows inside the box. This chaos can be firmly contained within the box, providing an external representation of the boundaries that this child so clearly needs. When s/he is comfortable with the box file, it may be appropriate to help sort out the chaos, possibly through life story work.

Drawing round the child

Children with a fragile sense of themselves and their personal boundaries may respond to this technique. The child lies flat on a large piece of paper on the floor, and is drawn round by the therapist. The child can then shade this picture of him- or herself, identifying the colours of his or her eyes and hair, and the clothes s/he is wearing. S/he can look at this picture and recognise it as him- or herself.

It can be illuminating to ask children to lie on their stomachs. The child has to try to identify what s/he looks like from behind. Children without clear physical boundaries often find this surprisingly difficult: they can colour those parts of themselves that they can touch, but shoulders, which they cannot reach, are unimaginable. Even when it is suggested that they look at other people from behind, and that their appearance is similar, they cannot own a part of themselves that they cannot see or touch.

A few children will be threatened by this technique. Children who have been sexually abused should be approached sensitively, as the appearance of an adult towering above them may be perceived as threatening. Practitioners should not use this technique with any child who does not participate willingly and with obvious pleasure; no child should ever be made to do anything s/he does not wish to.

How the body works

It is common for children to have fantasies about how their bodies work that bear little relation to reality. How food can be so pleasant at one end and unpleasant at the other is a source of amusement and enquiry. Without explanations, children will create answers for themselves. If they bleed they may believe that they are losing a vital, irreplaceable part of themselves. They need anatomical information. There are many good books which describe the processes within the body (Rayner, 1978; Gaffe, 1990). Children need clear descriptions that challenge the fantasies.

Children who have been sexually abused may need basic sex education (Bray, 1991). Although they have had sexual experience they may have no understanding of what was happening, and need information urgently. Ideally, parents or foster carers should educate children themselves, and be available to answer questions. However, many find this embarrassing, and the support of a therapist or social worker introducing the subject may be necessary. Books can help (Mayle & Robins, 1973; Gee, 1985), but openness and honesty with the inevitable questions is imperative.

Games to help children be more aware of their own bodies

Physical activity of any kind assists children to develop an awareness of the potential of their own bodies. Frequently, disturbed children cannot cope with the hurly-burly of the playground or organised games, and lack opportunities for physical exploration. Children with low self-esteem find it difficult to relax and enjoy the pleasure that can accompany exercise. They need time to rediscover the delights that physical sensations can bring.

Jennings (1993: pp. 37–41) often works with groups of children, and encourages them to roll each other gently across the floor. Children are asked to relax completely, facilitating movement. This is followed by their being as stiff and resistant as possible; both the child on the floor and the one pushing notice the physical difference between one game and another. This exercise can easily be transferred to individual therapy, provided the therapist is reasonably small and the child large enough to take turns at pushing.

In addition, some nursery games, such as *Row, row, row your boat*, provide opportunities for physical experience. Tactile materials such as clay and finger paint promote an awareness of physical sensations. Oaklander suggests working with clay with closed eyes, thinking about the slippery feel of the clay (1969: p. 75). Finger paints can be used to make hand- and footprints, and can prompt children to simply make a mess. Maintaining clear boundaries round this mess helps children understand physical containment, within which their own experience can be explored.

For many children, an inability to relax is a further difficulty. Children can be taught relaxation in the same way as adults, tightening and releasing muscles throughout the body, and finally feeling the easing of tension. Imagery can be helpful in enabling children to relax: as they lie or sit they can think of themselves on a warm sunny day (Koeppen, 1993). Oaklander suggests that children think of themselves as snowmen, standing alone in a garden and gradually melting (1969: p. 124).

Games to help survivors of abuse correct a distorted body image

The distortion of perception of sexually abused children is so common that it has gained the name of 'damaged goods syndrome' (Porter *et al.*, 1982: pp. 112–15; Faller, 1988: p. 291). Some children believe that they have been physically altered by the abuse, and people must know about it simply by looking at them (Byram *et al.*, 1995). Others believe that they may never be able to enjoy normal sexual relationships, nor have children. Believing that their bodies are impaired, many abuse themselves by self-harming activities such as arm cutting, or anorexia or bulimia (Herzog *et al.*, 1993; Miller *et al.*, 1993; Waller *et al.*, 1993), thus reinforcing a view of themselves as physically damaged.

Medical examinations, if undertaken sensitively, can challenge the child's view:

'The ability to state authoritatively that physical damage is absent or has been treated is a stepping-stone to convincing the child ...

that [s/he] ... has not been otherwise damaged by the sexual victi-
mization.'

(Porter *et al.*, 1982: p. 115)

Faller (1988) uses drawings to help children look more closely at
their views of their bodies. She encourages children to draw themselves,
noticing how many sexually abused children picture themselves without hands or limbs or sensory organs. She engages children in discussion about feelings of being damaged in some way, and challenges this
perception by encouraging children to change the picture themselves,
adding the missing part to make themselves whole (Faller, 1988: pp.
291–3).

The difficulties that survivors of sexual abuse may have in understanding their physical parameters may be linked to dissociative
defences being employed to survive the abuse. The psyche separates
from physical experience. These children cannot acknowledge their
own bodies without skilled help:

'To occupy a body filled with pain, gutted by pain, is to experience a
body which is finally, uninhabitable.'

(Young, 1992: p. 99)

Practitioners who find that the child cannot respond to techniques
aimed to restore a positive body image should consider the possibility
of a dissociative disorder.

Prolonged physical abuse may also lead children to question the
integrity of their bodily existence (Gardner *et al.*, 1990). Some children
have been so badly abused that they carry the scars with them for ever:
a broken leg may result in a permanent limp, or head injuries lead to
learning difficulties. These children live with the physical consequences
of abuse, as well as their feelings about it. They perceive themselves to
be imperfect and blemished; the strength and validity of these feelings
need acknowledgement before the child can find positive abilities to
build on.

Techniques to help the child make sense of his or her past and present

Many children referred for therapy have moved from home to home,
and from town to town, so often that they can no longer contain within
themselves an understanding of who they are and where they came
from. These children need an external representation of their personal
histories.

Life story work

During the past 15 years life story work has become an increasingly popular technique for helping children with disrupted histories. Children separated from their birth families lose a sense of identity which most of us take for granted. The process of piecing together a child's history and collecting it in book form is a valuable way of restoring that sense of identity. There is now a growing list of articles and booklets which offer ideas and encouragement to those undertaking this work (Connor *et al.*, 1985; Fahlberg, 1988c; Harrison, 1988; Ryan & Walker, 1993).

Before beginning life story work practitioners need to undertake thorough research into the child's history: this may involve many hours of reading files, but it is essential to understand the reality of this child's experience. Once this preparation is done, the book should be made with the child. It is the child's life story, and belongs to him or her alone.

The sharing of this understanding with the child can take many forms. Photographs are clearly important. Pictures of those who have cared for the child in the past can be stuck alongside the place in which they now live. The feelings that such pictures recall can be gently explored as the book is made (Berman, 1993). However, life story books are much more than photograph albums.

Maps, with drawings or cartoons, can help explain moves from one town to another. Visits are an integral part of this work. Past schools and foster carers are generally quick to ignore previous misdemeanours, and welcome children back. On one occasion, when I took Helen, a young woman with a very troubled history, to visit a family who had fostered her, the mother showed a treasured embroidery that Helen had made at school; the children (now young people themselves) recalled with laughter escapades which had clearly enraged the family at the time. Thus she could see that this family had fond memories of her time with them, as well as a realistic view of her challenging behaviour (Carroll, 1991).

Children need to know why as well as what happened. Such explanations should be given carefully, taking account of the child's feelings and beliefs about past and current carers. There is no escaping reality if a child has been abused, but children can begin to understand that there are pressures on parents that may lead them to behave in ways that they later regret (Ryan & Walker, 1993). Small children can learn that, although mummy may not be able to stop him or her being hurt, she still loves her child and wants the best for him or her.

Life story work can provide the vehicle to help children with different ethnic or cultural backgrounds explore their social experiences and achieve pride in their colour and history (Ryan & Walker, 1993). The practitioner must undertake thorough research into each child's racial origins, and share this knowledge with him or her.

Some children prefer particularly painful memories to be included in a separate section of the book. Children should feel free to choose with whom they share the most intimate details of their lives; this enables them to display past successes whilst keeping some aspects of their lives private.

For many children life story work has given meaning to an otherwise incomprehensible history. However, it uses the means of communication familiar to educated practitioners: words, diagrams and books. We are comfortable making order out of chaos by committing it to paper. Making a life story book with a child uses skills that are familiar to the adult (Carroll, 1993b). Children from homes where academic skills are not encouraged may be, at best, uncomfortable with such techniques; some will find them incomprehensible. Maps and flow charts that look so impressive in life story books are meaningless to small children unless accompanied by age-appropriate constructs providing explanations. For instance, I draw a large, simple map on a piece of paper, and put little wooden houses to represent the places where the child has lived; small figures sit by the houses, representing parents and carers. The child can move the small figure s/he knows as him- or herself from place to place, seeing that 'this is the place where s/he lived with Auntie Jean', and that both houses and people exist even though s/he is not with them.

Ecomaps

An ecomap (Fig. 6.5) can be a component of a life story book, and may be used to help any child who is confused about the number of adults involved in his or her life. It is described in detail by Fahlberg (1988c: pp. 218–21) and Ryan & Walker (1993: p. 38). Ecomaps are diagrams,

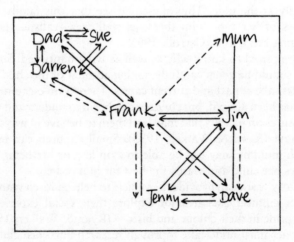

Fig. 6.5 Ecomap.

with the child in the centre, and all those who are, or have been involved in his or her care, drawn around him or her. Lines from one figure to another indicate feelings and difficulties in each relationship.

Fahlberg used ecomaps to prompt discussion of the child's perception of his or her history, and to detect misunderstandings. Accurate reasons for each move are included, challenging fantasies created by the child. Children are encouraged to express positive and negative aspects of each placement. Professional roles are clearly defined.

This is another technique well-suited to children and young people who are comfortable working with diagrams and maps. Those who have difficulty reading or writing will struggle to make sense of the diagram, and intellectual difficulties may overshadow any benefit the child may gain.

Sociograms

Sociograms (Fig. 6.6) have been developed by sociologists to show the cohesiveness of groups, and to heighten understanding of group processes. Redgrave (1987: pp. 63–9) has successfully adapted this technique to help children understand affectional patterns in their families. The names of all members of the child's family are written down, and the child encouraged to consider the strengths of feelings, both positive and negative, between them. Thus emotional bonds are displayed diagrammatically.

Redgrave (1987) illustrates the diagram with small houses to represent the various homes that family members live in. Small children cannot be expected to draw such a diagram unaided. They need prompting to think of all the people in their lives and how they feel about them. However, if the child can complete the sociogram alone, it can lead to fruitful discussion which reveals important attachments

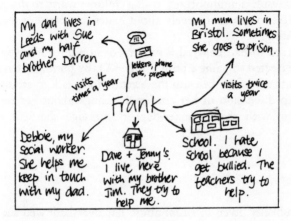

Fig. 6.6 Sociogram.

which may not be obvious in an initial assessment. A favourite aunt may emerge who can offer affection and warmth that is lacking in the rest of the family. It may also expose those individuals who have been least caring of the child.

This can be highly effective for children who fantasise that relationships in their families are perfect. On close scrutiny they can see that this is not so, and they must begin the task of accepting family relationships, flawed though they may be, as they really are.

Making posters

Children who struggle with reading and writing may warm to the opportunity of making posters, especially if large sheets of paper and plenty of paint are provided. The physical activity of painting may help to ease any discomfort the child may experience talking about sensitive issues.

Ideas for the titles of the posters include: What I Like About Myself (to help children begin to see themselves more positively), Who Can Help Me Now? (for children who have left the care of their natural families and are struggling to accept the help that is offered), Whose Fault Was It Really? (which challenges children's omnipotence and places responsibility for past abuse where it belongs), Friends Of My Parents (for children who believe that their parents have no-one to look after them except their children) and Don't Talk To Strangers (which can lead to discussions of self-protection and the child's right to feel safe). Practitioners should consider the difficulties of the individual child, and suggest a number of titles that might appeal (James, 1989: p. 208).

In my experience older children are less amenable to this technique, and need a more verbal intervention. However, provided the neatness of the end result is unimportant, young children warm to this approach and are able to talk more freely about issues that concern them whilst busy painting.

Ellie (aged 8) had enjoyed 9 months of non-directive play therapy when she elected to paint a poster (Fig. 6.7). By putting the number of her stepfather's house beneath the legend 'don't talk to strangers', she opened up discussion of her confused feelings about her own abuse contrasting with the 'stranger-danger' message she had heard in school.

The use of rituals

Recent publicity given to ritual abuse has overshadowed the positive aspects of rituals in western society.

Fig. 6.7 Ellie's poster.

'Across cultures and throughout history, rituals have provided forums for change and transformation, forums that give people a sense of comfort and control in a world that is mysterious and to a large degree incomprehensible. They are used to provide milestones that help to construct the reality of a person's, a family's, or a people's history; they are used to heal or to cause harm; they are used to ward off danger.'

(Hoorwitz, 1988: p. 297)

Traditionally, rituals facilitate the passage from one state to another: baptism, marriage, funerals; or they mark the passage of time: birthdays, Christmas, New Year. Each family develops its own traditions so that, within a general celebration of Christmas, there are many minor variations.

Children who move from one family to another rarely do so with the accompaniment of a ritual. Whilst strong feelings of grief and loss may be acknowledged, it is still hoped that children, resilient as so many are, will settle in a second family without too many difficulties. Too often, children have to adjust to third or fourth families, until permanent placements are found for them. Many cannot cope with the making and breaking of attachments that such changes bring.

Jewett (1984: pp. 17–18) has developed a candle ritual to help children in such circumstances. She suggests to a child that love is like a candle, and the first candle of love was lit by the mother's love when s/he was born. Other candles of love, for his or her father and other relatives, were lit gradually. Although s/he may no longer live with a birth family, these candles remain alight for as long as they are needed; from them s/he can light other candles if s/he wishes to. Thus, from that first candle, s/he will have as much love as s/he needs, and none are blown out until s/he is ready to do so.

Redgrave (1987: pp. 99–101) uses a similar technique which he calls loving and caring candles. He lights candles in much the same way as Jewett, describing the loving and caring feelings the child has for those who have been close to him or her. The child is asked to suggest which candle represents which person; if s/he no longer lives with them those candles are moved to a separate tray, and s/he can see that they are still burning.

I have found that many children believe that love is like cake: there is a limited amount and once every slice is used there is none left. Therefore, I extend Jewett's ideas and begin by cooking a cake with the child (which is fun), and then add the candles and discuss how my view of love differs from his or hers. Whilst the candles are still burning we can eat the cake.

However, I never use this technique with children who set fires or young survivors of ritual or sadistic abuse. Evidence is emerging that candles and fire can play a part in these rituals (Sinason, 1994), and this strategy will cause extreme anxiety.

For bereaved children, rituals can have special significance. Many families are not comfortable with children attending a funeral, and children may be unable to believe in the permanency of death. These children need help to create their own rituals to say 'goodbye', and the task of the therapist is to help each child to find a way that is meaningful to him or her (Crompton, 1990).

Techniques that help children express feelings

Five faces

Many workers begin with a pictorial representation of feelings: Jewett (1984: pp. 55–6) begins with five – sad, angry, happy, scared and lonely faces are drawn in circles or paper plates, and children are encouraged to think about them, and to pull appropriate faces. Gradually, the child learns that talking about feelings is acceptable.

Doyle (1990: pp. 43–4) begins with three empty face shapes, and asks each child to draw feelings in them. She has found that abused children tend to choose sadness, happiness and anger, which she uses to invite discussion of how these feelings are experienced by this child. Striker & Kimmel (1978), in *The Anti-Colouring Book*, also provide three face shapes, and prompt the child to draw by asking what people do with their faces to show how they are feeling.

Ryan & Walker (1993: p. 24) suggest using as many faces as the child permits; they use paper plates to draw expressions on, and hinge plates so they can be turned round to show both happy or sad feelings.

They encourage children to think about how people might be feeling inside when their facial expressions appear mixed.

Colour your life

This technique is designed to help children think about their feelings, and to express them verbally (O'Connor, 1988: pp. 251–8). They are asked to consider an emotion and express it in colour; for instance, red is often associated with anger, and blue with sadness. The child is given a large sheet of paper, and asked to fill it with all the feelings s/he has had in her life: the worker might suggest that if s/he has felt happy for about half his or her life, then half the paper should be a happy colour. As the child paints or colours, the worker encourages verbalisation of the feelings s/he is illustrating.

James (1989: p. 196) uses a comparable technique to help children think carefully about how their feelings can change. She facilitates the matching of colours to feelings, and asks children to paint one circle to illustrate how they feel now, and another to show how they felt on a previous, traumatic, occasion. Further circles are added for children to illustrate how they think other family members might be feeling.

One further variation, also developed by James (1989: p. 196), uses a long piece of wallpaper, which represents the child's life. As s/he thinks about the feelings that s/he has had at different times s/he paints different coloured circles. James suggests that it is wise to keep quiet while children do this, and seek discussion only when they have finished painting. Left to work in silence, the child reaches feelings that would be lost if there were interruptions. I only use small circles for children with difficulty recognising boundaries; I find one long piece of wallpaper (and plenty of newspaper) a constructive, if messy, alternative.

List of feelings

Fahlberg has identified over 180 different feelings that people may experience from time to time (1988c: pp. 202–3). Too often, subtle emotions such as nervousness, unease, boredom, temptation, or embarrassment are forgotten when discussing feelings with children. Fahlberg uses this list to help social workers explore their own feelings as well as those of their young clients. It is a valuable reminder of the range of emotional responses we can expect from children.

James (1989: pp. 108–9) has developed a technique to help children explore their feelings and understand ambivalence. She has a large basket of marker pens, and a number of small squares of paper with different emotions written on them. Children are asked to identify an event, and think about the feelings associated with it, placing a number of pens in the paper to indicate the strength of feeling. For instance, if a child is feeling extremely angry with a tinge of regret, a large pile of pens will be placed on the 'angry' paper, and a few on 'regret'.

I have adapted this technique for use with young adolescents. I encourage them to write as many different feelings as they can recall on small pieces of paper. I then ask them to consider the feelings associated with one incident, and rank them in order of strength. I illustrate this by describing an event in my own life which prompted strong feelings at the time, such as a minor road accident, and share my own responses. One 13 year old came to understand her ambivalence at living in a children's home, when she identified her mixed feelings of sorrow at the separation from her mother and relief at being free from fraternal sexual pestering.

Elliott (1987) creates an 'emotional barometer' for each child, with a smiling face at one end indicating that the child feels 'better than great', and tears at the other to describe 'super pits' (p. 192). She asks children to consider how they feel at the beginning of each session, marking this on the 'barometer'; this ensures that the practitioner takes account of the child's emotional state during each session, as well as introducing emotion as a valid topic of consideration. I have found this particularly useful with children who are prone to mood swings.

Garbage bag

When children have settled into therapeutic play, James introduces the 'garbage bag' (James, 1989: pp. 167–70). She brings a brown paper bag to the session, and fills it with unpleasant rubbish: used tissues, old food from the fridge, etc. She suggests to the child that living with unresolved memories of trauma is like carrying a garbage bag all the time, and the only way to leave these feelings behind is to talk about them. She enables children to write a brief line about everything in the past that has troubled them, and puts this in a separate bag, which she keeps. Agreement is reached that they will talk about items in the bag for a set time during each session, until the child is ready to throw each piece of paper away: one day the bag will be empty and the child ready to face the future unencumbered. James explains to children:

> 'You'll always remember those things that have happened to you, but you can get so that you don't feel like it's a big smelly mess that you always have to carry around with you. You can just leave it behind, and move on with your life.'

> (1989: p. 170)

Articulate children, who can understand that talking about problems makes them manageable, can respond well to this technique. For some, the gradual emptying of the bag is tangible evidence of progress and provides the encouragement they need to continue with therapy. Others cannot understand the symbolism, and regard the initial introduction to the garbage bag as evidence that their worker is more disturbed than they are!

Focusing techniques

Focusing centres on the concept that feelings are bodily experiences, and understanding the nature of physical responses to feelings enables children and young people to effect changes in those responses (Neagu, 1988: pp. 266–93). It is a technique that is taught in six steps:

(1) The child records on audio tape all those aspects of his or her life that upset or worry him or her; the tape is played back and s/he is asked to associate feelings with each item.
(2) The child is asked to select the item which causes him or her greatest difficulty.
(3) The child considers his or her physical sensations when s/he thinks about this difficulty, painting or drawing pictures to help describe these feelings.
(4) The child is encouraged to think of words that describe these physical reactions, e.g. shaky, jumpy.
(5) The child is helped to look at what makes him or her feel jumpy, or shaky, and to consider the physical response to the words. S/he is not asked to alter these reactions, but to understand them.
(6) Further consideration and experiencing of the feelings gradually helps them to lose their impact (Neagu, 1988: pp. 270–72).

This is a highly skilled process. However, it is helpful to remember that emotions are experienced physically, and there are occasions when enabling children to identify the connection between feelings and reactions is valuable. Children who set fires often experience a buzz of excitement before an incident. If they can be taught to recognise this trigger, and seek help or other satisfactory experiences at this time, a fire may be averted (Bumpass *et al.*, 1983). The physical response of some sexually abused children indicates that they can contain bodily memories of abuse, which can be introjected as nausea by their workers (Sinason, 1988).

Special issues for children who have survived sexual abuse

Children who have been sexually abused have specific difficulties which must be addressed by those who seek to help them. A detailed study of the problems faced by these children is beyond the scope of this book; practitioners working with them need a thorough understanding of child sexual abuse and its consequences (Sgroi, 1982; Doyle, 1987; Bannister, 1988; Wattam *et al.*, 1989; Faller, 1988, 1990).

There are 10 impact and treatment issues which may be addressed during therapy:

(1)   'Damaged goods' syndrome.
(2)   Guilt.
(3)   Fear.
(4)   Depression.
(5)   Low self-esteem and poor social skills.
(6)   Repressed anger and hostility.
(7)   Impaired ability to trust.
(8)   Blurred boundaries and role confusion.
(9)   Pseudomaturity coupled with a failure to accomplish developmental tasks.
(10)   Self-mastery and control (Sgroi, 1982: p. 109).

Not all issues need the intervention of a therapist: a child's lack of social skills may be addressed by foster parents, who gently teach him or her to use the toilet in private. Inability to trust can best be repaired by experiencing a long-term relationship in which there is no abuse of power. Children who are fearful need these feelings acknowledged and understood by those who care for them; they may be attended to both at home and in the therapeutic session.

Other issues are rightly addressed in therapeutic play. Children may find it impossible to express anger freely at home. In a play session they can begin to explore open expression of anger. I have found clay bombs to be particularly effective (James, 1989: pp. 165–6): wet clay, dropped or thrown from a height, makes a satisfying splat; a model can be made of the person or event that has caused the child to be angry and bombs dropped on them.

It is common for sexually abused children to feel isolated; this is often countered by forming groups of young survivors, where they can share experiences and understand their common problems. James (1989: pp. 96–8) invites children to guess what other sexually abused children worry about: this takes for granted that this child's experience is not unique, and the therapist is familiar with his or her difficulties. It may also prompt questions about abuse and its consequences which the therapist can answer honestly.

Although sexually abused children share common concerns, the abuse will have individual meanings for this child, living in this family. In addition, understanding of the abuse will change for the child as s/he matures, and further help should be offered to treat issues as they emerge. A 5 year old is unlikely to have concerns about the impact of abuse on sexuality, but such worries may overwhelm him or her as an adolescent.

It is impossible to overestimate the challenge of working with sexually abused children (Wyatt & Powell, 1988). The manifestations of their distress are so diverse, and the emotional demands they place on their workers so extensive, that practitioners need training, supervision and support. There are numerous detailed case studies of successful interventions with child survivors of sexual abuse (Hunter, 1986; Harper, 1989; Ellis *et al.*, 1990; Bray, 1991; Gil, 1991; Strand, 1991), which offer hope to children and their therapists.

Practitioners differ in their therapeutic approach to sexually abused children. Bannister (1988, 1989) begins by enabling children to act out the abuse, generally prompted by dolls or puppets. Bradbury (1987) feels that overt expression of anger is pivotal to recovery. Deblinger *et al.* (1990) undertook research which illustrates the effectiveness of cognitive behavioural treatment, in which children were taught coping strategies for abuse-related memories and behaviours, and preventive measures for the future. Dellar (1989) relied on games to prompt expression of feeling.

A small number of children who have been sexually abused will have suffered ritual or sadistic abuse (Sinason, 1994). The tales that these children tell are truly horrifying. The behavioural manifestations of their distress can be extreme. It is important that their dreadful stories are believed, for the worker who deals with his or her own feelings by denial compounds the disturbance of an already grossly damaged child.

Morrison (1988) emphasises that sexually abused children face the same hazards of childhood as their peers: they must attend school, and most continue to live in families.

'The most fundamental principle of work with victims of [child sexual abuse] is not to approach them as though they are a unique species of client whose needs are radically different from those of other young people.'

(Morrison, 1988: p. 312)

Young survivors of sexual abuse have many ordinary, childish issues to consider, as well as intrusive memories of the past.

Survivors of sexual abuse need to learn how to keep themselves safe in the future. This is raised in many schools, where children are taught to think about touches that they enjoy and others that make them feel uncomfortable, and their right to have control over their bodies. 'Kidscape' has published a number of story books and other materials to help those addressing this issue. These programmes are designed to help children recognise potentially abusive situations and seek appropriate help. However, it should never be implied that children are ever accountable for abuse; it is adults who should care for and protect children and who must take responsibility for the harm they cause.

Practical aids

Many children are more familiar with modern technology than their workers; however, computers, video games and cameras as well as books, story telling and board games can all form a valuable component to therapeutic work with children and young people.

Computers

Children who find personal contact difficult may be able to express themselves through computers. Word processing programs enable children to write and rewrite the stories of their lives, until they are comfortable with its reality. Drawing pictures on computers offers a similar opportunity to reshape the image until the desired result is achieved. Writing or drawing on computer can be immediately satisfying, and children with low self-esteem can be proud of their results. Children who feel powerless are rewarded by the control experienced when they work on computers.

Many children enjoy playing computer games. This can be a solitary or competitive activity. Many games involve the child enacting scenes of considerable violence, which in themselves may be abhorrent; however playing such games may bring relief to the child who struggles with guilt over violence in his or her fantasies. Less aggressive games can also bring the satisfaction and self-esteem for children who struggle to achieve in other areas. Gardner (1991) joins children in Nintendo™ games, recognising that these are an integral part of the world for children; they can encourage children to develop problem-solving strategies, to release and control aggression, as well as obvious qualities such as improving hand–eye co-ordination. More importantly, children like them; this alone is good enough reason to explore their therapeutic value.

However, some children will retreat into playing on a computer to escape from interactions with other children or adults. Computers have no feelings; thus children with a limited ability to express emotions avoid opportunities to take emotional risks if too much emphasis is given to a computer.

The Bridge Child Care Development Service has produced a computer program entitled *My Life in Words and Pictures*; it is an imaginative and original therapeutic tool. It includes programs enabling the child to create stories and pictures, and can be a valuable contribution to life story work. The material is multi-cultural, and particularly helpful for children with limited verbal skills or disabilities.

Regrettably, I know significantly less about computers than most children referred for therapy, even those under 5. Many children enjoy sharing their skills, although some become frustrated by my lack of ability. I know that colleagues who are familiar with the technology find ways to use it imaginatively.

Video equipment and photographs

Video equipment can by used imaginatively in children's therapy. The delight of the child who produces a film for him- or herself can be extremely rewarding. However, children are unlikely to keep such films to themselves, and will show them to friends and relatives. It is therefore not a good medium with which to explore painful material; it is much more effective in affirming self-esteem.

There are a number of videos used in group therapy with children that may be applicable in individual work. Children who cannot listen to a fairy story may be familiar with the film version. Gil, at a conference in Reading in September 1994, described showing a little girl a video of herself to help her understand the processes that were evident in her play. This child was stuck in the repetitive play, with dissociative interludes, that is common in survivors of trauma. She had no insight into the significance of her play; but when she saw the video she could link material in the play with past experience, and this brought with it enlightenment and emotional relief.

Photographs are more useful for practitioners trying to explore more private material:

'Photos are tangible documents of actual times and events that have really happened in front of the camera and thus can be discussed as the equivalent of ... that actuality.'

(Weiser, 1988: p. 346)

Photographs are a reminder of real events. They bring with them feelings about that event: people tend to take photographs of relatives, friends or incidents that were important, and that significance is recalled when the photograph is considered again at a later date. Most people's photographs are intensely personal, representing a private reality captured on film. Looking at past photographs with children can prompt memories and feelings that would otherwise remain unexplored.

Going out and taking photographs with children can be an enlightening experience (Berman, 1993). Armed with a simple camera (complicated technology can detract from the therapeutic value of picture taking), children look at the world as something worth recording:

'As photographs are representations of how we see the world, and how we choose to interpret it to others and ourselves, they convey nonverbally how we perceive and create meaning. They are very real to people ... and take on a real living quality at times (as when we remove the snapshot of an ex-friend or love from our albums or wallet, when we grieve the photos lost in a house fire or if a purse or wallet is stolen).'

(Weiser, 1988: p. 350)

Children with a fragile sense of themselves can learn to look through the viewfinder of a camera and record what they see. These pictures form an essential part of who the child is; it is a record of his or her view of the world. Darkroom techniques are not difficult to learn, and children who have the opportunity to develop and print their own pictures gain enormous self-esteem when mastering this process.

I have used the taking of photographs as an introduction to using a box file. Children who are very resistant to therapy require an unconventional approach in order to engage them. Adolescents who resist intimacy may find it reassuring to hide behind the lens of the camera. The taking of photographs, and subsequent examination of them, can provide an initial activity on which other techniques can be built.

Books, stories and story telling

Many practitioners have shelves full of books designed to help children with specific problems. Cattanach (1992) includes an annotated bibliography of children's books, which cover most of the issues that worry children (pp. 152–9; see also Ward, 1989, Appendix 1; McMahon, 1992: pp. 217–20; the BAAF, Children's Society, *Letterbox Library* and the *Being Yourself* catalogues). In addition, familiar fairy tales contain elements of children's fantasies, and their satisfying endings bring hope of resolution to children whose inner worlds are chaotic. By creating a medium in which these fears and fantasies can be given life and mastered, the writers of fairy stories have understood each child's need to personify good and evil, and to experience both (von Franz, 1974; Ekstein, 1983). In addition to the contributions of western authors, practitioners should also look to writers from other countries where fables and stories have developed that reach the inner worlds of children (Cattanach, 1994b). Gersie & King (1990) include a rich collection of stories from all over the world which reflect the preoccupations and fantasies of children.

However, there remain issues that are not provided for by the literature available. I recall working with one small boy whose father was in prison during the riots in Strangeways. Having seen the news, this child believed that Daddy lived on a roof! He was unconvinced by my reassurance, and I could find no book to help him. The only solution for this child was a visit to the prison.

For other children, workers may need to tell the stories themselves. This is not as difficult as it seems at first; children soon remind a worker who has wandered from the title, and the delight of a child when they hear of a fantasy figure who has faced difficulties comparable to his or her own and survived is rewarding in itself. The only basic rule is to have some idea where the story is going before commencing, and remembering that all stories have a beginning, a middle and an end. The moral or lesson of the story should emerge clearly from its conclusion.

Other therapists join children in mutual story telling (Gardner, 1971, 1986a; Brandell, 1988). This involves therapist and child joining together to discover a story; this can be done by taking turns to complete a sentence, or one taking over when the other becomes 'stuck'. For instance, I invited Anne, aged 7, to join me in a story:

Jo: 'Once upon a time there was a little rabbit called...'
ANNE: 'Flopsy. She lived with her mummy and daddy in a little hole under a tree...'
Jo: 'One day, when she got up in the morning...'
ANNE: 'There was no-one else in the house...'

Flopsy's efforts to feed herself, and acknowledgement of her physical and emotional hunger, enabled Anne to tell her own story without uncontainable anxiety. I helped to steer her towards a happy ending.

Therapists need to be aware of the influence of television and films on children's stories. Rose (1995) discovers useful metaphors in popular programmes which create powerful images for children. Other practitioners encourage children to write, or tape record, their stories, and suggest alternative endings which offer more hope than the child's gloomy conclusion. Oaklander (1969) invites children to tell stories about the pictures they have drawn, thus expanding on work done in another medium. One of the joys of story telling is its ability to fit flexibly into almost any material with which the child is working.

Board games

Nickerson & O'Laughlin (1983) comment that many children are familiar with board games, which provide a recognisable context in which anxiety can be contained and explored. Children who struggle to maintain boundaries respond to the need for rules and turn-taking. Games such as *Monopoly* and the *Game of Life* encourage fantasy about life experiences, and can be used to prompt discussions about poverty, helplessness and power. Children who are particularly resistant to therapy or are highly anxious may sit comfortably playing a game.

Redgrave (1987) is imaginative in his application of board games. All his games are made with the child, and apply to his or her unique circumstances. With one boy he made a game which he called *The Marathon Walk*. The child had decided that his goal was to return to live with his mother; between the start of the game and the final goal the therapist created several large road blocks, some of which were temporary hindrances which could be overcome, while others were permanent blockages which required the child to consider another route to his eventual goal. With another child, Redgrave created walls crossing the board, indicating to the child that this route might be impassable.

With a third child he created a *Hill of Waiting and Planning*, to help describe the process of finding a permanent placement for the child.

Philip, aged 8, had experienced his parents' divorce as a young child, and subsequent erratic behaviour by his mother. His worker constructed a *Game of Feelings*, with a dial on which different feelings were written, and a central spinner which rotated; worker and child took turns with the spinner, and had to act out or verbalise the feelings selected by the spinner (Price, 1991: p. 241). This enabled Philip to identify the confusing feelings that were causing him such problems.

For those who struggle to create such games themselves, the *Being Yourself* catalogue includes a number of non-competitive games that can help children to think about themselves. The *Stop, Relax and Think* game helps to teach children self-control in a non-threatening way. The *Up and Down with Feelings Game* includes a board with a grid of line-drawn faces representing various emotions, with different feeling words round the outside. The underlying message of this game is that there are no right or wrong feelings, and hurt emotions can be changed. The *Safely Home* game encourages children to consider how to respond to the dangers that can beset them between school and home. Kaduson & Finnerty (1995) demonstrate the value of structured board games in promoting co-operative behaviour in children with attention deficit hyperactivity disorder.

Contributions from art, drama and music therapists

Workers can learn from colleagues in other fields, particularly art, music and drama. Few practitioners will have the ability to improvise on a piano or glockenspiel with sufficient skill to mirror the child's feelings or projections. Music therapists use all forms of sound and rhythm to communicate with children. For them, the musical instrument takes the place of Winnicott's transitional object (Bunt, 1994); it can be touched, smelled, looked at and heard. It can contain the child's private feelings and fantasies and can be the bridge between therapist and child, providing the means of communication between them. Many workers include items such as tambourines, drums and shakers in their toy cupboards. Small children in particular love the noise and rhythms they make, and this natural interest can help to engage the child in therapy. Young children love singing and dancing, and offer the worker a 'concert' of new songs they have learned at school. Others are readily soothed by music, which can help to comfort a child at the end of a stressful session. However, if the practitioner finds that any child spends all the time using music in the sessions, a referral to a skilled music therapist is recommended: since music is his or her chosen means of communication s/he needs a practitioner skilled in this field.

Art therapists also share Winnicott's notion of the activity occurring in external space, where inner and outer reality meet. The child is introduced to the materials and told that s/he is free to use them as s/he chooses. This prompts spontaneous expression of feeling in which unconscious images appear, mingling external reality with images from the child's inner world.

> 'Children's drawings are literally recordings of their vitality and life: the drawings are structures in themselves, yet simultaneously refer to events and objects outside themselves, and it is to this dimension of "meaning" that therapists ... should attend.'
>
> (Arguile, 1992: p. 141)

Art therapy has traditionally been used to help clients with limited communicative abilities to express themselves (Liebmann, 1990). However, it can also offer hope to disturbed or unhappy children (Fielden, 1990; Arguile, 1992; Trent, 1992). They, too, are provided with materials for painting, drawing and modelling, and given the opportunity to express themselves freely. The act of painting or moulding clay can itself be therapeutic; a succession of pictures can help both practitioner and child reach a deeper understanding of his or her difficulties (Burgess & Hartman, 1993). Current technology can also be utilised; children who may be reluctant to use tactile materials may warm to computer graphics (Johnson, 1993).

Many art therapists have psychoanalytic training and experience which enables them to comprehend and interpret unconscious material that is presented in the child's pictures (DiLeo, 1983; Johnson, 1987; Furth, 1988). Few play workers are comparably trained. However, an understanding of the development of children's drawings is helpful (Strauss, 1978; Thomas & Silk, 1990); very young children begin with circular scribbles, which slowly develop into recognisable people. Few children make accurate representations of objects on paper until early adolescence. Some children find it easier to represent themselves in cartoon form (Crowley & Mills, 1989).

Many books which offer guidance on the treatment of abused children include illustrations of their drawings (Oaklander, 1969; Gil, 1991; Webb, 1991; Cattanach, 1994b). Moore (1994) highlights the difference between the drawings of children who have been ritually or sadistically abused from other forms of abuse. I normally offer drawing and painting materials to children alongside other toys. Some children may concentrate on artistic activities, finding it a satisfactory means of expression. If the worker already has a warm relationship with the child, consultation from an art therapist may help the child to make full use of this medium. Alternatively, if the worker lacks any innate artistic flair, a referral should be considered.

Art involves not only painting and drawing: it can also be a three-dimensional activity. Ideally, boxes, glue and sticky tape can be provided for modelling, as well as clay, playdough or plasticine. Many children are highly creative with a wide variety of materials, and produce imaginative models that give personal satisfaction. The aim of this activity is not to produce a beautiful model, but to enable the child to express him- or herself. One boy with a borderline psychosis spent one session creating a *Star Ship Enterprise*: an invitation to join him in his journey 'where no man has gone before'.

Although Jennings' book is entitled *Playtherapy with Children* (1993) many of her ideas stem from her background in drama. She highlights the place of role play in the normal development of children, and advocates that this natural stage should be harnessed by the practitioner to prompt the development and exploration of roles and fantasies. Jennings has developed an extensive range of techniques to help children who have failed to negotiate earlier stages successfully. Children who did not explore their worlds sensorially as young children are physically constrained when older. Exercises which bring them in touch with bodily sensations recreate the delight of infancy and release energy and enthusiasm. Once children reach the stage at which roles develop naturally, the therapist makes the materials available to enable the child to explore his or her most terrifying fantasies in safety. By assuming roles, children can project fears and feelings into another persona, and experience them as another would. The expression of feeling is cathartic, and the real identity of the child remains intact.

Lucy, a 9 year old who had left the care of her single mother after many years of severe physical abuse and neglect, began by enjoying a unchallenging games of 'shops'. In time she included a robber (a role she generally took herself), who stole the contents of the shop. By exploring the power of the robber in role, and returning to her 9-year-old self at the end of each session, Lucy could enjoy the power of the aggressor and still resume her childish identity with ease. Cattanach (1994a) affirms the role of dramatherapy as its working on the boundary between 'me' and 'not me' (Winnicott, 1971). Throughout the drama, the 'me' of the child remains distinct, whilst assuming the role of 'not me' through which s/he can experiment with feelings that could not otherwise be faced.

Summary

This chapter has included a number of focused techniques, aimed at solving a particular problem, or meeting a particular need. Some children, with specific difficulties or circumstances which require direct intervention, respond well to such techniques. An initial assessment may help to define therapeutic goals, and thus the choice of an appropriate intervention(s). The practitioner may begin by selecting a method to encourage rapport between adult and child, or encourage the child to illustrate his or her understanding of current circumstances. Some children need help to explore unconscious fantasies, while others focus on techniques to facilitate understanding of external reality, past or present.

Additional inspiration can be found in allied professions: art, music and drama therapists. Cameras, books, computers or board games all have a place in helping troubled children.

Throughout every session, awareness of the feelings the child is expressing, either directly through an activity or indirectly through projections, is important. Without attention to these emotions, the child will feel that therapeutic play is something that is done to him or her, rather than a journey which s/he and the therapist travel together. Focused interventions should be congruent with the child's view of the world, and help bring understanding and insight to it.

Chapter 7
Challenges in Therapeutic Play

Introduction

However skilled the worker, and however extensive the range of techniques at his or her disposal, there is no evading the fact that some children are easier to treat than others. Therapeutic play is not a panacea; it is not a solution for every child. Some reject help altogether; others are so paralysed with anxiety or memories of past abuse that the relationship offered to them is intolerable.

It is now widely accepted that children who have experienced abuse, disaster, separations from their birth families or other trauma benefit from skilled help. Moustakas (1973) advocated play therapy for children struggling with familiar challenges of childhood, such as the arrival of a new baby. I rarely offer help to such children unless they exhibit symptoms indicating serious difficulties. Nevertheless, Moustakas has helped to highlight the emotional demands placed on children. Given the stress of family life, and the expectation that children will attend and enjoy school, it is not surprising that children who experience additional traumas become disorientated and disturbed. Many who care for them confirm that skilled intervention is needed.

Not all children agree. Some respond with aggression or passive resistance; others retreat into regression or withdrawal. To comprehend their hostility requires an understanding of the child's view of the world.

Children who dissociate, or those who are unintegrated, pose special difficulties for the worker. Many have had a particularly difficult start in life, and without help will continue to experience emotional disorders well into adulthood. It is crucial that the worker makes the effort to understand the child's experiences; only then will his or her behaviour make sense.

Many of the techniques in this book are best employed with latency-aged children: those at primary and junior schools. However, very young children and adolescents are also referred from time to time; workers need to adapt their skills to meet the needs of these client groups. Those helping disabled or sick children should approach their work from the same premise: try to understand this child's experience, and use this understanding to promote a healthy adjustment to individual circumstances.

The timing of therapy

I have no list of contra-indications, such as those defined by West (1992: p. 30). She feels it is inappropriate to offer play therapy to:

- Children with severe learning difficulties;
- Those who struggle to distinguish fantasy from reality;
- Those with learned maladaptive behaviours resulting from family dysfunction;
- Children on the verge of major life change;
- Those currently involved in investigations into allegations of abuse;
- Children under 4 or older than 11;
- Those whose safety is not assured.

Whilst I do not share such a list of contra-indications, I agree that there are occasions when therapy is inappropriate, and the child's behaviour is not projection, but a legitimate way to reject help.

It is not always appropriate to bring a child for therapy week after week when the feelings that s/he expresses are so negative. It is essential to look to other stresses in the child's life, to assess whether these are enough for him or her to cope with at the moment (Dyke, 1987).

Crompton (1991) stresses the importance of ensuring that children are not coerced into therapeutic play when not ready to do so. She recalls being invited, when visiting an agency for the first time, to use a set of Russian dolls to illustrate her personal relationships. Unwillingly, she agreed:

> 'I did not wish to face those memories, at that time, in that place, with that person. I had consented but felt that my consent had been unfree. I felt manipulated and invaded and for a long time I felt angry. I learned a great deal but not, I think, what had been intended.'

> (Crompton, 1991: p. 32)

We can all learn from this experience: whilst it is valid to test resistance and assess the extent to which anxiety underlies the child's behaviour, no child should be made to face unbearable feelings or memories.

It is unwise to begin exploring feelings from the past when a child has major changes in circumstances on the horizon. Children need a consistent, reliable environment which will accept and nurture them throughout the process of therapy, before they can consider accepting help. Changes of school or foster home demand too much for them to cope with therapeutic play as well. In these instances the social worker should try to support those caring for the child while s/he settles, and wait until s/he feels safer.

West (1990) underlines the difficulties of working with children 'in limbo': living in short-term placements (which too often last a year or more), waiting for stable plans to be made and agreements about a permanent placement kept. She emphasises the profound distress and confusion experienced by these children:

> 'Compound ... issues of attachment, loss, lack of self-esteem, powerlessness, with guts and feelings that churn around, and with word and thought processes that are inadequate, with grown-ups telling you what to do and feel (or what not to do and feel), and we might begin to glimpse something of the experiences of children in limbo.'
>
> (West, 1990: p. 11)

West stresses that these children are often expected to cope with exploration of feelings about the past, life story work to provide an explanation of events, and express clear opinions about their hopes for the future. It is too much. In my opinion, we should concentrate on finding ways to help these children tolerate current anxieties, leaving discussion of past pain until the child is settled. However, Family Makers and other organisations which find adoptive placements for abused children disagree: they regard intensive work with a child prior to a move as appropriate preparation, and regard it as too late to wait until they have formed secure attachments in their new homes.

It is legitimate for children to express resistance to facing painful feelings associated with trauma (Hurley, 1991). Some deny the actuality of the event; others cannot accept the reality of the feelings that go with it. Bereaved children may refuse to accept the permanence of loss associated with death (Segal, 1984), and are alarmed by the prospect of therapeutic play which may challenge this belief. It is common for children to avoid the experience of fear by omnipotent denial (Copley & Forryan, 1987). Abused children no longer living with their birth families may reject help, believing that feelings associated with the abuse have been left behind. Some children may, reluctantly, agree to attend sessions, but refuse to mention the past (Gil, 1991). Occasionally a child will continue for many months in superficial and anxiety-avoiding activities indicating a deep resistance to facing feelings from the past (Bow, 1993).

For some children, the time, or the therapist, may be wrong. S/he may be unable to say that s/he cannot talk to a woman who reminds him or her of an aunt, or to insist that, right now, s/he wants to forget about the past. Such children are consistently resistant before play sessions, finding unlikely excuses why s/he cannot possibly attend today. They glower throughout their sessions, and slam the door with relief when they leave. For these children, the timing, or the worker, may be the wrong person in the wrong place at the wrong time.

The child needs to leave knowing that s/he has been listened to: 'I can see that coming to see me is making you unhappy, and so you don't need to come any more if you don't want to. But I shall never forget you. If you ever change your mind I shall be here and I shall want to see you.'

The behaviour of these children contrasts sharply with those who always arrive promptly, are angry if the worker is a minute late, and join him or her readily. The session may be characterised by verbal abuse, mayhem created with the materials, ensuring that the therapist experiences the full range of the child's overwhelming feelings, and then s/he is reluctant to leave. This is emotionally demanding for the worker, but the needs of the child are being met.

The angry child's view of the world

Hostile, aggressive children are notoriously difficult to help:

'Although diagnostic labels are important, one might say that it is not so much by their . . . labels that these children are known, but by their violently disruptive behaviour and their extreme resistance to remedial efforts.'

(Willock, 1983: p. 387)

They are so challenging to treat that one writer even concluded that:

'Attempts to treat these patients almost always fail.'

(Berman, 1964: p. 24)

Both authors were writing some years ago; however, little attention has been given to the needs of these highly aggressive children, and they continue to be a challenge to any practitioner.

These children have learned to see the world as hostile, and they respond in kind. The last thing they can recognise, let alone respond positively to, is someone offering to help. It is natural to be alarmed by these children: many have a history of violence, and there appears no reason why they should stop now. However, practitioners should be aware that fears for their personal safety may be projections; it is important to remain calm with such children, in order to help quieten their panic.

Some children, demanding that I remove myself, can provoke strong rejecting feelings. It is human to respond to a child repeatedly telling you to 'F*** off', to want to do just that. This is how every adult in his or her life has behaved; it is how s/he expects the worker to behave.

Other children project waves of unexpected rage. Again, these feelings belong to the child, and to other relationships. At the time, it may be difficult to remain sufficiently objective to recognise this. It is easy to sympathise with a child whose experiences have been traumatic, but to admit to anger with him or her is much harder. At some point, most children need to show the extent of their unhappiness. Aggressive, defiant children tend to do this by ensuring that the worker feels it. They will insist that the practitioner is useless, and it is a waste of time coming. There are times when one believes that s/he is right. It is often difficult to carry on caring, and continue to believe that acceptance of the child in the face of this onslaught is what s/he needs and will eventually respond to.

Occasionally one meets a child who is difficult to like. Professionals meeting to discuss his or her progress struggle to find pleasant attributes. It is not our role to like or dislike the child: it is imperative to accept him or her as s/he is. S/he will almost certainly despise him- or herself. A therapist who persists with positive comments will not be believed.

Directive techniques are rarely effective with hostile children. Asked to draw or play a game they turn away or become verbally abusive. Active interventions require a degree of co-operation which these children find impossible. Non-directive techniques, which begin by accepting the child's hostility as a valid response to his or her circumstances, may be successful.

Practitioners should be aware of the significance of parental management when assessing hostile children. Research shows a significant link between harsh or inconsistent parenting and aggressive behaviour (Utting, 1994). Such families need behavioural interventions to teach alternative ways of coping with conflict. Behavioural management programmes, set up at home and giving clear guidance to parents or foster carers to manage behaviour constructively, attend to the problem effectively. Parents are taught to seek appropriate behaviour to praise and reward, and techniques for managing challenging behaviour without resorting to verbal or physical aggression. When followed rigidly, these programmes reinforce attachment behaviour in both adult and child; the consequent improvement in family relationships together with behavioural changes generally brings a significant decrease in aggression. Individual treatment offered to these children reinforces the belief that the child is the problem; parents or foster carers must be helped to manage the behaviour positively if the child is to change (Webster-Stratton, 1985; Train, 1993; Utting, 1994).

Working with withdrawn, silent children

Withdrawn, silent children offer as many challenges as aggressive ones. The worker needs to understand their reticence. Some children require psychiatric assessment of their silence. The child may be clinically depressed; the effort of speech has become more than s/he can manage (Goodyer, 1983; Shaffer, 1985). Disorders such as deafness, autism, aphasia and elective mutism all require a medical diagnosis and the therapeutic play worker must work alongside other professionals ensuring that all the child's needs are met.

There are many reasons to explain the silence of children:

> 'Some children are silent because they are resentful about seeing the therapist, some are frightened, some would like to talk but don't know what to say, and some really prefer to sit quietly rather than to do something else.'

> (Reismann, 1973: p. 105)

Unless the worker can ascertain the reason for the silence, s/he cannot respond appropriately.

The primary consideration is the child's view of silence. This may be the only peaceful place where s/he can escape from adult demands and expectations. The practitioner who disturbs this reverie with words devalues the capacity for pleasure s/he is discovering within him- or herself.

For some, silence reflects anxiety. Overwhelmed by waves of feelings that s/he cannot control, the child retreats from all relations, and becomes helpless. Non-directive practitioners respond by accepting the silence, perhaps reflecting the child's anxiety and sitting quietly until s/he can relax and begin to play. The child alone is responsible for choosing to converse or remain quiet. Reismann recounts cases of children who respond to this approach (1973, pp. 104–105); one persisted in saying nothing throughout her play sessions, while her behaviour at home improved. Although this may sound simple, sitting in silence and remaining in contact with a child is extraordinarily difficult:

> 'Despite the seeming ease of doing nothing, it is difficult to sit with a child who is quiet and motionless for about an hour, if for no other reason than that the therapist is likely to drift off into reverie or suffer the effects of boredom.'

> (1973: p. 106)

Some children use silence to mask extreme anger. Unable to express rage, they turn it on themselves. Silence may be used punitively, indicating defiant refusal to join the relationship. Their difficulties mirror those of aggressive children: when they speak it is often with a torrent of abuse. Once engaged in therapy, these children often use silence to provoke anxiety in the therapist. On one occasion Josie, a 9-year-old survivor of sexual abuse, punished me for taking a holiday over

Christmas (in spite of her session being on Christmas Day!) by announcing that I was to spend the session in prison: she told me to sit on a chair facing the wall and refused to speak for 50 minutes. I struggled to remain sensitive to her feelings of abandonment, but recognised a sense of great personal injustice; it would have been easier to day-dream rather than remain in touch with such uncomfortable feelings (Carroll, 1995a).

Occasionally, silence reflects life at home. Mollie, aged 8, lived with a seriously depressed mother who responded verbally only when Mollie misbehaved. There was no chatter in the home. From the first session it was clear that she expected me to remain silent. I felt it important that she saw me as different from her mother; I reflected her anxiety about talking, and persisted in a running commentary about what she was doing – looking out of the window, picking at her fingers, etc. At the same time I played idly with the playdough. For half an hour Mollie was turned away from me, unable to indicate that she was listening. Then she reached for a crumpled bag of sweets from her coat pocket and offered me one: she had begun to communicate. Although she remained silent throughout many of her subsequent sessions, I learned to understand her extensive non-verbal vocabulary.

Children such as Mollie, who have not learned to deal with conflict in the safety of their own families, are unable to assert themselves appropriately; they respond to adult authority with silence or aggression. They cannot manage any situation which requires negotiation or compromise. We should seek techniques which will enable the child to understand and practise more appropriate conflict-solving behaviours, whilst avoiding being judgemental about past aggression.

Working with children with delayed emotional development

Some children are referred for help by adults concerned that their behaviour corresponds to that of a much younger child; they cannot conform to the expectations of their chronological age. Many families are endlessly patient with these children, accepting that they have no control over their immaturity. However, at school, both teachers and other pupils can make life extremely difficult. Many of these children cannot concentrate for long, and become disruptive and demanding in the classroom; in the playground they stand alone, or are enticed by other children to misbehave.

It is necessary to maintain a clear distinction between genuinely regressive behaviour and manifestations of the child's need for a secure attachment (Bowlby, 1980a). Johnson stresses that regression is a normal response to trauma:

'Under severe stress, children attempt to master the situation by reverting to behaviour patterns that were successful in earlier developmental stages. This represents a search for a comfort zone.'

(1991: pp. 51–52)

Thus they return to behaviours with which they are familiar, and fail to meet developmental challenges. In a family in which this behaviour is misunderstood punitive responses to the child's regression can cause further distress and confusion. In time, the behaviour becomes entrenched, and sensitive management as well as therapeutic play is needed to prompt the resumption of normal development.

The first task of the practitioner is to understand the reason for any emotional delay. O'Connor (1991) emphasises the importance of assessment and treatment of delayed development. He comments that children of different ages respond to trauma in different ways: children under 2 can recover from an isolated, traumatic event, and it may have very little impact on later functioning. However, when trauma is experienced repeatedly during the first few years of life, children may be fixated in a state where dangerous situations are undifferentiated. Feeling permanently vulnerable, they are always prepared to defend themselves from perceived attack. Prolonged distress becomes part of the child's world.

Fiona had been cared for by her grandmother since infancy; when she was 4 years old she moved to live with her mother and stepfather. She struggled to cope with the loss of her grandmother, and to make attachments to two adults whom she barely knew. As she began to settle, step-siblings arrived. Fiona's behaviour deteriorated; the family were offered a range of interventions: family therapy, behaviour management, individual counselling. Eventually, Fiona left the family and lived in long-term foster care. At the age of 12 she was referred to me. Fiona played easily, with a vivid imagination and ability to gain relief from symbolic expression of feelings. However, she was functioning as a 4 year old; it was very clear that the arrival of siblings, just as she was forming attachments in her new home, had been more than she could bear, and her development had been arrested at this point. An understanding foster mother, and play therapy which helped her to explore feelings of jealousy and rejection, enabled her to make rapid progress.

Many of these children are highly anxious, and cannot tolerate any direct reference to their distress. They need the worker to respond to their infant needs before they can begin to consider feelings associated with subsequent events. The child's earliest unmet needs must emerge and be acknowledged in the context of therapy, and progress made from there. As the child progresses s/he will face and master experiences that have hindered his or her development. Sally (see Chapter 5) regressed to infancy during her therapy, representing her abuse at the age of 4 symbolically, and emerged relatively unscathed as a healthy 5 year old. Fiona (see above) began by exploring issues of basic trust, and went on to master feelings of profound rage at past rejections. Eventually, these feelings subsided, and she began to talk in a mature and realistic way about life with her mother and stepfather.

Working with unintegrated children

Unintegrated children, those who have not achieved a state of wholeness and understanding of themselves as a cohesive individual (Dockar-Drysdale, 1968; Winnicott, 1986), require skilled therapeutic intervention. For many of these children only a community in which their special needs are understood and catered for can begin to attend to their profound difficulties (Dockar-Drysdale, 1990).

However, there are insufficient therapeutic places for the children needing them, and therapeutic play workers are likely to meet these children from time to time. Practitioners who suspect that a referred child may not have achieved integration should seek consultation with a child psychiatrist. A therapeutic team, consisting of the child's carers (who will need respite from the chaotic demands of the child from time to time), possibly a social worker and child psychiatrist, the child's teachers and therapist, must act consistently to offer the context of security in which s/he can achieve a sense of personal identity. Mutual support for all involved, with external supervision and consultation, is essential if the needs of the child are to be met.

Unintegrated children cannot contain experiences in a meaningful way; events and relationships remain disconnected from each other. A colleague caring for such a child once described it as like working with a sieve: he kept pouring in positive experiences in the hope that one day the holes would clog up and the child hold on to them! Children with no cohesive sense of self cannot contain the therapeutic experience from week to week; more frequent sessions may help. Some children respond to gentle reminders of their play in previous sessions, with the worker providing the containing link between one experience and the next. Any indication that the child can connect one session with the next should be seen as progress.

Michelle spent her early years with her drug-dependent mother moving from home to home, with occasional stays with foster parents when her mother was in prison. Her social worker was reluctant to remove her from the care of her mother, who was clearly attached to her daughter. However, her mother was deeply involved in drug culture, and care for Michelle was haphazard. Although there was no direct allegation of sexual abuse, she was a highly sexualised child, and it was known that many different men had stayed in the home. When she finally left the care of her mother (having been discovered by her social worker scavenging for food when her mother was unconscious) at the age of 6, her behaviour was bizarre. Her foster mother was prepared for a child who could not use a knife or fork, but not for one who rushed endlessly round the house, went to throw herself out of windows, and who was unable to distinguish fantasy from reality. A second foster home, which had been well prepared for the problems Michelle would present, was found, and she was offered therapeutic play when she was 7. In non-directive play sessions she looked for solitude; she seemed to seek a quiet place inside herself. However, a sudden rush of anxiety would send her running round the room, flinging toys indiscriminately, in evident panic. As she was not harming anyone, I elected to sit quietly until she settled. Then she retreated again into silence. It was months before she could externalise her chaos, engaging in play that could begin to heal her.

The professional team working with Michelle recognised that, ideally, she needed a therapeutic placement if the extreme deprivation and disturbing experiences of her infancy were not to leave her permanently scarred. However, such a placement was not available, and the presence of an enthusiastic and committed foster mother led to her remaining within the home. An extensive professional team continued to address her needs for several years; eventually she was able to disclose sadistic abuse by a number of men.

Working with children who dissociate

It is common for children, in the face of overwhelming emotions, to dissociate from them. If children had to face the reality of their feelings on a daily basis, they would be unable to continue to function at home or school. In order to survive, they believe that these feelings (and sometimes the abuse that gives rise to these feelings) do not exist (James, 1989). By denying the reality of abuse, the child can deny the psychological and physical pain associated with it. Children learn to trigger this defence whenever the abuse occurs. It is a highly effective process which enables children to carry on with their lives through apparently unbearable trauma (Johnson, 1991; Wilson *et al.*, 1992).

However, once removed from the abuse, many of these children continue to dissociate when faced with anything unpleasant. A minor reprimand from a foster mother can be met with a blank stare, and the child will have no recollection of what has been said. Responsibility for extreme behaviour can even be denied by the child (Kelsall, 1994).

Persistent dissociation is serious, and requires psychiatric consultation. There is some disagreement as to the precise definition of dissociative disorder, and the symptoms associated with it (Piper, 1994). However, most practitioners feel that there is a continuum of symptoms, from mild absences to extreme denial of reality. At its most severe, it emerges as multiple personality disorder (James, 1989; Putnam, 1993). Whilst accurate assessment of dissociative traits by a child psychiatrist is necessary, it is helpful for the therapist to be aware of associated symptoms:

- Spontaneous trance states, when the child stares into space;
- Use of another name;
- A claim not to be him- or herself or a claim of dual identity;
- Referring to him- or herself as 'we';
- Change in ability to perform tasks;
- Denial of behaviour that has been observed by others;
- Change in vision, handwriting, or style of dress;
- Drastic changes in behaviour, unexplained outbursts, disorientation;
- Hearing voices;
- Loss of time;
- Drawing self as multiple persons;
- Feeling remote from the environment, or describing surroundings as being altered;
- Getting lost when walking a familiar route (James, 1989: pp. 104–105).

For children with severe dissociative problems the prognosis is poor; many will need psychiatric support for much of their lives. Skilled intervention is needed for children and young people with multiple personalities, if they are to be spared the distress that this condition can bring in adulthood (Schreiber, 1975; McElroy, 1992).

Help may be sought for children whose disorders are less severe by carers or teachers concerned about their behaviour, or about the child's denial of his or her traumatic history. Wilson *et al.* (1992) describe the advantage of a non-directive approach for dissociative states. Children can explore inner conflicts connected with past events symbolically, without explicitly facing the events themselves:

'Whilst the therapist should have the ability to talk about the child's symbolic play in order to make the play more conscious for the child, the child himself does not necessarily need to talk about it. The child can work through the conflicts symbolically and in this way re-integrate them in a healthy way.'

(1992: pp. 184–5)

Whilst agreeing that some children need to verbalise an experience in order to make it real, others can absorb the meaning of that reality if they have explored it extensively in play. James disagrees. She writes that:

'As much as possible within a given child's capability, dissociative experiences and disowned parts of their identity and consciousness must be brought into the treatment environment, where they can be safely contained, while the therapist assists the child towards integration. Experiences and feelings which remain hidden behind amnesias or dissociative barriers are interpreted by the child as too overwhelming or too dangerous to acknowledge.'

(James, 1989: p. 107)

James describes a number of exercises which she uses to encourage acknowledgement and open expression of feeling, as a necessary precursor to understanding the cause of pain. She exhorts practitioners to approach issues relating to the child's past directly; workers who avoid raising painful aspects of the child's history are introjecting the child's belief that they are too distressing to contemplate.

Whilst James's optimism is encouraging, practitioners should remain sensitive to children who dissociate. If a child can disengage from reality at will, it is not surprising if s/he does so when reprimanded, or when the worker suggests that some things have happened in the past that s/he wishes to ignore. Practitioners who insist on facing such children with the reality of past abuse may struggle against rigid denial. This insistence may, in itself, become abusive. No child should experience unnecessary pain: if s/he does not feel strong enough to face reality, s/he should not be made to do so. Moore (1994), who helps survivors express their feelings about past abuse through drawings, also recommends caution: the child may be able to express him- or herself on paper, but interpretation of drawings by bringing attention to their abusive aspects may be experienced by the child as retraumatising.

Working with very young children and adolescents

West (1992) believes that child-centred play therapy is most appropriate for children between the ages of 4 and 11. Oaklander (1969) regards 5 as young for therapeutic play, believing that children presenting disturbance at that age are reflecting pathology in the family. However, both very young children and adolescents are referred from time to time, and the worker needs to consider an appropriate response.

It is a challenge to try to understand the world of small children, and to communicate with them:

'We should bring an equal amount of professionalism and expertise to communicate with babies and toddlers as we would to an adult or older child.'

(Carroll & Williams, 1988: p. 20)

Too often, adults assume that small children cannot understand what is happening, and therefore have no feelings about it. However, those who have studied babies and small children testify how rich and varied their emotions are, and how effectively they communicate with those who will listen (Harris, 1975; Leach, 1977; Richards, 1980).

Small, pre-verbal children, separated from their families following abuse, pose special problems for those who care for them. Rarely are they offered explanations for their sudden removal from home and arrival in an unknown family. For the child, his or her world has turned upside-down.

It is difficult, but not impossible, to offer very young children simple clarification about what is happening to them. It takes time, patience and imagination (Petrie, 1989). Since play is the child's natural means of communication, adults wishing to talk with them should use toys to illustrate his or her words. With one little girl, unavoidably separated from siblings as well as her parents, I took small buildings, cars and people, and re-enacted what had happened using the toys. I showed her that all her family still existed, even though she could not see them, and her sisters were safe with Auntie Jane, her parents had gone to a special place to help them stop being naughty, and she was living with Auntie Anne. This child could not ask questions, but her uncertainty had been reflected in her behaviour. Using play, I illustrated her concerns, and gave her some answers.

Explaining therapeutic play to small children may be almost impossible. The introduction that is needed for an older child is incomprehensible to a 3 year old. I generally tell small children that I come to see children who have been hurt; we play together and this helps them to feel better. Directive techniques help in providing explanations. However, non-directive therapy enables small children to use toys to express feelings and experience mastery in a world that bewilders them.

Stephen, who was 3 when I first met him, had been severely neglected and abused; his misery was evident in his constant screaming and nightmares. During his first few sessions, Stephen was hyper-alert, and unable to settle. Gradually, he began to manipulate the toys, but insisted on putting the cars on top of each other and bouncing them up and down, and then looking hopelessly at me. Knowing the extent of his abuse, and the efforts he was making to communicate with me, I decided to offer him anatomically explicit dolls. These came with me in my toybag, along with everything else: they prompted Stephen to illustrate his experiences graphically, to his obvious relief. He was then able to direct his anger at the mother doll, and to show his distaste for anything that was dirty. Slowly his mood lifted: he began to smile, and eventually to laugh (Carroll, 1993b).

Music is a particularly useful resource to use with very young children. Bunt (1994) comments on the interest in music and rhythm that is evident in fetuses *in utero*, which extends to the fascination of the baby to the noises around him or her, from the gentle lullaby to the roar of the hoover. Bunt recounts her work with a 5-month-old girl, cared for by a foster mother after inadequate parenting from her alcohol- and heroin-addicted mother. This child was extremely tense, crying constantly. However, she became fascinated by a pair of Indian bells, which distracted her from her discomfort long enough for the crying to cease. Gradually, she was introduced to a wider range of sounds, and, through them, she was able to relax and communicate with her foster family. Few therapeutic play workers have the skill, or range of instruments, that are available to the music therapist; however, they should not forget the natural interest of small children in sounds and rhythms.

In contrast, many adolescents respond to focused interventions more readily than non-directive techniques. Overwhelmed with the confusion and uncertainty that is a normal feature of adolescence, they need the focus of directive methods if therapy is not to submerge in their diffuse and ever changing feelings.

Practitioners working with adolescents are likely to introject some of the adolescent chaos. It is necessary for the worker to return these feelings to the young person, to enable him or her to understand and tolerate conflicts without expressing them in behaviour (Hoxter, 1964).

Many adolescents have been unable, for various reasons, to play freely as young children. Some have lacked encouragement, cultural permission, or space, or were not safe enough in their home environment to relax and play. Lack of toys does not mean that children do not play: with imagination and facilitative adults children can use almost anything. However, a secure environment, in which exploration and discovery are encouraged, where children are given private space to explore fantasies and social time to enjoy making friends, are all components of satisfactory childhood play. Children who have missed these times are impoverished: it is extremely difficult to recreate the spontaneity of childhood in adolescence.

Foster carers, aware of this loss, often refer older children for therapeutic play, hoping to make up for missed opportunities in the past, and provide a stepping stone towards maturity. Many of the young people who have not had the chance to play have distorted thought processes; they cannot think clearly about the past nor envisage the future. Thus they are at the mercy of impulses and drives, with no restraining thoughts to help modify behaviour. With the sexual and aggressive urges that beset all adolescents, it is not surprising that the behaviour of many deprived of play opportunities in childhood is so extreme. In theory, regressive play could offer the chance to make up for missed experiences, and provide the basis for an internal mechanism to understand events, promoting a more constructive response to daily life.

Wilson *et al.* (1992) offer non-directive play therapy to adolescents; they provide a fully equipped playroom, saying that they conduct all their work in this room. The young person is free to talk or play as s/he wishes. Their experience is that adolescents can relax and play, if given permission to do so. They describe the play of a 14-year-old boy, referred for therapy after his father had abandoned the family, playing with wild animals and puppets. He was able to express feelings symbolically by giving the puppets characters. Only when this play reached its conclusion could he verbalise some of his feelings (p. 151).

In my experience, many adolescents are deeply affected by the attitude of their peers. Yvonne, aged 14, was functioning as a much younger child both at home and at school; initially she enjoyed her sessions and used the materials imaginatively. Then another young person in her children's home made a disparaging remark about play being babyish, and she was never able to relax and enjoy herself freely again.

Those adolescents who cannot respond to the opportunity of non-directive play therapy may find more directive techniques attractive. Some enjoy making and playing board games; others engage readily in making books or working with computers. There is a clearly defined purpose to the activity, which is explained beforehand and agreed with the young person. There is a reason for attending sessions, and a goal in sight. Art, drama or music therapies, which can apply equally to children, adolescents and adults, may be appropriate (Liebmann, 1990; Waller & Gilroy, 1992; Bunt, 1994; Jennings *et al.*, 1994). Through such therapies young people believe they have joined the adult world, but still find childish means of expression. Fantasies can be expressed in paint; aggression can emerge through clay; role play can externalise experiences and prompt expression of feeling; young people can make music, or soothe themselves listening to it.

It is common for adolescents to refuse help. Therapy can be successful only with a willingness to accept help by the young person. Therapy is a journey that worker and client take together, and both should travel willingly. Whilst the door is left open for adolescents who reject treatment, their right to do so must be respected.

However, when faced with adolescents who are abusing others, I would make extensive efforts to overcome resistance and engage the young person in therapy. The Family Law Reform Act (1969) and the Children Act (1989) are unclear as to whether young people under 16 can be made to attend for treatment (Freeman, 1994). Practitioners may hold a private view of the rights of young people, and be unwilling to promote the value of therapy with a young person who is particularly resistant. It is not easy to weigh the harm likely to be perpetrated in the future if the young person does not receive help against the right s/he has to refuse. It is a decision which should be taken by a professional team and not by the therapeutic play worker alone.

Practitioners assessing young people who sexually abuse younger children should develop skills in assessing the severity of the young person's behaviour (Dey & Print, 1992), and be familiar with the techniques which challenge that behaviour and promote healthy expression of sexuality (Salter, 1988). The behaviour of the young bully needs assessment and modification, to enable him or her to make fulfilling relationships without misusing power (Lane, 1992; Tattum, 1993). Research into the treatment needs of these young people is incomplete. Further work is essential before any practitioner can approach this work confident that his or her intervention will prevent further harm (Bentovim *et al.*, 1991; Report of the Committee of Inquiry into Children and Young People who Sexually Abuse Other Children, 1992).

Those working in this field should seek further training and skilled supervision and support. The evidence of adult perpetrators of abuse, disclosing the history of their aberrant behaviour (Faller, 1988; Doyle, 1994), indicates that young people engaging in severe sexual abuse of younger children will continue to be a danger to those weaker than themselves for many years. Many of these young people have themselves been abused, and the treatment they receive must make the connection between past abuse and current behaviour (Gil & Johnson, 1993). Programmes developed in America (Johnson & Berry, 1989), offering individual and group therapy to children under 13 who have abused those younger than themselves, stress the importance of involving families in reinforcing the message that such behaviour is unacceptable. In the UK, the Young Abusers Project also approaches the problems posed by these young people by addressing individual, familial and societal issues, believing that only by attending to every aspect of the young person's life can their behaviour be modified (Williams, 1994).

Working with children in hospital, and children with disabilities

There is a growing recognition of the play requirements of children with special needs. However, with the reduction of facilities in NHS hospitals, it is now less common to find play specialists on children's wards in hospitals, bringing toys which provide opportunities for the child to express his or her anxiety about medical procedures. These practitioners have developed particular skills in enabling children to cope with a hospital stay with minimal trauma. They also recognise the child's need to experience autonomy, all the more difficult within the confines of a hospital ward (McMahon, 1992).

Those working in hospitals are familiar with the impact of illness on children, and common behavioural and emotional consequences. There is evidence that play aids the recovery of sick children (Sylva, 1993). Children may have deep fears concerning separation from familiar surroundings, and fantasies about illness and possibly death. Feelings from earlier separations may make this hospital stay all the more traumatic. It is common for children to be angry that they should suffer in this way when classmates are healthy. Wayne, aged 7, who had recovered from meningitis, was unable to cope with his extreme anger at the severity of his illness, which contrasted with the relief of his family that he had survived. He welcomed four sessions, in which the meaning of the illness was fully explored, and he was able to leave this rage behind.

Inventiveness may be needed to create a space where play can be uninterrupted. Children who must remain in bed need the privacy of closed curtains to exclude other children; the worker may need to discuss the work fully with medical staff to ensure that they give the child the privacy s/he needs.

Practitioners working with dying children require specialist skills and close supervision and support (Judd, 1989; Crompton, 1990). These children need help to express their fears and fantasies, both about their own future and that of their families. The worker should be contained as safely as the child if s/he is to confront the suffering of these children without denial. Practitioners able to work in this field are rewarded by the evident courage of children, who, given the space, time and understanding, face the most painful feelings and emerge at peace with themselves.

There is a growing awareness of the play needs of children with disabilities (Campion, 1991; Hellendoorn, 1994a & 1994b). The requirements of these children are disparate. The origin of each child's difficulties, and the personal meaning of this disability for him or her, will vary on each occasion (Donovan & McIntyre, 1990). Those born disabled will have a different emotional perception of their problems from those injured through accident or illness. Similarly, each family responds differently, and there is a wide variation in the provision of community resources.

Art therapists have long understood the needs of disabled children and adults (Arguile, 1992); music therapy is offered to adults and children with mental health difficulties, who can express themselves in rhythms or songs (Oldfield & Feuerhahn, 1986; Bunt, 1994). Jennings' understanding of the need of the infant to experience him- or herself fully through embodiment play (1993), can be applied to children with disabilities needing help to explore their full physical potential (Haines, 1983).

Practitioners can therefore draw on the experience of other disciplines when working with disabled children. However, most children can use a range of toys and materials to express themselves. Those who care for them may complain that they are often angry and dissatisfied;

they need a forum where their grief at the loss of normal abilities and its impact can be understood. Sinason (1992) has worked extensively with young people with severe disabilities, and admires the courage with which they are able to tell their stories. The rage of young bodies trapped in helplessness is often denied; when it can be heard the child is freed to express him- or herself fully.

Children with sensory deficits can benefit from therapeutic play. The child with a hearing loss may welcome non-directive techniques, which give him or her the opportunity to escape from endless pressure to communicate, and retreat into a silent world where s/he can be herself. The worker who is skilled at non-verbal communications can join that world, and share the experience of hearing loss. Practitioners working with visually impaired children should pay special attention to the provision of materials which give tactile pleasure and can be easily recognised, and ensure that these are always placed where the child can find them easily.

Some disabled children need to be taught to play; a structured programme devised for the individual child, can help to improve play skills (McConkey, 1994). Planet produce a range of materials designed to stimulate disabled clients of all ages (see Appendix 3).

Many of these children have been labelled as 'stupid' or 'lazy'; they have internalised this view of themselves and continue to present it to the external world. They respond to a space where difficulties are explored without being judged. These children are aware that they cannot achieve the same results as their classmates; some are subjected to bullying which causes further difficulties. It may take time, and patience, to understand the child's comprehension of his or her difficulties. Some children will cease trying; it is easier to be thought stupid than to try and to fail (Sinason, 1992). Others hide their difficulties, producing challenging behaviour in the classroom rather than be seen by other children to be struggling. Children with multiple disabilities may lack the physical capacity to play, and have never been given permission to express themselves. Sessions may need to be adult-led (Nakken *et al.*, 1994), especially for children whose disabilities are such that spontaneous responses are impossible. Nevertheless, all children have the right to express feelings and to explore the world; practitioners should make efforts to empower them to do so.

Few children with learning difficulties achieve their full potential, and the therapeutic process should be structured to maximise competence (Donovan & McIntyre, 1990). For example, in a one-to-one situation, the child may complete a complex task that is impossible amid the distractions of the classroom. The child may believe a family myth that he or she cannot achieve; opportunities to succeed may unlock abilities of which no-one was previously aware. Play has been shown to be an effective introduction to speech therapy for children with a language delay (Mogford-Bevan, 1994). Therapeutic play techniques have been applied to adults with learning difficulties, who are able to express themselves symbolically but whose language skills are limited (Hellendoorn, 1994a).

Play approaches have even been attempted with psychotic and autistic children (Alvarez, 1992; van Berckelaer-Onnes, 1994); this is a highly specialised field, and practitioners should seek expert advice before agreeing to offer therapeutic play to these children. Whilst their play needs should not be overlooked, their view of the world is so unlike that of other children that the help they receive should address a need for normal experiences, in the knowledge that they will not be normally understood.

The value of having fun

Given the misery with which therapeutic play workers become familiar, it is easy to forget the right of each child to enjoy him- or herself and have fun. Play itself is intrinsically pleasurable. Laughter can be therapeutic, and may not always be a defence against intolerable pain but a genuine expression of humour. Some children use humour frequently, in an effort to protect themselves. One 10-year-old boy was extremely quick to tell a joke if the material in his play became too painful: it was his way of telling me that I was too close for comfort. By my respecting this defence, he was able to face difficult matters in his own time, with the relief of humour when he needed it. On one occasion he was so genuinely funny that I lost control with laughter; he responded with delight that he had entertained me so effectively.

Humour is a valid defence against pain. Bass & Davis describe an adult survivor of sexual abuse who was concerned about her use of humour to avoid facing distress; her counsellor replied:

'Humour is only one way of dealing with tragedy. Other people destroy themselves or others, or they start fires or they drink themselves to death. Of all the possible ways there are to deal with pain, you have chosen the one that ... affirms life with laughter.'

(1988: pp. 46-47).

Lowenfeld, in her study of children's play, explored its comic element. She concluded that:

'Laughter is the great healer, as it is the peacemaker among peoples, and when it is not malicious it is both the creator and the outer evidence of sanity.'

(Lowenfeld, 1935: p. 280)

Cattanach (1994b), describing her work with an adolescent, illustrates how therapy expands from healing into laughter. The joy of laughing together is as therapeutic as the pain of cathartic tears.

O'Connor sees the promotion of the child's ability to have fun as a primary goal of therapy:

'All play therapy shares a common goal: the re-establishment of the child's ability to engage in play behaviour as it is classically defined. Specifically, this means that the play therapist seeks to maximise the child's ability to engage in behaviour which is fun, intrinsically complete, person-orientated, variable, flexible, non-instrumental, and characterised by a natural flow ... Play therapists universally recognise that treatment has been successfully completed when the child demonstrates an ability to play with joyous abandon – this is what makes play therapy unique.'

(1991: p. 6)

Summary

Many of the children referred for therapeutic play present particular challenges to the worker. Whilst many of these children are challenging for all those around them, without an understanding of the child's experiences it is impossible to begin to meet his or her needs. Some children are so hostile, or their conduct so bizarre, that only by knowing details of past events can current behaviour make sense. These children may express themselves through overt aggression, or total withdrawal. Those abused as infants, with no emotional security on which to found a personality, are unintegrated. Others dissociate from current reality, in an effort to block out memories of past abuse.

Young children and adolescents also pose difficulties for the therapeutic play worker. Efforts should be made to communicate with them, and to hear their stories.

Sick or disabled children are also referred for therapeutic play. This is a specialised field, and only a brief outline of this rewarding work has been included in this chapter.

Many children referred for therapeutic play cannot relax and have fun. If the worker fails in his or her efforts to engage the child in life story work, if a non-directive approach has led to sullen rejection of practitioner and materials, and if all the child-centred techniques at his or her disposal have been exhausted, s/he should look again at the child and consider whether this intervention, although apparently unsuccessful, has released his or her emotions sufficiently to raise a smile. The child who can laugh and cry will be healthier than one who can only weep.

Chapter 8

Closing Procedures; and Looking after the Worker

Introduction

For many children, therapeutic play is the opportunity they need to make sense of events or circumstances, master confusing and distressing feelings, and leave the past behind. Without skilled intervention, they would continue to carry the past, like perpetual luggage dragging behind them at every turn.

This final chapter brings together two vital issues that are central to any therapeutic intervention. A worker who cannot care for him- or herself cannot offer appropriate care to the children s/he seeks to help. Attention to personal needs, in the form of appropriate training, support and supervision, ensures that relationships with children remain professional. When practitioners can ensure that their own needs for warmth and intimacy, and for professional recognition and support, are fully met, they will offer a truly therapeutic relationship to each child. This guarantees that the termination of these relationships can be effected positively for both worker and child.

The closing of any intervention needs as much preparation as the beginning: each ending is another loss, and children whose lives have been characterised by separations will grieve for the conclusion of another relationship. However, therapeutic play cannot continue for ever; and workers should consider the meaning of terminating this relationship for this child.

Terminating therapy

Practitioners who engage in focused work seldom have difficulty determining when therapeutic play should come to an end. If goals are clearly defined at the outset their attainment will be clear to both practitioner and child, and termination should come easily. Some techniques, such as life story work, come to a natural end when the child's life has been perused in depth. Some work is time-limited, and both practitioner and child are prepared for the work to cease after the allotted time.

Non-directive play therapists, or those whose work is not naturally time-limited, find the decision to terminate therapeutic play more problematic. The closing of therapy requires as thorough consideration as its assessment. Timing is crucial; and the implications for every child are different.

Reismann concludes that principles of termination are of equal importance to other practice issues. He believes that:

'The therapist negotiates termination with the client when he believes that the advantages of ending the meetings out-weigh what may be gained by their continuance.'

(Reismann, 1973: p. 67)

There are always additional matters that can be addressed in therapeutic play. Although the child may seem well adjusted, future events such as a change of school could cause further anxiety and the therapist may judge additional support to be essential. Family relationships may remain a cause of stress and unhappiness, and the worker may feel that the child continues to need someone who holds him or her in unconditional regard.

However, there are risks in continuing therapeutic play. During the course of treatment it is normal for children to become dependent on the worker (Freud, 1965). While a child is highly dependent I often seek an opportunity to tell him or her that I understand how important these sessions are now, but one day s/he will feel better and will not want to come any more. Most children respond with disbelief. As feelings are resolved, his or her dependency lessens, and s/he becomes more involved with friends and other interests outside the playroom. The practitioner who continues to work beyond this point can lead a child to believe that there is something wrong with him or her, that s/he is frail or lacks the ego strength to cope with the normal stresses of childhood. Therapeutic play should promote emotional well-being, not undermine it.

Many children seem to outgrow therapeutic play (O'Connor, 1991). They lose the self-absorption of earlier sessions, and begin to discuss family news, relate tales of events at school or adventures with friends. It becomes clear that the child can think about matters that do not directly relate to him- or herself. It is time to consider ending.

Each practitioner has his or her own words which s/he uses to introduce the notion that it is time for therapy to end. I gently remind children of the problems they had when they first came to see me, and comment on how proud I am of the changes they have made. I recall the comment I made weeks or months before, that the day would come when they no longer need to see me. I follow by saying that I do not think we need to meet for much longer, and invite the child to comment. I have been impressed by the number of children who respond with enthusiasm; one child even said he had been thinking the same thing but did not like to say it for fear of hurting my feelings!

I always allow several sessions to work through residual feelings the child may have; it is impossible to prescribe how long this may take. Stephen, aged 3, (see Chapter 7) responded to my suggestion that he no longer needed me to visit by piling all the toys in front of him, throwing them one-by-one into a heap behind him, and striding purposefully out of the room (Carroll, 1993b). This unequivocal response is unusual; most children need several sessions to adjust to the ending of therapeutic play. Few can tolerate a prolonged goodbye, and young children may cope well with just 2 weeks preparation.

For some children the ending of their play sessions can reflect earlier, painful losses. Those who have been bereaved may find the ending of the therapeutic relationship revives feelings of grief and loss (Carroll, 1995b). It is unavoidable that many feelings raised during previous weeks or months will be mirrored in this separation. Occasionally, this final parting is the trigger that prompts the child to face the reality of his or her bereavement. Gillian, a 12 year old whose mother had died, was unable to think about her loss until therapy drew to a close: losing her therapist activated feelings about the death of her mother and were dealt with in the final stages of therapy (Copley & Forryan, 1987: p. 164).

Occasionally, a child will ask for therapeutic play to end. Often, s/he is right. Jack (see Chapter 5), aged 5, whose inner world was populated by monstrous figures, greeted me one day with a huge smile on his face, announcing that his 'monsters had all gone'. I could see that they had; he no longer needed me and responded well to the loving care of an adoptive family. We enjoyed a final session together, and I left him confident that he would continue to flourish. Another child, aged 11, asked if he could stay at school on Tuesdays from now on, because they were beginning a new topic. I knew that, if school work was more inviting than play sessions, it was definitely time to stop.

However, it is possible that the child's expressed wish for therapeutic play to come to end can be seen as a 'flight into health', a defence against releasing threatening feelings (Haworth, 1982b); the worker has to make a judgement as to the validity of the child's claim to feel better. I find the principle of Reismann, that therapeutic play ends when the benefits of ending outweigh those of continuing, invaluable. If the child is determined that s/he no longer wishes to continue, and is able to express that wish assertively, s/he will sabotage efforts the practitioner may make to keep him or her attending play sessions. The door should be left open for the child to return; if s/he is avoiding facing feelings from the past they are likely to recur, possibly when s/he has the strength to consider them fully.

It is common for children to use the final few play sessions to recap on activities of the previous months or weeks (Haworth, 1982b). It can feel as if the entire content of therapeutic play has been crammed into those final minutes. The purpose of such play is to reinforce internalised understanding, to reassure the psyche, and to confirm mastery. This play needs acceptance without comment.

I always make a celebration of our final session. The nature of this varies from child to child, but I ensure that something different happens, to underline that this is not the same as other sessions and the child cannot avoid saying goodbye. Often, this celebration takes the form of a small snack; with a few children I have spent our last hour together in Macdonald's. I try to ensure that it is a hopeful session, full of optimism for the future and confirmation of the child's courage to make such progress in his or her therapy that s/he is ready to face the future, finding appropriate support from family and friends.

West (1984) approaches the termination of therapeutic play slightly differently. She comments, rightly, on the paucity of literature about ending therapy with children. She understands the closing of therapy, as Reismann does, to be a logical progression in the child's therapy. However, she pays special attention to the process of separation, regarding it as a bridging phase, one in which:

'child and therapist are freed to let go of each other without prejudicing the outcome of therapy.'

(West, 1984: p. 49)

West concentrates on those cases where the ending of therapy can be planned. She looks for indications that feelings that emerge in the transference relationship between child and therapist have been resolved, no longer hindered by emotions from early experiences but rooted in the here and now. She also seeks evidence that relationships the child has with family and friends can offer effective support and care, and that s/he has discovered satisfaction in age-appropriate activities.

Having identified this stage, West begins to decrease the frequency of sessions, allowing both worker and child the opportunity to let go of each other gradually. Although she allows for different patterns of ending, allowing for the myriad needs of children, she stresses the importance of a gradual separation giving space for both adult and child to resolve feelings at the inevitable parting.

My experience is slightly different from West's. I have found that, for most children, three or four weekly sessions, in which the child's progress is confirmed and feelings about the coming separation can be aired, are plenty to allow both child and practitioner to part comfortably. However, there are always exceptions. Children who are dependent on the routine of play sessions, or for whom the relationship with the worker has been particularly restorative, may need the gentle bridging process described by West if they are to accept the ending of therapeutic play without seeing it as a rejection.

If the child has made progress, and I can see him or her able to enjoy life, I rarely struggle on a personal level to bring his or her play sessions to an end. It is only on those occasions when the timing of closure is taken out of my hands that I find ending difficult: when the child is moved suddenly to a foster home too far away, or funding for therapeutic play is no longer available. On these occasions it is important that I discuss my feelings fully in supervision, to ensure that they do not enter my relationship with the child.

There was one other child who caused me considerable distress: this boy was moving to a therapeutic community. It was the right placement for him, and we had ample time to prepare for the parting. What I had not expected was the depth of projected sadness that he would leave behind: he waved happily as he was driven away, leaving a secretary and play therapist in tears!

Training, support and supervision

Understanding of the value and limitations of therapeutic play has developed rapidly in recent years. There are burgeoning training courses in play therapy now available (see Appendix 2). The British Association of Play Therapists (see Appendix 1) are in touch with new courses as they are developed. Whilst short courses offer an introduction to the techniques and skills involved, it is important to take the time to study the subject in depth and achieve an appropriate qualification before undertaking extensive work with children.

Each practitioner looks for something different from training. It is important that the training selected expands on previous knowledge, not simply confirming it. The social worker who has attended several courses on the needs of the abused child needs to extend his or her comprehension of the value of play; the practitioner with drama therapy training may need help to understand the needs of the abused child. Since the experience and training needs of those undertaking this work are so disparate, it is impossible to be prescriptive.

However, there is a body of knowledge that is essential. Every therapeutic play worker needs a thorough understanding of child development, both emotional and physical, and must be fully aware of the pivotal part played by play in this development. S/he should comprehend the process of therapeutic play, and be well prepared for the pain of children that emerges through their play. Some courses, notably those based in drama therapy, seek to expand the adult's play repertoire, enabling him or her to role play with conviction (Cattanach, 1994b). Others pay greater attention to expanding the practitioner's understanding of psychodynamic processes.

Play therapy courses also include a detailed study of the work of Axline and Moustakas, and other non-directive practitioners, whose work underpins much current practice. They include other play therapy methods, expanding the repertoire of the worker to ensure that their approach can be fully child-centred. In addition, the experiences of abused children and those with psychiatric and physical disabilities are considered. Playing with children may appear simple; however, enabling children to experience play as healing is extremely complex, and training facilitates understanding of that complexity as well as developing appropriate skills.

Therapeutic work with children is immensely stressful (Sainsbury, 1994). It cannot be tolerated alone: no individual practitioner should consider undertaking this work without adequate support. This includes colleagues who may not need to know the intimate details of a child's play, but can offer a timely cup of coffee after eventful sessions, and be understanding of a need to express projected feelings.

Each individual practitioner has his or her own ways to relieve stress and maintain an equilibrium: workshops to address this issue underline the importance of meeting personal needs before those of clients. Long walks, hot baths, glasses of wine, playing with one's own children, all help to keep the therapist in touch with his or her own reality and not drowning in the projections of young clients. Jennings (1993) describes this as the therapist keeping alive his or her own ability to play: finding times when s/he can pursue creative or physical activities whose sole purpose is the provision of pleasure. These pursuits are personally renewing, and sufficient time made available to enjoy them regularly promotes individual well-being as well as the emotional resources to cope with the demands of working with troubled children.

Attention to spiritual needs may be important. For some, this is easily met within orthodox religion. However, even those with a clear faith can have belief in a caring god tested by the tales of degradation and distress told by so many children. Practitioners working with abused children may need help to find personal solutions to the conflict between the evidence of human cruelty with which s/he works, and a wish to deny that such injustices exist. The task of continuing to hear and to believe the stories that children tell, whilst keeping a part of oneself unsullied by the overflow of their feelings, is never fully complete. There are times of overwork, or a particularly stressful case, when the world feels full of evil. These are the occasions when taking time to attend to oneself is especially important.

Laughter is often the most effective restorative. A sense of humour is essential, and no practitioner should avoid finding the funny side of his or her work. Occasionally such laughter releases feelings pent up from sessions, even when tears may appear more appropriate than sniggering. A sense of humour, and awareness of the ridiculous, helps to restore equilibrium. In addition, it is common for a child to ask his or her therapist to join in an absurd game, and self-consciousness is unhelpful. An ability to forget the normal constraints of adulthood and join in the fun of a session can confirm a child's ability that it is acceptable to pursue pleasure. Practitioners who cannot find ways to laugh outside play sessions will find it difficult to join the laughter within them.

Cattanach (1992) recognises that therapeutic play with distressed children can become 'addictive'; there is a thrill in surviving the negative feelings that are projected one's way, and being part of a child's journey towards health. However, practitioners who concentrate solely on this work can be overwhelmed by the distress they must face every day, and lose a realistic, life-affirming approach to children:

'The therapist becomes damaged and such "addiction" can induce total burn out. In this state of "addiction" perspectives become confused and the therapist is unable to tolerate the pain and suffering of her clients so tries to alleviate it all. She becomes afraid of making mistakes and thinks that taking care of herself is somehow bad for the children.'

(Cattanach, 1992: p. 147)

Gil (1991) shares Cattanach's concern for the therapist who concentrates on working solely with children who have been abused, and recommends that s/he seeks other work to balance the stress that accompanies helping such children.

The British Association of Play Therapists emphasises that all qualified and practising play therapists should undergo a period of personal therapy, in order to understand the influence of childhood experiences, and to separate private feelings from those introjected during therapeutic play. Some practitioners seek on-going therapy to address this issue, finding it beneficial to continue to consider personal needs in a therapeutic context. Few agencies are prepared to pay for such counselling, and therapists have to meet the cost themselves.

A personal therapist can also help the practitioner who is considering whether s/he has the qualities and experience that would enable him or her to undertake this stressful work. Those abused as children can expect occasions when the pain of children will revive personal memories; this should not disbar them from this work, but resolution of individual feelings is a prerequisite to helping others. Therapeutic play is not for healing the worker's inner child; the needs of that child must be met elsewhere. Others, whose childhood was less painful, may yet find the acute distress of children difficult to tolerate. It is not easy to walk the tightrope of openness to the child's projections without being overwhelmed by them.

Axline lists her recommendations as to the basic requirements for all therapists:

'They should have a genuine respect and interest in the child as a total person. They should have patience and understanding of the

complexities of the child's inner world. They should kno[w] [them-]
selves well enough to be willing and able to serve the child's [...]
without emotional involvement. They should have sufficient obje[c-]
tivity and sufficient intellectual freedom to set up tentative hypoth-
eses ... – with adequate flexibility to adjust their thinking and
responses to further enhance the child's self-discovery. They should
have sensitivity, empathy, a sense of humour, and a light touch
because the child's world is variable, delicate, full of movement,
lights, shadows, rhythm, poetry and grace.'

(1982b: p. 124)

This seems a little like the perfect person! Many may feel they cannot
live up to such high ideals. However, such a list can give the therapist
areas to think about, and aspirations to aim for.

The British Association of Play Therapists, formed in 1992, is
developing procedures to offer on-going professional support to practitioners throughout Britain. Many feel very isolated. At present, the
Association provides a regular newsletter, but hopes to develop a
professional journal with well-constructed research. In addition, the
annual conference is an opportunity to meet others committed to
helping children through play.

Good supervision is crucial (Banks & Mumford, 1988; Wilson *et al.*,
1992; Pritchard, 1995). Not all agencies have experienced consultants
available, and skilled help has to be sought elsewhere. The worker
should look for:

'[an] ideal supervisor [with] a constellation of abilities which assist in
the integration of the . . . worker's knowledge, understanding, sen-
sitivities and existing competencies, while facilitating a learning
process which both illuminates present and past experiences and
enables competent professional judgements.'

(Ash, 1994: p. 21)

Such consultants are not easy to find; if a skilled, experienced
supervisor is not available locally, practitioners may find a child
psychotherapist or child psychiatrist able to offer appropriate help.
Supervision should also address the emotions and responses of the
practitioner, as s/he contains those of the child (Ash, 1994; Cattanach,
1994b). The supervisor needs to be flexible, as the nature and focus of
supervision may change as the practitioner becomes more experienced
(Hawkins & Shohet, 1989).

If there are sufficient practitioners working together, supervision in
groups can be immensely supportive, and provide the medium in which
less experienced or confident practitioners can learn effectively. The
collective support of such a group balances the isolation of the work.
Such groups must be confidential; the details of sessions remain within

It is a forum for individuals to explore per-
therapy may have caused them, and to
relationships. This can only be achieved if
gh degree of trust, and there is considerable

istinguished from case management: this is an
vity, undertaken by a team leader who is
k undertaken by the whole team (Cattanach,
ment addresses practical issues; supervision
attends to the details of therapy and the feelings that arise with them
(Sawdon & Sawdon, 1995). For many practitioners, the same individual, often a line manager, fulfils both functions. However, there are
occasions when personal issues may need thorough exploration without a concern that this may have an adverse effect on any career plans.
In addition, such supervisors have to tread the tightrope between
empowerment of the practitioner and control of his or her work. These
issues need honest exploration, and any conflicts resolved to the
satisfaction of both supervisor and worker.

Conclusion

This book has addressed the question of what I do; how I assess the
needs of children, and the techniques employed to meet those needs.

I share Axline's belief that children contain within themselves the
ingredients for health; that they can recover from distressing experiences and live enriched and satisfying lives:

> '[Play]therapy is based upon the assumption that the individual has
> within himself, not only the ability to solve his own problems satis-
> factorily, but also [a] growth impulse that makes mature behaviour
> more satisfying than immature behaviour.'

(1969: p. 15)

The experience of abuse is certainly traumatic, and its consequences
can be extremely severe. Neither should the impact of bereavement,
serious illness or disability ever be underestimated. It may seem that
many of these children are intent on self-destruction. Their behaviour
seems to confirm a compulsion to recall past traumas, rather than leave
them behind (Terr, 1990). However, given the space to think, the time
of an adult who seeks only the child's well-being, and confirmation of
his or her own value as an individual, irrespective of past events, the
child can and will seek recovery.

Occasionally I meet a child who challenges this belief, who persis-
tently retains self-destructive behaviours despite all my efforts. It is
tempting, in these circumstances, to seek someone to blame: it was not

an appropriate referral, the child has an organic malfunction which influences his or her conduct, s/he is still having contact with his or her mother which is reinforcing destructive behaviour. Whilst such a response is natural, it does not solve the problem for this child. It may be that I do not have the skills to meet his or her needs; this does not imply that these needs cannot be met and my task may be to help find an agency or placement that is able to help him or her.

Believing as I do that even the most disturbed children need not remain locked in destructive behaviour patterns, it follows that they have a right to receive the help and care that they crave. Abused children can be separated from abusers, and found a family to care for them. However, they carry the luggage of abuse with them, and will continue to do so unless helped to leave it behind. Many children traumatised by disasters, bereavement or serious illness cannot abandon the feelings that accompany that trauma without help.

I recall working with a 5-year-old boy who had been sexually abused by his grandfather and an uncle, and was displaying chaotic behaviour in his foster home. In his play he told me that he was going on holiday, and collected every item in the playroom to represent his luggage. Week after week he devoted his time to carrying this luggage round the playroom: he never reached a destination since so much time was spent keeping his luggage together. Eventually he heard me comment that I thought he was carrying a lot of luggage in his head; he gave me a delighted smile of recognition and was able to move on to a different activity.

Distressed children have the right to have their unhappiness acknowledged and their stories heard. They need someone who will listen to them, who can accept and contain the reality of the past, and free them to discover optimism in the present. Without this help they remain locked into feelings and behaviours from earlier events or circumstances, which they continue to carry into adult relationships and experiences. Some children even appear to grow taller as therapy progresses; it seems as if they have carried all their cares on their shoulders, and once these begin to lift they can stand tall and look the world in the eye.

The number of children who would benefit from this help is clearly vast. There are too few practitioners to meet the needs of all traumatised children who would benefit from therapeutic play. We cannot reach them all. There remain many whose needs will go unrecognised, and who will continue to struggle with unhappiness long after the trauma is over. As practitioners we must do the best we can to help those who reach us.

However, we can also highlight the plight of so many children whose needs are misunderstood or ignored (Miller, 1987, 1992). If resources can be found to help them now, the misery that they carry can be alleviated; and all our children offered the chance of happiness that, at present, is offered to so few. Although others may seek to deny their pain, we must not do so. There are adults who wish to believe that, for children, the past is best forgotten; we know it is not that easy. We also know that there are solutions, given the will to find them.

It is beyond the resources of most therapeutic play workers to plead for those children for whom help is not available. Most need their energy to care for the children already referred to them. Nevertheless, as more training courses are developed, and the British Association of Play Therapists is able to expand, the valuable skills of therapeutic play workers will be increasingly recognised, and more children will be referred. When we are asked: 'What do you actually do?' we should reply as fully as possible, bringing to public awareness the scope of our work and its role in healing hurt children.

Therapeutic play can bring light to children who live in darkness; smiles to children who can only cry; and inner peace to replace turmoil. This contribution to human happiness should never be dismissed as 'just playing'.

Appendix 1

The British Association of Play Therapists

The British Association of Play Therapists was founded in 1992, by a group of practitioners who had trained together. The aims of the Association are:

- To promote an understanding and awareness of play therapy.
- To provide a support network for play therapists.
- To provide information on relevant training.
- To compile a directory of full and associate members.
- To provide a list of members able to offer supervision.
- To offer a forum for discussion of professional issues.
- To regularly distribute a journal/newsletter.

The Association seeks to promote recognition of the value of play therapy as a valid intervention in the care of troubled children, and promotes the importance of adequate training and supervision for practitioners. Consequently, in order to qualify for full membership, practitioners should have undertaken specific training, receive regular supervision, and had personal therapy. Associate membership is offered to all other applicants. Enquiries should be sent to:

The British Association of Play Therapists,
PO Box 97,
Wallingford,
OX10 0EB

Appendix 2

Training Courses

There is a growing number of training courses which address therapeutic work with children. Readers are advised to approach the Association of Play Therapists for up-to-date information.

Practitioners should look carefully at course content, and consider whether it covers those aspects that are of importance to the individual or her agency.

The following institutions offer training which includes therapeutic work with children:

Department of Community Studies
Faculty of Education and Community Studies
University of Reading
Bulmershe Court
Earley
Reading RG6 1HY
Telephone: 01734 318851
Fax: 01734 352080

Roehampton Institute
Digby Stuart College
Roehampton Lane
London SW15 5PH
Telephone: 01959 523535
Fax: 01959 533858

The Training Office
The Tavistock Clinic
120 Belsize Lane
London NW3 5BA
Telephone: 0171 435 7111
Fax: 0171 794 8741

Department of Social Policy and Social Work
University of York
Heslington
York YO1 5DD
Telephone: 01904 432629
Fax: 01904 433475

Social workers can find additional information on post-qualification courses applicable to their work from:

Central Council for Education and Training in Social Work
4th Floor
Derbyshire House
St Chad's Street
London WC1 8AD
Telephone: 0171 278 2455
Fax: 0171 278 2934

Practitioners wishing to work in hospitals should make enquiries from:

National Association of Hospital Play Staff
40 Brunswick Square
London WC1N 1AZ

Further information for courses for occupational therapists can be obtained from:

British Association of Occupational Therapists
6–8 Marshalsea Road
London SE18 1HL
Telephone: 0171 357 6480
Fax: 0171 357 1353

Art therapists should make enquiries from:

British Association of Art Therapists
11a Richmond Road
Brighton
East Sussex BN2 3RL

British Institute for the Study of Arts in Therapy
Christchurch
27 Blackfriars Road
London SE1

Appendix 3
Useful Addresses

The following organisations can offer materials, guidance and support to practitioners working with children:

British Agency for Adoption and Fostering
Skyline House
200 Union Street
London SE1 0LY
Telephone: 0171 593 2000
Fax: 0171 593 2001

Being Yourself catalogue, available from:

The Old Bakery
Charlton House
Dour Street
Dover CT16 1ED
Telephone: 01304 226800/226900
Fax: 01304 226700

Children's Hours Trust
8 Wallace House
Caledonian Estate
10 Caledonian Road
London N7 8TL

Children's Society
Edward Rudolf House
Margery Street
London WC1X 0LJ
Telephone: 0171 837 4299
Fax: 0171 837 0211

Kairos
53 Ferriby Road
Hessle
Hull HU13 0HS
Telephone: 01482 649839
Fax: 01482 647377

Save the Children
Cambridge House
Cambridge Grove
London W6 0LE
Telephone: 0181 741 4054
Fax: 0181 741 4506

Kidscape
152 Buckingham Palace Road
London SW1W 9TR
Telephone: 0171 730 3300
Fax: 0171 730 7081

Letterbox Library (for multicultural and non-sexist children's books):

8 Bradbury Street
London N16 8JN
Telephone: 0717 226 1633
Fax: 0171 226 1768

The Bridge Child Care Development Service
First Floor
34 Upper Street
London N1 0PN
Telephone: 0171 704 2386
Fax: 0171 704 2387

Planet
Save the Children
Cambridge House
Cambridge Grove
London W6 0LE
Telephone: 0181 741 4054
Fax: 0181 741 4506

Bibliography

Ainsworth, M.D.S., Blehar, M.C., Waters, E. & Wall, S. (1979) *Patterns of Attachment: A Psychological Study of the Strange Situation.* Lawrence Erlbaum and Associates, Hillsdale, NJ.

Ainsworth, M.D.S. (1989) Attachment beyond infancy. *American Psychologist,* **44,** 709–16.

Aldgate, J. & Simmonds, J. (eds) (1988) *Direct Work with Children: A Guide for Practitioners.* Batsford/BAAF, London.

Allan, J. & Berry, P. (1987) Sandplay. *Elementary School Guidance and Counselling,* **21,** 300–306. Reprinted in *Play Therapy Techniques,* (eds C.E. Schaefer & D.M. Cangelosi). pp. 117–123. Aronson, London and New Jersey.

Alvarez, A. (1992) *Live Company.* Routledge, London and New York.

American Psychiatric Association (1987) *Diagnostic and Statistical Manual of Mental Disorders,* 3rd edn. Washington DC.

Ammen, S. (1994) The good-feeling-bad-feeling game. In: *Handbook of Play Therapy, Vol. 2: Advances and Innovations,* (eds K.J. O'Connor & C.E. Schaefer). pp. 283–94. Wiley, New York.

Amster, F. (1982) Differential uses of play in treatment of young children. In: *Play Therapy: Dynamics of the Process of Counselling Children,* (ed. G.L. Landreth). pp. 33–45. Charles C. Thomas, Illinois.

Arguile, R. (1992) Art therapy with children and adolescents. In: *Art Therapy: A Handbook,* (eds D. Waller & A. Gilroy). pp. 140–54. Open University Press, Buckingham.

Ariel, S. (1992) *Structured Family Playtherapy.* Wiley, New York.

Arlow, J.A. & Kadis A. (1946) Finger painting. *American Journal of Orthopsychiatry,* **16,** 134–46. Reprinted in *Play Therapy Techniques,* (eds C.E. Schaefer & D.M. Cangelosi). pp. 161–75. Aronson, London and New Jersey.

Ash, E. (1994) Taking account of feelings. In: *Good Practice in Supervision: Statutory and Voluntary Organizations,* (ed. J. Pritchard), Jessica Kingley Publishers, London & Bristol, Pa.

Association of Play Therapists Newsletter (1995) Definition of play therapy, issue 3.

Axline, V. (1964) *Dibs: In Search of Self. Personality Development in Play Therapy.* Riverside Press, Harmondsworth.

Axline, V. (1969) *Play Therapy.* Ballantine Books, New York.

Axline, V. (1982a) Entering the child's world via the play experience. In: *Play Therapy: Dynamics of the Process of Counselling Children,* (ed. G.L. Landreth). pp. 47–57. Charles C. Thomas, Illinois.

Axline V. (1982b) Non-directive play therapy procedures and results. In *Play Therapy: Dynamics of the Process of Counselling Children*, (ed. G.L. Landreth). pp. 120–29. Charles C. Thomas, Illinois.

Aylward, G.P. (1985) Understanding and treatment of childhood depression. *Journal of Paediatrics*, 107(1), 1–9.

Banks, E. & Mumford, S. (1988) Meeting the needs of workers. In: *Direct Work with Children: A Guide for Practitioners*, (eds J. Aldgate & J. Simmonds). pp. 101–10. Batsford/BAAF, London.

Bannister, A. (1988) Monster-man has gone. *Community Care*, November, 21–2.

Bannister, A. (1989) Healing action – action methods with children who have been sexually abused. In: *Child Sexual Abuse: Listening, Hearing and Validating the Experiences of Children*, (eds C. Wattam, J. Hughes & H. Blagg). pp. 78–94. Longman, London.

Bannister, A., Barrett, K. & Shearer, E. (1990) *Listening to Children – The Professional Response to Hearing the Abused Child*. Longman, London.

Barker, P. (1981) *Basic Family Therapy*. Granada, London.

Bass, E. & Davis, L. (1988) *The Courage to Heal: A Guide for Women Survivors of Child Sexual Abuse*. Cedar Mandarin Press, London.

Beitchman, J.H., Zucher, K.J., Hood, J.E., DaCosts, G.A., Akamn, D. & Cassavia, E. (1992) A review of the long-term effects of child sexual abuse. *Child Abuse and Neglect*, 16, 101–18.

Ben (1991) *Things in My Head*. Colour Books, Dublin.

Bentovim, A., Vizard, E. & Hollows, A. (1991) *Children and Young People as Abusers: An Agenda for Action*. National Children's Bureau, London.

van Berckelaer-Onnes, I.A. (1994) Play training for autistic children. In: *Play and Intervention*, (eds J. Hellendoorn, R. van der Kooij & B. Sutton-Smith). pp. 173–83. State University of New York Press, New York.

Bergmann, A. (1993) To be or not to be separate: the meaning of hide-and-seek in forming internal representations. *Psychoanalytic Review*, 80(3), 361–75.

Berman, L. (1993) *Beyond the Smile: The Therapeutic Use of the Photograph*. Routledge, Guildford.

Berman, S. (1964) Techniques of treatment of a form of juvenile delinquency, the antisocial character disorder. *Journal of the American Academy of Child Psychiatry*, 2, 24–52.

Bion, W.R. (1962) *Learning From Experience*. Heinemann, London.

Bixler, R.H. (1982) Limits are therapy. In: *Play Therapy: Dynamics of the Process of Counselling Children*, (ed. G.L. Landreth). pp. 173–90. Charles C. Thomas, Illinois.

Black, D. (1987) Depression in children. *British Medical Journal*, 294, 462–3.

Bow, J.N. (1993) Overcoming resistance. In: *The Therapeutic Powers of Play*, (ed. C.E. Schaefer). pp. 17–44. Aronson, New York.

Bowlby, J. (1959) *Child Care and the Growth of Love*. Penguin, Harmondsworth.

Bowlby, J. (1969) *Attachment and Loss, Vol.1 Attachment*. Hogarth Press, London.

Bowlby, J. (1980a) Caring for children. In: *A Secure Base: Clinical Applications of Attachment Theory*, (ed. J. Bowlby), Lecture 1. pp. 1–19. Routledge, London.

Bowlby, J. (1980b) The origins of attachment theory. In: *A Secure Base:*

Clinical Applications of Attachment Theory, (ed. J. Bowlby), Lecture 2. pp. 20–38. Routledge, London.

Bowyer, L.R. (1970) *The Lowenfeld World Technique*. Pergamon Press, Oxford.

Bradbury, A. (1987) Anger as therapy. *Community Care*, November, 20–21.

Brandell, J.R. (1988) Story telling in child psychotherapy. In: *Innovative Interventions in Child and Adolescent Therapy*, (ed. C.E. Schaefer). pp. 9–42. Wiley, New York.

Bray, M. (1991) *Poppies on the Rubbish Heap – Sexual Abuse: The Child's Voice*. Cannongate, Edinburgh.

Brummer, N. (1988) White social workers/black children: issues of identity. In: *Direct Work with Children: A Guide for Practitioners*, (eds J. Aldgate & J. Simmonds). pp. 75–86. Batsford/BAAF, London.

Bumpass, E.R., Fagelman F.D. & Brix, F.J. (1983) Interventions with children who set fires. *American Journal of Psychotherapy*, 27, 328–45.

Bunt, L. (1994) *Music Therapy: An Art Beyond Words*. Routledge, London.

Burgess, A. & Hartman, C.R. (1993) Children's drawings. *Child Abuse and Neglect*, 17, 161–8.

Byram, V., Wagner, H.L. & Waller G. (1995) Sexual abuse and body image distortion. *Child Abuse and Neglect*, 19(4), 507–10.

Campion, J. (1991) *Counselling Children*. Whiting & Birch, London.

Carlson, N. (1990) *I Like Me*. Puffin Books, London.

Carroll, J. (1991) Piecing it together. *Community Care*, January 26–7.

Carroll, J. (1993a) Play therapy or life story work. *Association of Play Therapists Newsletter*, 1(1), 7–13.

Carroll, J. (1993b) Play therapy with very young children. *Association of Play Therapists Newsletter*, 1(2), pp. 3–8.

Carroll, J. (1994) The protection of children exposed to marital violence. *Child Abuse Review*, 3(1), 6–14.

Carroll, J. (1995a) Reaching out to aggressive children. *British Journal of Social Work*, 25, 37–53.

Carroll, J. (1995b) Non-directive play therapy with bereaved children. In: *Interventions with Bereaved Children*, (eds S. Smith & M. Pennells). Jessica Kingsley Publications, London.

Carroll, J. & Williams, P. (1988) Talking to toddlers. *Community Care*, January, 20–22.

Cassidy, J. & Berlin, L.J. (1994) The insecure/ambivalent pattern of attachment: theory and research. *Child Development*, 64, 971–91.

Cattanach, A. (1992) *Play Therapy with Abused Children*. Jessica Kingsley Publications, London.

Cattanach, A (1994a) Dramatic play with children: The interface of dramatherapy and play therapy. In: *The Handbook of Dramatherapy*, (eds S. Jennings, A. Cattanach, S. Mitchell, A. Chester & B. Meldrum). pp. 133–44. Routledge, London and New York.

Cattanach, A. (1994b) *Play Therapy: Where the Sky Meets the Underworld*. Jessica Kingsley Publications, London.

Cervi, B. (1995) Gimme shelter. *Community Care*, 1065, 16–17.

Cipolla, J., McGown, D.B. & Yanulis, M.A. (1990) *Communicating Through Play Techniques for Assessing and Preparing Children for Adoption*. BAAF, London.

Claman, L.(1980) The squiggle-drawing game. *American Journal of Psychotherapy*, 34, 414–25. Reprinted in *Play Therapy Techniques* (eds C.E. Schaefer & D.M. Cangelosi). pp. 178–89. Aronson, London and New Jersey.

Connor, T., Sclare, I., Dunbar D. & Elliffe J. (1985) Making a life story book. *Adoption & Fostering*, 9(2), 32–5, 46.

Conway, A. (1994) Trance-formations of abuse. In: *Treating Survivors of Satanist Abuse.*, (ed. V. Sinason). Routledge, London.

Cook, J.L. & Sinker, M. (1993) Play and the growth of confidence. In: *The Therapeutic Powers of Play*, (ed. C.E. Schaefer). pp. 65–80.

Cooper, C. (1992) Beating the crime. *Community Care*, 932, 12–13.

Copley, B. & Forryan, B. (1987) *Therapeutic Work with Children and Young People*. Robert Royce, London.

Covitz, J. (1986) *Emotional Child Abuse: The Family Curse*. Sigo Press, Boston.

Crompton, M. (1990) *Attending to Children – Direct Work in Social and Health Care*. Edward Arnold, London.

Crompton, M. (1991) Invasion by Russian dolls: on privacy and intrusion. *Adoption & Fostering*, 15, 31–3.

Crowley, R. & Mills, J.C. (1989) *Cartoon Magic: Using Characters to Help Children Solve Their Problems*. Magination Press, New York.

Davenport, G.C. (1991) *An Introduction to Child Development*. Collins, London.

Davies, B. (1991) Responses of children to the death of a sibling. In: *Children and Death*, (eds D. Papadatou & C. Papadatos). pp. 125–33. Hemisphere Publishing Corporation, London and New York.

Davis, M. & Wallbridge, D. (1983) *Boundary and Space: An Introduction to the Work of D.W. Winnicott*. Karnac Books, London.

Deblinger, E., McLeer, S. & Henry, E. (1990) Cognitive behavioural treatment for sexually abused children suffering post-traumatic stress: preliminary findings. *Journal of the American Academy of Child and Adolescent Psychiatry*, 29(5), 747–52.

De Domenico, G. (1994) Jungian play therapy techniques. In: *Handbook of Play Therapy, Vol 2: Advances and Innovations*, (eds K.J. O'Connor & C.E. Schaefer). pp. 253–82. Wiley, New York.

Dellar, S. (1989) Working with sexually abused children through games – ideas from practice. *Practice*, Spring, 66–79.

Department of Health (1988) *Protecting Children: A Guide for Social Workers Undertaking a Comprehensive Assessment*. HMSO, London.

Department of Health and Social Security (1984) *Guidance for Guardians ad litem in the Juvenile Court*. HMSO, London.

Dey, C. & Print, B. (1992) Young children who exhibit sexually abusive behaviour. In: *From Hearing to Healing: Working with the Aftermath of Sexual Abuse*, (ed. A. Bannister). pp. 57–81. Longman/NSPCC, Hong Kong.

DiLeo, J.H. (1983) *Interpreting Children's Drawings*. Brunner/Mazel Publishers, New York.

Dockar-Drysdale, B. (1968) *Therapy in Child Care*. Longman, London and Harrow.

Dockar-Drysdale, B. (1990) *The Provision of Primary Experience*. Free Association Books, London.

Donker-Raymaker, T. (1982) Beeldcommunicatatie bij een rouwproces. Quoted in Hellendoorn J. Imaginative playtechniques in psychotherapy with children. In: *Innovative Interventions in Child and Adolescent Therapy*, (ed. C.E. Schaefer). pp. 43–65. Wiley, New York.

Donovan, D.M. & McIntyre, D. (1990) *Healing the Hurt Child: A Developmental-Contextual Approach*. Norton, London and New York.

Doyle, C. (1987) Helping the victims of sexual abuse through play. *Practice*, 1, 27–38.

Doyle, C. (1990) *Working with Abused Children*. BASW/Macmillan, London.

Doyle, C. (1994) *Child Sexual Abuse: A Guide for Health Professionals*. Chapman & Hall, London and Glasgow.

Doyle, J.S. & Stoop, D. (1991) Witness and victim of multiple abuses: collaborative treatment of 10-year-old Randy. In: *Play Therapy with Children in Crisis: A Casebook for Practitioners*, (ed. N. Webb). pp. 111–42. Guilford Press, New York.

Dyke, S. (1987) Saying 'no' to psychotherapy: consultation and assessment in a case of sexual abuse. *Journal of Child Psychotherapy*, 13(2), 65–79.

Ekstein, R. (1983) Play therapy for borderline children. In: *Handbook of Play Therapy*, (eds C.E. Schaefer & K.J. O'Connor). pp. 412–18. Wiley, New York.

Elliott, S. (1987) The emotional barometer. *Elementary School and Guidance Counselling*, 21, 312–17. Reprinted in *Play Therapy Techniques*, (eds C.E. Schaefer & D.M. Cangelosi). pp. 191–6. Aronson, London and New Jersey.

Ellis, P.L., Piersmath, H.L. & Grayson, C.E. (1990) Interrupting the re-enactment cycle: psychotherapy of a sexually traumatized boy. *American Journal of Psychotherapy*, 44(4), 525–35.

Erikson, E. (1977) *Childhood and Society*. Triad/Granada, Suffolk.

Esman, A.H. (1983) Psychoanalytic play therapy. In: *Handbook of Play Therapy*, (eds C.E. Schaefer & K.J. O'Connor). pp. 11–20. Wiley, New York.

Excell, J.A. (1991) A child's perception of death. In: *Children and Death*, (eds D. Papadatou & C. Papadatos). pp. 87–103. Hemisphere Publishing Corporation, London and New York.

Fahlberg, V. (1988a) Attachment and separation. In: *Fitting the Pieces Together*, (ed. V. Fahlberg). pp. 9–73. BAAF, London.

Fahlberg, V. (1988b) Child development. In: *Fitting the Pieces Together*, (ed. V. Fahlberg). pp. 75–179. BAAF, London.

Fahlberg, V. (1988c) Helping children when they must move. In: *Fitting the Pieces Together*, (ed. V. Fahlberg). pp. 181–288. BAAF, London.

Fahlberg, V. (ed.) (1991) *Residential Treatment – A Tapestry of Many Therapies. For the Staff of Forest Heights Lodge*. Perspective Press, Indianapolis.

Faller, C.K. (1988) *Child Sexual Abuse. A Manual for Diagnosis, Case Management and Treatment*. Macmillan, London and Basingstoke.

Faller, C.K. (1990) *Understanding Child Sexual Maltreatment*. Sage Publications, California.

Faust, J. & Burns, W.J. (1991) Coding therapist and child interaction: progress and outcome in play therapy. In: *Play Diagnosis and Assessment*, (eds C.E. Schaefer, K. Gitlin & A. Sandgrund). pp. 633–89. Wiley, New York.

Fielden, T. (1990) Art therapy as part of the world of dyslexic children. In: *Art*

Therapy in Practice, (ed. M. Liebmann). pp. 104–13. Jessica Kingsley Publishers, London.

von Franz, M.L. (1974) *Shadow and Evil in Fairytales*. Spring Publications, Dallas.

Freeman, M. (1994) Removing rights from adolescents. *Adoption & Fostering*, 17(1), 14–21.

Freud, A. (1946) *The Psychoanalytic Treatment of Children*. Hogarth Press, London.

Freud, A. (1965) *Normality and Pathology in Childhood*. Penguin, Harmondsworth.

Freud, S. (1905) Fragment of an analysis of a case of hysteria. *Standard Edition*, 17. Hogarth Press, London (1953).

Freud, S. (1920) Beyond the pleasure principle. *Standard Edition, 18*. Hogarth Press, London (1953).

Furth, G.M. (1988) *The Secret World of Drawings: Healing Through Art*. Sigo Press, Boston.

Gaffe, J. (1990) *The Human Body and How It Works*. Kingfisher Books, London.

Garbarino, J. (1993) Challenges we face in understanding children and war: a personal essay. *Child Abuse and Neglect*, 17, 787–93.

Garbarino, J. & Scott, F.M. (1989) *What Children Can Tell Us: Eliciting, Interpreting and Evaluating Information from Children*. Jossey-Bas, San Francisco.

Gardner, J.E. (1991) Nintendo games, originally published as Can Mario Brothers help: Nintendo games as an adjunct in psychotherapy with children. *Psychotherapy: Theory and Research*, 28, 667–70. Reprinted in *Play Therapy Techniques*, (eds C.E. Schaefer & D.M. Cangelosi). pp. 273–80. Aronson, London and New Jersey.

Gardner, R.A. (1971) Mutual storytelling. *Acta Paedopschiatrica*, 38, 253–62. Reprinted in *Play Therapy Techniques*, (eds C.E. Schaefer & D.M. Cangelosi). pp. 199–209. Aronson, London and New Jersey.

Gardner, R.A. (1986a) Treating oedipal problems with the mutual storytelling technique. In: *Handbook of Play Therapy*, (eds C.E. Schaefer & K.J. O'Connor). pp. 355–68. Wiley, New York.

Gardner, R.A. (1986b) Checkers. In: *Game Play: Therapeutic Use of Childhood Games*, (eds C.E. Schaefer & A. Reid). pp. 215–32. Wiley, New York. Reprinted in *Play Therapy Techniques*, (eds C.E. Schaefer & D.M. Cangelosi). pp. 247–62. Aronson, London and New Jersey.

Gardner, R.M., Gardner, E.A. & Morrell, J.A. (1990) Body image of sexually and physically abused children. *Journal of Psychiatric Research*, 24(4), 313–21.

Gee, R. (1985) *Facts of Life*. Usbourne, London.

Gersie, A. & King, N. (1990) *Storymaking in Education and Therapy*. Jessica Kingsley Publishers, London.

Gil, E. (1991) *The Healing Power of Play – Working with Abused Children*. Guilford Press, London and New York.

Gil, E. & Johnson, T.C. (1993) *Sexualised Children: Assessment and Treatment of Children Who Molest*. Launch Press, America.

Gill, T. (ed.) (1996) *Electronic Children*. National Childrens' Bureau, London.

Ginott, H.G. (1961) *Group Psychotherapy with Children: The Theory and Practice of Play Therapy*. McGraw Hill, New York.

Ginott, H.G. (1982a) A rationale for selecting toys in play therapy. In: *Play Therapy: Dynamics of the Process of Counselling Children*, (ed. G.L. Landreth). pp. 145–52. Charles C. Thomas, Illinois.

Ginott, H.G. (1982b) Therapeutic interventions in child treatment. In: *Play Therapy: Dynamics of the Process of Counselling Children*, (ed. G.L. Landreth). pp. 160–72. Charles C. Thomas, Illinois.

Ginott, H.G. (1982c) Play therapy: the initial session. In: *Play Therapy: Dynamics of the Process of Counselling Children*, (ed. G.L. Landreth). pp. 201–16. Charles C. Thomas, Illinois.

Goetze, H. (1994) Processes in person-centred play therapy. In: *Play and Intervention*, (eds J. Hellendoorn, R. van der Kooij & B. Sutton-Smith). pp. 63–76. State University of New York Press, New York.

Goodyer, I. (1983) The recognition and management of the depressed child. *Maternal and Child Health*, September, 381–3.

Griff, M.D. (1983) Family play therapy. In: *Handbook of Play Therapy*, (eds C.E. Schaefer & K.J. O'Connor). pp. 65–75. Wiley, New York.

Guerney, L.F. (1983) Client-centred (non-directive) play therapy. In: *Handbook of Play Therapy*, (eds C.E. Shaefer & K.J. O'Connor). pp. 21–64. Wiley, New York.

Haines, H.M. (1983) The value of play. *Handicapped Living*, May, 12–15.

Hale, R. & Sinason, V. (1994) Internal and external reality: establishing parameters. In: *Treating Survivors of Satanist Abuse*, (ed. V. Sinason). pp. 273–84. Routledge, London and New York.

Hall, L. & Lloyd, S. (1989) *Surviving Sexual Abuse: A Handbook for Helping Women Challenge their Past*. Falmer Press, New York.

Handford, M. (1988) *Where's Wally?* Walker Books, London.

Harper, J. (1989) The watcher and the watched. *Adoption & Fostering*, 13(2), 15–21.

Harris, M. (1975) *Thinking about Infants and Young Children*. Clunie Press, Perthshire.

Harris, P.(1989) *Children and Emotion*. Blackwell Science, Oxford.

Harris-Hendricks, J., Black, D. & Kaplan, T. (1993) *When Father Kills Mother: Guiding Children Through Trauma and Grief*. Routledge, London.

Harrison, J. (1988) Making life books with foster and adopted children. In: *Innovative Interventions in Child and Adolescent Therapy*, (ed. C.E. Schaefer). pp. 377–99. Wiley, New York.

Hartman, C.R. & Burgess, A.W. (1993) Information processing of trauma. *Child Abuse and Neglect*, 17, 47–58.

Hawkins, P. & Shohet, R. (1989) *Supervision in the Helping Professions*. Open University Press, Milton Keynes.

Haworth, M.P. (1982a) Limits and the handling of aggression. In: *Play Therapy: Dynamics of the Process of Counselling Children*, (ed. G.L. Landreth). pp. 157–9. Charles C. Thomas, Illinois.

Haworth, M.P. (1982b) Termination. In: *Play Therapy: Dynamics of the Process of Counselling Children*, (ed. G.L. Landreth). pp. 254–6. Charles C. Thomas, Illinois.

Haworth, M.R. & Keller, M.J. (1964) The use of food in therapy. In *Child Psychotherapy: Practice and Theory*, (ed. M.R. Haworth). pp. 330–37. Harper Collins, New York.

Hellendoorn, J. (1988) Imaginative play techniques in psychotherapy with children. In: *Innovative Interventions in Child and Adolescent Therapy*, (ed. C.E. Schaefer). pp. 43–65. Wiley, New York.

Hellendoorn, J. (1994a) Play therapy for mentally retarded children. In: *Handbook of Play Therapy, Vol. 2: Advances and Innovations*, (eds K.J. O'Connor & C.E. Schaefer). pp. 249–79. Wiley, New York.

Hellendoorn, J. (1994b) Imaginative play training for severely retarded children. In: *Play and Intervention*, (eds J. Hellendoorn, R. van der Kooij & B. Sutton-Smith). pp. 113–22. State University of New York Press, New York.

Hellendoorn, J., van der Kooij, R. & Sutton-Smith, B. (eds) (1994) *Play and Intervention*. State University of New York Press, New York.

Herzog, D.B., Staley, J.E., Carmody, S., Robbins, W.M. & van der Kolk, B. (1993) Childhood sexual abuse in anorexia nervosa and bulimia nervosa: a pilot study. *Journal of the American Academy of Child and Adolescent Psychiatry*, 32(5), 962–6.

Hipgrave, T. (1985) A time of changes. *Community Care*, June, 17–19.

Hoorwitz, A.N. (1988) The therapeutic use of rituals with children. In: *Innovative Interventions in Child and Adolescent Therapy*, (ed. C.E. Schaefer), pp. 297–315. Wiley, New York.

Hoxter, S. (1964) The experience of puberty. *Journal of Child Psychotherapy*, 1(2), 13–25.

Hunter, M. (1986) The monster and the ballet dancer: a four-year-old's view of sexual abuse. *Journal of Child Psychotherapy*, 12(2), 29–39.

Hunter, M. (1994) Working with the past. *Adoption & Fostering*, 17(1), 31–6.

Hurley, D.M. (1991) The crisis of paternal suicide: case of Cathy, aged four-and-a-half. In: *Therapy with Children in Crisis: A Casebook for Practitioners*, (ed. N. Webb). pp. 237–53. Guilford Press, New York.

Irwin, E.C. (1983) The diagnostic use of pretend play. In: *Handbook of Play Therapy*, (eds C.E. Schaefer & K.J. O'Connor). pp. 148–73. Wiley, New York.

Irwin, H.J. (1994) Proneness to dissociation and traumatic childhood events. *Journal of Nervous and Mental Diseases*, 182(8), 456–60.

James, B. (1989) *Treating Traumatized Children*. Lexington Books, Toronto.

James, B. (1994) *Handbook of Attachment Trauma Problems in Children*. Lexington Books, New York.

Jehu, D., Klassen, C. & Grazen, M. (1985–6) Cognitive restructuring of distorted beliefs associated with childhood sexual abuse. *Journal of Social Work and Human Sexuality*, 4, 49–69.

Jennings, S. (1993) *Playtherapy with Children: A Practitioner's Guide*. Blackwell Science Ltd, Oxford.

Jennings, S., Cattanach, A., Mitchell, S., Chesner, A. & Meldrum, B. (1994) *The Handbook of Dramatherapy*. Routledge, London and New York.

Jewett, C. (1984) *Helping Children Cope with Separation and Loss*. Batsford Academic, Guildford and Kings Lynn.

Johnson, D.R. (1987) The role of the creative arts therapies in the diagnosis and treatment of psychological trauma. *The Arts in Psychotherapy*, 14, 7–13.

Johnson, K. (1991) *Trauma in the Lives of Children*. Macmillan, Basingstoke.

Johnson, R.G. (1993) High tech play therapy. In: *Play Therapy Techniques*, (eds C.E. Schaefer & D.M. Cangelosi). pp. 281–6. Aronson, London and New Jersey.

Johnson, T. & Berry, C. (1989) Children who molest: a treatment programme. *Journal of Interpersonal Violence*, 4, 185–203.

Judd, D. (1989) *Give Sorrow Words: Working with the Dying Child*. Free Association Books, London.

Kaduson, H.G. & Finnerty, K. (1995) Self-control game: interventions for Attention Deficit Hyperactivity Disorder. *International Journal of Play Therapy*, 4(2), 15–29.

Kalff, D. (1980) *Sandplay*. Sigo Press, Santa Monica.

Kelsall, M. (1994) Fostering the ritually abused child. In: *Treating Survivors of Satanist Abuse*, (ed. V. Sinason). pp. 94–9. Routledge, London and New York.

Kempe, R.S. & Kempe, C.H. (1978) *Child Abuse*. Fontana/Open Books, Shepton Mallett.

Kerr, A., Gregory, E., Howard, S. & Hudson, F. (1990) *On Behalf of the Child: The Work of the Guardian ad litem*. Venture Press, Rochester.

Klein, M. (1937) *The Psychoanalysis of Children*. Hogarth, London.

Klein, M. (1955) The psychoanalytic play technique. *American Journal of Orthopsychiatry*, 25, 223–37. Reprinted in *Play Therapy: Dynamics of the Process of Counselling with Children*, (ed. G. Landreth). pp. 74–91. Charles C. Thomas, Illinois.

Koeppen, A.S. (1993) Relaxation training for children. In: *Play Therapy Techniques*, (eds C.E. Schaefer & D.M. Cangelosi). pp. 235–43. Aronson, London & New Jersey.

Kottman, T. (1994) Adlerian play therapy. In: *Handbook of Play Therapy, Vol. 2: Advances and Innovations*, (eds K.J. O'Connor & C.E. Schaefer). pp. 3–26. Wiley, New York.

Kurtz, P.D., Gaudin, J.M., Wodarski, J.S. & Howling, P.T. (1993) Maltreatment and the school-aged child: school performance consequences. *Child Abuse and Neglect*, 17, 581–9.

Landreth, G.L. (ed.) (1982) *Play Therapy: Dynamics of the Process of Counselling Children*. Charles C. Thomas, Illinois.

Landreth, G.L. (1991) *Play Therapy: The Art of the Relationship*. Accelerated Development Inc, Indiana.

Lane, D.A. (1992) Bullying. In: *Child and Adolescent Therapy: A Handbook*, (eds D.A. Lane & A. Miller). pp. 138–56. Open University Press, Buckingham.

Lane, D.A. & Miller, A. (eds) (1992) *Child and Adolescent Therapy: A Handbook*. Open University Press, Buckingham.

Leach, P. (1977) *Baby and Child*. Michael Joseph, London.

Liebmann, M. (ed.) (1990) *Art Therapy in Practice*. Jessica Kingsley Publishers, London.

Lowenfeld, M. (1979) *The World Technique*. George Allen and Unwin, London.

Lowenfeld, M. (1935, 1991) *Play in Childhood*. Mackeith Press, London.

McConkey, R. (1994) Families at play: interventions for children with developmental handicaps. In: *Play and Intervention*, (eds J. Hellendoorn, R. van der Kooij & B. Sutton-Smith). pp. 123–32. State University of New York Press, New York.

McElroy, L.P. (1992) Early indicators of pathological dissociation in sexually abused children. *Child Abuse and Neglect*, 16, 833–46.

McMahon, L. (1992) *A Handbook of Play Therapy*. Routledge, London.

Mapp, S. (1994) Video nasties. *Community Care*, May, 22–3.

Maxime, J.E. (1993) The therapeutic importance of racial identity in working with black children who hate. In: *How and Why Children Hate: A Study of Conscious and Unconscious Sources*, (ed. V. Varma). pp. 94–112. Jessica Kingsley Publishers, London and Philadelphia.

Mayle, P. & Robins, A. (1973) *Where Did I Come From? The Facts of Life Without Any Nonsense and With Illustrations*. Macmillan, London.

Miljevic-Ridjicki, R. & Lugomer-Armano, G. (1994) Children's comprehension of war. *Child Abuse Review*, 3(2), 134–44.

Miller, A. (1987) *The Drama of being a Child, and the Search for the True Self*. Virago, London.

Miller, A. (1992) *Breaking Down the Wall of Silence: To Join the Waiting Child*. Virago, Reading.

Miller, A.F., McCluskey-Fawcett, K. & Irving, M. (1993) The relationship between childhood sexual abuse and the onset of bulimia nervosa. *Child Abuse and Neglect*, 17(2), 305–13.

Mitchell, R.R. & Friedman, H.S. (1994) *Sandplay: Past, Present and Future*. Routledge, London and New York.

Mogford-Bevan, K.P.(1994) Play assessment for play-based intervention: a first step with young children with communication difficulties. In: *Play and Intervention*, (eds J. Hellendoorn, R. van der Kooij & B. Sutton-Smith). pp. 157–72. State University of New York Press, New York.

Mollon, P. (1994) The impact of evil. In: *Treating Survivors of Satanist Abuse*, (ed. V. Sinason). pp. 136–47. Routledge, London and New York.

Mook, B. (1994) Therapeutic play: from interpretation to intervention. In: *Play and Intervention*, (eds J. Hellendoorn, R. van der Kooij & B. Sutton-Smith). pp. 39–52. State University of New York Press, New York.

Moore, J. (1994) Lethal weapon. *Community Care*, April, 20.

Moore, M.S. (1994) Common characteristics in the drawings of ritually abused children and adults. In: *Treating Survivors of Satantist Abuse*, (ed. V. Sinason). pp. 221–41. Routledge, London and New York.

Morrison, J. (1988) Working with sexual trauma: some principles of individual therapy with adolescent and pre-adolescent victims of child sexual abuse. *Practice*, Winter, 311–25.

Moustakas, C. (1973) *Children in Play Therapy*. Aronson, New York.

Moustakas, C. (1982) Emotional adjustment and the play therapy process. In: *Play Therapy: The Dynamics of Counselling Children*, (ed. G.L. Landreth). pp. 217–32. Charles C. Thomas, Illinois.

Moyles, J.R. (1989) *Just Playing? The Role and Status of Play in Early Childhood Education*. Open University Press, Milton Keynes and Philadelphia.

Mullender, A. & Morley, R. (eds) (1994) *Children Living with Domestic Violence*. Whiting and Birch, London.

Nakken, H., Vlaskamp, C. & van Wijck, R. (1994) Play within an intervention for multiply handicapped children. In: *Play and Intervention*, (eds J. Hellendoorn, R. van der Kooij & B. Sutton-Smith). pp. 133–44. State University of New York Press, New York.

Neagu, G.V. (1988) The focussing technique with children and adolescents. In: *Innovative Interventions in Child and Adolescent Therapy*, (ed. C.E. Schaefer). pp. 266–93. Wiley, New York.

Newson, E. (1983) Play therapy: an alternative language for children and their social workers. *Foster Care*, December, 16–17.

Newson, E. (1992) The barefoot play therapist: adapting skills for a time of need. In: *Child and Adolescent Therapy: A Handbook*, (eds D. Lane & A. Miller). pp. 89–107. Open University Press, Buckingham.

Nickerson, E.T. & O'Laughlin, K.S. (1983) The therapeutic use of games. In: *Handbook of Play Therapy*, (eds C.E. Schaefer & K.J. O'Connor). pp. 174–88. Wiley, New York.

Nicol, A.R., Smith, J., Kay, B., Hall, D., Barlow, J. & Williams, B. (1988) A focussed casework approach to the treatment of child abuse: a controlled comparison. *Journal of Child Psychiatry and Psychology*, 29(5), 703–11.

Oaklander, V. (1969) *Windows to Our Children*. Real People Press, Utah.

Oaklander, V. (1994) Gestalt play therapy. In: *Handbook of Play Therapy, Vol 2: Advances and Innovations*, (eds K.J. O'Connor & C.E. Schaefer). pp. 143–56. Wiley, New York.

O'Connor, J.K. (1988) The colour-your-life technique. In: *Handbook of Play Therapy*, (eds C.E. Schaefer & K.J. O'Connor). pp. 251–8. Wiley, New York.

O'Connor, J.K. (1991) *The Play Therapy Primer*. Wiley, New York.

O'Connor, K. (1994) Ecosystemic play therapy. In: *Handbook of Play Therapy, Vol. 2: Advances and Innovations*, (eds K.J. O'Connor & C.E. Schaefer), pp. 61–84. Wiley, New York.

O'Connor, K.J. & Schaefer, C.E. (eds) (1994) *Handbook of Play Therapy, Vol. 2: Advances and Innovations*. Wiley, New York.

O'Hagan, K. (1993) *Emotional and Psychological Abuse of Children*. Open University Press, Buckingham.

Oldfield, A. & Feuerhahn, C. (1986) Using music in mental handicaps: helping children with handicaps and providing support for their parents. *Mental Handicap*, 14, 10–14.

Owusu-Bempah, J. (1994) Race, self-identity and social work. *British Journal of Social Work*, 24(2), 123–36.

Palmer, P. (1992) *Liking Myself*. Little Imp Publications, California.

Perry, L. & Landreth, G. (1991) Diagnostic assessment of children's play therapy behaviour. In: *Play Diagnosis and Assessment*, (eds C.E. Schaefer, K. Gitlin & A. Sandgrund), pp. 643–62. Wiley, New York.

Petrie, P. (1989) *Communication with Children and Adults: Interpersonal Skills for those Working with Babies and Children*. Edward Arnold, London.

Piaget, J. (1952) *The Origins of Intelligence in Children*. Norton, New York.

Pinney, R. (1983) *Bobby, Breakthrough of an Autistic Child*. Harvill Press.

Pinney, R. (1990) *Children's Hours, Special Times for Listening to Children*. Obtainable on request from Children's Hours Trust (see Appendix 3).

Piper, A., Jr (1994) Multiple personality disorder. *British Journal of Psychiatry*, 164, 600–612.

Porter, F.S., Blick, L.C. & Sgroi, S. (1982) Treatment of the sexually abused child. In: *Handbook of Clinical Intervention in Child Sexual Abuse*, (ed. S. Sgroi). pp. 109–45. Lexington Books, Lexington, Mass.

Powell, A.S. (1991) The idealisation of therapy: fantasy versus reality in clinical practice. *British Journal of Psychiatry*, 159, 850–56.

Price, J.E. (1991) The effects of divorce precipitate a suicide threat: the case of Philip, aged 8. In: *Play Therapy with Children in Crisis: A Casebook for*

Practitioners, (ed. N.B Webb). pp. 219–36.Guilford Press, New York &
London.

Priest, K. (1985) Adolescents' response to parents' alchoholism. *Social Casework: The Journal of Contemporary Social Work,* November 533–539.

Pritchard, J. (ed.) (1995) *Good Practice in Supervision: Statutory and Voluntary Organizations.* Jessica Kingsley Publishers, London & Bristol, Pa.

Putnam, F.W. (1993) Dissociative disorders in children: behavioural profiles
and problems. *Child Abuse and Neglect,* 17, 39–45.

Pynoos, R.S. & Eth, S. (1984) *The child as witness to homicide. Journal of
Social Issues,* 2(4), 72–8.

Rayner, C. (1978) *The Body Book.* Scholastic Children's Books, London.

Redgrave, K. (1987) *Child's Play: 'Direct Work' with the Deprived Child.*
Boys' and Girls' Welfare Society, Cheadle.

Reismann, J.M. (1973) *Principles of Psychotherapy with Children.* Wiley, New
York.

Report of the Committee of Inquiry into Children and Young People who
Sexually Abuse Other Children (1992) National Children's Homes,
London.

Reynolds-Mejia, P. & Levitan, S. (1990) Counter-transference issues in the in-
home treatment of child sexual abuse. *Child Welfare League of America,*
69(1), 53–61.

Richards, M. (1980) *Infancy: The World of the Newborn.* Harper & Row
Publishers, London.

Roberts, J. (1993) The importance of self-esteem to children and young people
separated from their families. *Adoption and Fostering,* 17(2), 48–50.

Roberts, R.E.I. (1994) The trials of an expert witness. *Journal of the Royal
Society of Medicine,* 87, 628–31.

Robertson, J. (1952) *A two-year-old goes to Hospital* (film). Concord Films
Council, Ipswich; University Film Library, New York.

Robinson, B.E. (1989) *Working with Children of Alcoholics.* Lexington Books,
Lexington, Mass.

Rogers, C.R. (1951) *Client-Centred Therapy.* Constable, London.

Rose, A. (1995) Metaphor with an attitude: the use of 'Mighty Morphin Power
Rangers' television series as a therapeutic metaphor. *International Journal of
Play Therapy,* 4(2), 59–72.

Rosenbluth, D. (1970) Transference in child psychotherapy. *Journal of Child
Psychotherapy,* 2(4), 72–8.

Ryan, T. & Walker, R. (1993) *Making Life Story Books,* 2nd edn. BAAF,
London.

Ryan, V. & Wilson, K. (1995a) Non-directive play therapy as a means of
recreating optimal socialization patterns. *Early Development and Parenting,*
4(1), 29–38.

Ryan, V. & Wilson, K. (1995b) Child therapy and evidence in Court Pro-
ceedings. *British Journal of Social Work,* 25, 157–72.

Ryan, V. & Wilson, K. (1996) *Case Studies in Non-Directive Play Therapy.*
Balliere Tindall, London.

Sainsbury, E. (ed.) (1994) *Working with Children in Need.* Jessica Kingsley
Publishers, London & Bristol, Pa.

Salter, A. (1988) *Treating Child Sex Offenders and Victims.* Sage Publications,
London and California.

Sandford, L.T. (1991) *Strong in the Broken Places: Overcoming the Trauma of Childhood Abuse*. Virago, Reading.

Sawdon, C. & Sawdon, D. (1995) The supervision partnership: a whole greater than the sum of the parts. In: *Good Practice in Supervision: Statutory and Voluntary Organizations*, (ed. J. Pritchard). pp. 3–19. Jessica Kingsley Publishers, London & Bristol, Pa.

Schaefer, C.E. (ed.) (1988) *Innovative Interventions in Child and Adolescent Therapy*. Wiley, New York.

Schaefer, C.E. (1993) *The Therapeutic Powers of Play*. Aronson, New York.

Schaefer, C.E. (1994) Play therapy for psychic trauma in children. In: *Handbook of Play Therapy, Vol. 2: Advances and Innovations*, (eds K.J. O'Connor & C.E. Schaefer). pp. 297–318. Wiley, New York.

Schafer, C.E. & Cangelosi, D.M. (eds) (1993) *Play Therapy Techniques*. Aronson, London and New Jersey.

Schaefer, C.E. & O/Connor, K.J. (eds) (1983) *Handbook of Play Therapy*. Wiley, New York.

Schafer, G.E. (1994) Games of complexity: reflections in play structure and play intervention. In: *Play and Intervention*, (eds J. Hellendoorn, R. van der Kooij & B. Sutton-Smith). pp. 77–85. State University of New York Press, New York.

Schmidtchen, S. (1994) Stimulating and guiding children's spontaneous learning in play therapy. In: *Play and Intervention*, (eds J. Hellendoorn, R. van der Kooij & B. Sutton-Smith). pp. 53–62. State University of New York Press, New York.

Schreiber, F.R. (1975) *Sybil*. Penguin, Harmondsworth.

Segal, H. (1986) *Introduction to the Work of Melanie Klein*, 2nd edn. Hogarth Press, London.

Segal, R.M. (1984) Helping children express grief through symbolic communication. *Social Casework*, 25(10), 590–99.

Sgroi, S. (1982) *Handbook of Clinical Intervention in Child Sexual Abuse*. Lexington Books, Lexington, Mass.

Shaffer, D. (1985) Depression, mania and suicidal acts. In: *Child and Adolescent Psychiatry: Modern Approaches*, (eds M. Rutter & L. Herzov). pp. 698–707. Blackwell Science, Oxford.

Sinason, V. (1988) Smiling, swallowing, sickening and stupefying: the effect of sexual abuse on the child. *Psychoanalytic Psychotherapy*, 3(2), 97–111.

Sinason, V. (1992) *Mental Handicap and the Human Condition: New Approaches from the Tavistock*. Free Association Books, London.

Sinason, V. (ed.) (1994) *Treating Survivors of Satanist Abuse*. Routledge, London and New York.

Sinason, V. & Svensson, A. (1994) Going through the fifth window – other cases rest on Sundays. This one didn't. In: *Treating Survivors of Satanist Abuse*, (ed. V. Sinason). pp. 13–21. Routledge, London and New York.

Singer, D.G. (1994) Imagery techniques in play therapy with children. In: *Play and Intervention*, (eds J. Hellendoorn, R. van der Kooij & B. Sutton-Smith), pp. 85–98. State University of New York Press, New York.

Singer, J.L. (1994) The scientific foundations of play therapy. In: *Play and Intervention*, (eds J. Hellendoorn, R. van der Kooij & B. Sutton-Smith). pp. 27–38. State University of New York Press, New York.

Sjolund, M. & Schaefer, C.E. (1994) The Erica method of sand play diagnosis and assessment. In: *Handbook of Play Therapy, Vol. 2: Advances and Innovations*, (eds K.J. O'Connor & C.E. Schaefer). pp. 23–52. Wiley, New York.

Sloss, J. (1978) Play therapy for maladjusted children. *Social Work Today*, 9(46), 14–15.

Sloves, R.E. & Peterlin, K.B. (1994) Time-limited play therapy. In: *Handbook of Play Therapy, Vol. 2: Advances and Innovations*, (eds K.J. O'Connor & C.E. Schaefer). pp. 27–60. Wiley, New York.

Sluckin, A. (1981) Behavioural social work with encopretic children, their families and school. *Child Care, Health and Development*, 7, 67–80.

Smith, P.K. & Cowie, H. (1991) *Understanding Children's Development*. Blackwell Science, Oxford.

Strand, V.C. (1991) Victim of sexual abuse: case of Rosa, aged 6. In: *Play Therapy with Children in Crisis: A Casebook for Practitioners*, (ed. N. Webb). pp. 69–91. Guilford Press, New York.

Strauss, M. (1978) *Understanding Children's Drawings*. Rudolf Steiner Press, London.

Striker, S. & Kimmel, E. (1978) *The Anti-Colouring Book*. Hippo Books, London.

Stubbs, P. (1989) Developing anti-racist practice – problems and possibilities. In: *Child Sexual Abuse – Listening, Hearing and Validating the Experiences of Children*, (eds C. Wattam, J. Hughes & H. Blagg). pp. 95–121. Longman.

Sutton-Smith, J.L. (1994) The foundations of play therapy. In: *Play and Intervention*, (eds J. Hellendoorn, R. van der Kooij & B. Sutton-Smith). pp. 3–22. State University of New York Press, New York.

Sylva, K. (1993) Play in hospital: when and why it's effective. *Current Paediatrics*, 3, 247–9.

Tattum, D. (1993) *Understanding and Managing Bullying*. Heinemann, Oxford.

Terr, L. (1990) *Too Scared to Cry*. Basic Books, New York.

Thomas, G.V. & Silk, A.M.T. (1990) *An Introduction to the Psychology of Children's Drawings*. Harvester Wheatsheaf, New York.

Thompson, N. (1993) *Anti-Discriminatory Practice*. Macmillan, Basingstoke.

Tizard, B. & Phoenix, A. (1994) Not such mixed up kids. *Adoption and Fostering*, 18(1), 17–22.

Train, A. (1993) *Helping the Aggressive Child: How to Deal with Difficult Children*. Souvenir Press, London.

Trent, B. (1992) Art therapy can shine a light into the dark history of a child's sexual abuse. *Journal of the Canadian Medical Association*, 146(8), 1412–17.

Utting, D. (1994) War and peace. *Community Care*, April, 29-30.

Waller, D. & Gilroy, A. (eds) (1992) *Art Therapy: A Handbook*. Open University Press, Buckingham.

Waller, G., Hamilton, K., Rose, N., Sumra, J. & Baldwin, G. (1993) Sexual abuse and body-image distortion in eating disorders. *British Journal of Clinical Psychology*, 32, 350–52.

Ward, B. (1989) *Good Grief: Exploring Feelings, Loss and Death with Under 11s, A Holistic Approach*. Good Grief, Uxbridge.

Waterhouse, S. (1987) *Time for Me*. S. Waterhouse, 34, Bell Lane, Byfield, Northants.

Waters, E., Posada, G., Crowell, J. & Lay, K.L. (1994) The development of attachment: from control system to working models. *Psychiatry*, 57, 32–42.

Wattam, C., Hughes, J. & Blagg, H. (eds) (1989) *Child Sexual Abuse – Listening, Hearing and Validating the Experiences of Children*. Longman, London.

Webb, N. (1991) *Play Therapy with Children in Crisis: A Casebook for Practitioners*. Guilford Press, New York.

Webster-Stratton, C. (1985) The effect of father involvement in parent training for conduct problem children. *Journal of Child Psychology and Psychiatry*, 26(5), 801–10.

Weinrib, E.L. (1983) *Images of the Self: The Sandplay Therapy Process*. Sigo Press, Boston.

Weiser, J. (1988) Phototherapy: using snapshots and photo-interactions in therapy with youth. In: *Innovative Interventions in Child and Adolescent Therapy*, (ed. C.E. Schaefer). Wiley, New York.

West, J. (1983) Play therapy with Rosie. *British Journal of Social Work*, 13, 645–61.

West, J. (1984) Ending or beginning: discussion of the theory and practice of termination procedures in play therapy. *Journal of Social Work Practice*, 1(2), 9–65.

West, J. (1990) Children 'in limbo'. *Adoption & Fostering*, 14(2), 11–15.

West, J. (1992) *Child-Centred Play Therapy*. Edward Arnold, London.

Wilkes, C.R. (1987) Management of affective disorders in children. *Update*, 617–24.

Williams, M. (1994) The young abusers project. *Young Minds Newsletter*, 18, 12–13.

Willock, B. (1983) Play therapy with the aggressive, acting-out child. In: *Handbook of Play Therapy*, (eds C.E. Schaefer & K.J. O'Connor). pp. 387–411. Wiley, New York.

Wilson, K., Kendrick, P. & Ryan, V. (1992) *Play Therapy: A Non-Directive Approach for Children and Adolescents*. Balliere Tindall, London.

Winnicott, D.W. (1971) *Therapeutic Consultations in Child Psychiatry*. Hogarth Press, London.

Winnicott, D.W. (1974) *Playing and Reality*. Pelican, Harmondsworth.

Winnicott, D.W. (1986) *Home is where We start from*. Norton, New York.

Woltmann, A.G. (1950) Mud and clay. In: *Personality-Symposium of Topical Issues*, (ed. W. Wolff). pp. 35–50. Grune Stratton Inc. Reprinted in *Play Therapy Techniques*, (eds C.E. Schaefer & D.M. Cangelosi). pp. 141–57. Aronson, London and New Jersey.

Wyatt, G.E. & Powell, G.J. (eds) (1988) *The Lasting Effects of Sexual Abuse*. Sage, London.

Young, L. (1992) Sexual abuse and the problem of embodiment. *Child Abuse and Neglect*, 16, 89–100.

Yule, M. & Williams, R.M. (1992) The management of trauma following disasters. In: *Child and Adolescent Therapy: A Handbook*, (eds D. Lane & A. Miller). pp. 157–76. Open University Press, Buckingham.

Index